COLLEGE SACRAMENTAL THEOLOGY

COLLEGE SACRAMENTAL THEOLOGY

BY

REV. ANTHONY F. ALEXANDER
Priest of the Diocese of Cleveland

DEPARTMENT OF THEOLOGY
John Carroll University

Author of COLLEGE APOLOGETICS
and COLLEGE MORAL THEOLOGY

HENRY REGNERY COMPANY
CHICAGO, 1961

Nihil Obstat

REV. EDWARD B. BRUEGGEMAN, S.J.
Censor Librorum

Imprimatur

ALBERT GREGORY CARDINAL MEYER, D.D.
Archiepiscopus Chicagiensis

November 14, 1960

© *1961 Henry Regnery Company, Chicago, Illinois*
Manufactured in the United States of America
Library of Congress Catalog Number 61-11083

To

REV. ROBERT A. BONNELL

and

REV. VINCENT P. HAAS

PRIESTS, GENTLEMEN, LOYAL FRIENDS

this book is affectionately dedicated

Contents

	Preface	ix
I	THE AUTHORITY OF THE CHURCH	1
II	SACRAMENTS IN GENERAL	24
III	BAPTISM	48
IV	CONFIRMATION	76
V	HOLY EUCHARIST	93
VI	HOLY MASS	111
VII	HOLY COMMUNION	135
VIII	PENANCE	152
IX	EXTREME UNCTION	194
X	HOLY ORDERS	210
XI	MATRIMONY	231
	EPILOGUE	262
	Bibliography	265
	Index	267

Preface

THE KNOWLEDGE of theology has transcendent merit insofar
as it deals with the deepest, most personal, and most practical
values in education and in life. Yet often enough Catholic
adults appear to settle for relatively a youngster's grasp of the
catechism in coping with the mature religious needs of their
personal lives and occupational duties. In today's tough,
secular-minded world this result of an incomplete schooling
inevitably puts the individual's faith at a disadvantage. In a
parallel case, a man's business or professional practice would
obviously be handicapped if supported merely by an adoles-
cent's experience of relevant facts, skills, and wisdom. The
Catholic in question, however, may be quite unaware of any
missing experience in his religio-theological training.

The college course-sequence in theology has the same merit
and underlying necessity for the student as any other subject
in liberal education. Accordingly, it carries forward its con-
tributing theological disciplines much as any adult knowledge
and competency are matured by collegiate experience. The
process implies both new depth and a new capacity for inte-
grating the theoretical and practical considerations involved
at each level of theology, whether the level be catechetical or
otherwise. Thus, in contrast to the frankly catechetical ap-

proach of grade school and the principles-orientation of high school religion classes, college presents theology in set terms as a science.

What this means is suggested by the following points of scientific theological method. For example, the theologian is concerned to define terms and situations and to analyze them dispassionately. He is interested in historical backgrounds and personalities. He is sensitive to the real need of verifying the true facts among the tortuous and frequently unreliable data of religious history. For him the rhythms of cause and effect, the counterpointing of tradition and progress, the forging of objective judgment amidst the alarms of free-wheeling controversy and impugned authority become matters not only of flat scientific appraisal, however, invariably they also involve the personal insights and value judgments of human prudence. Accordingly, theological study is at the same time a science and an art working together in deliberate process to illuminate, point, and systematize religious truth. The ideal result is a security of intelligence and spirit grounded upon sincere inquiry, thoroughgoing evidence, and convincing truth.

Manifestly, there is a gap between the actual needs of the college student, however, and the further requirements of the professional theologian. The latter is naturally equipped with more sophisticated tools and experience in the areas of languages, philosophy, and scripture than the undergraduate student has available. Accordingly, the effective college textbook profits much, as in the present instance, from the skillful adaptation of theological science to the typical experience and academic stance of the college student. In joining this third textbook, *College Sacramental Theology*, to his well-regarded books in apologetics and moral theology, Father Alexander again does the Catholic college student a good turn.

Undoubtedly, in the ordering of the many insights and areas of theology to each other as a whole, the values and implications of the sacraments make sacramental theology into the most distinctively Catholic treatise of all. Dealing as they do with the principal and ordinary means of grace, the sacraments represent seven ironclad contracts between God and the individual Catholic soul whereby divine Life and divine ways become our actual possession under appropriate dispositions and conditions. In contrast to other preparatory treatises of theology which are mainly historical or theoretical in nature, sacramental theology in concept is eminently a practical subject calling for personal decisions and eliciting good habits. In the present textbook this practical orientation is furthered, moreover, by the resourceful and unusual combination of both dogmatic and moral aspects of sacramental theology in one presentation. The challenge is clearly to the college instructor to make over the student's academic contact with the power sources, the energies, and vitality of Christian life, as represented by this course, into a personal opportunity for a loving and vital relationship with God, author and end of these dynamic instrumentalities.

JOSEPH F. DOWNEY, S.J.

Dean, College of Arts and Sciences

John Carroll University

October, 1960

COLLEGE SACRAMENTAL THEOLOGY

OUTLINE OF APOLOGETICS

God
—
Soul

Religion—

Natural

Supernatural—Historical Evidence—Christianity—Gospels—
Integrity
Authorship
Historicity

Jesus
—
Christ

Claimed Divinity

Proved Divinity—

Miracles— Teach—Supernatural—Supernatural—Supernatural—Religion
Prophecies   Goal   Life

Faith 1. True | —All Men
2. Immutable
Morals 3. Indispensable | —All Ages

Church—

People
Officials
Means
Goal

Four
Marks
of
Identification

=

A. Permanent
B. Visible
C. Non-Copiable

1. Peter—
2. Universal—
3. Unity—
4. Sanctity—

Time
Place
Doctrine
Government
Founder
Doctrines
Members

—Roman
—Catholic
—One
—Holy

Infallibility of

Act
Faith

I

The Authority of the Church

§ 1. *Before beginning a detailed study of the sacraments, we should review the arguments for holding that the Catholic Church teaches by Divine Authority.*

For discovering the truth about the sacraments, there is no substitute for the clear, sure voice of Holy Mother, the Church. It is impossible to drive a wedge between the teaching authority of Christ and the teaching authority of His Church. The two are one. A person cannot logically accept one without accepting the other, for Christ said to His Church, "He who hears you, hears me, and he who rejects you, rejects me." (Luke 10:16) When Christ founded His Church, He knew full well that in time there would arise many spurious agencies masquerading as His Church. There would be great danger that sincere persons would be deceived by these false churches. It was imperative that the True Church be clearly identified, and so Christ stamped fool-proof, easily-seen marks of identification on it. It is time well spent for us to review the arguments for the divinity and infallibility of the Roman Catholic Church. To be sure, these arguments will be merely sketched in this chapter. They are fully amplified in textbooks of apologetics.[1]

Some have advocated a different approach to teaching truth

1

and refuting error. They have urged that we refute heresies on the sacraments with weapons designated by those heretics who propounded the heresies. Heretics accept Sacred Scripture but reject Sacred Tradition as a font of divine revelation. To allow heretics to lay down the criteria for the discovery of truth is to assign to them a prominence that they do not deserve. We should not allow ourselves to be side-tracked into partial battles over particular truths. Rather, we should fix the discussion on the one fundamental question and reduce multiple inquiries to a single element, namely, Church authority.

§ 2. *There is a strong historical reason for emphasizing the authority of the Church in refuting the heresies which attack the sacraments.*

During the first fifteen centuries of the Christian era, there were comparatively few heresies attacking the Church's teaching on the sacraments. But in the Sixteenth Century, the leaders of the Protestant revolt inaugurated a general campaign against them. They rejected practically every one of the Church's dogmas on this subject. The sudden and sweeping character of these denials indicated much more than what appeared on the surface. Let us compare these errors with the Christological heresies of the early centuries. The ancient errors were advanced by men like Apollinaris, Eutyches, and Theodore of Mopsuestia. The early heretics did not seek merely to refute a doctrine taught by the Church. They sought to replace it with a doctrine of their own and tried to fortify their position with clever philosophical arguments. It took several centuries for some of their errors to become full-blown. The heresies taught by the leaders of the Protestant revolt consisted of a string of denials scarcely fortified by solid intellectual arguments. There was a reason for this too. At least one reason was the desire to teach doctrines opposed to what the Catholic Church taught. The simplest way to do this was merely to deny. There is some basis to suspect that the real target was not the sacraments. It was the Church. The heretics were trying to discredit the Church by attacking her teachings. The only way to turn back the present day version of the Sixteenth Century heretics is to prove the teaching authority and infallibility of the Church. In doing so, we need not appeal to faith. We shall sketch the chain of inquiries proving that the Roman Catholic Church was founded by Christ to teach revealed truth, and *a fortiori* to teach the truth about the number, nature, and purpose of the sacraments.

§ 3. *There are five ways to prove the existence of God by use of reason unaided by revelation.*

Apologetics assumes nothing, not even the existence of God. St. Thomas Aquinas showed that there are at least five complete philosophical proofs for the existence of God.[2] He labeled them the ways from motion, causality, contingency, degrees of perfection, and design. Space does not permit us to include all of them here. One is sufficient. Let us choose the proof from motion. (1) The starting point of this proof is that there are things in existence which move. A bird flies, a dog runs, a meteorite hurtles through space, and so forth. (2) Motion is more than movement from place to place. More accurately, it is any progressive acquiring of a perfection, so that a student learning, a tree growing, a man growing old are also examples of motion. (3) An object cannot move and be at rest at the same time and in the same respect, for motion is the absence of rest and rest is the absence of motion. (4) If an object now at rest is to move, it must acquire this perfection from an external object which has it to give. Being at rest, it clearly cannot give itself something that it does not have. If the object moves, it has a "received" motion. (5) A series of subordinated movers cannot of themselves account for the initial presence of motion, for the whole series has a "received" motion. (6) We must conclude that the perfection called motion was first imparted to the series by a Being outside the series. That Being must possess "unreceived" perfection. Since His perfection is unreceived, He always had it, He has no beginning. Since He had no beginning, He is eternal. Since He is necessarily eternal, He is infinite. Since He is infinite, He is the Being we call God. Therefore God exists.

§ 4. *The existence in man of a spiritual immortal soul can be proved by the use of reason unaided by revelation.*

If the Bible had never been written and the Church had never been founded, we could still prove the existence of the soul by philosophical arguments. We sketch one of them here. Man is able to think. He sees a concrete object such as an auto in external reality. It has many notes that particularize it and set it apart from other autos. It has its own color, model, style, and so forth. When a person perceives this object he forms an image of it in his brain. That image has all the notes that the object had in objective existence. We call this image a percept. But man has a power by which he can strip away the individuating notes from an image and grasp only the nature of an object. A nature is that which makes a thing what it is. To be an auto, a vehicle need not be of a particular make or model. All it need have is the nature of an auto. When a person knows an essence stripped of individuating notes, he has formed a concept or an idea. Let us now compare a percept with a concept. A percept fits only one object because it has individuating notes. A concept fits all the objects in a class because it embodies an essence without individuating notes. Since a percept is individual, it must be concrete or material. But since a concept is universal, it must be abstract or nonmaterial. Only a material power can form a percept. We call this power the brain. Only a non-material power can form a concept. We call it the intellect. Since the intellect is a non-material power, it must be rooted in a non-material or spiritual substance called the soul. Since the soul is non-material, it does not have parts. Death is the break-down of a thing into its component parts. The soul has no parts, and consequently it cannot break-down or die.

§ 5. *Man's inescapable desire to be perfectly happy indicates an inescapable duty to practice religion.*

The conclusion that man must practice religion is based on a series of premises. (1) One of the most uniform traits of human behavior is man's desire to be happy. A person is happy when he possesses that which is good or desirable. It may be a good of the material order or of the non-material order. The first is exemplified by such things as wealth or power. The second by such things as knowledge or truth. Man seeks happiness by every one of his deliberate and free acts. Even when he submits to something painful, he looks upon it as a stepping stone to happiness. (2) The craving to be happy is part of man's natural equipment. He is born with it and never outgrows it. He does not acquire it by education, nor does he lose it with old age. (3) Partial goods can at best produce a partial happiness. If they satisfy a person in one respect, they leave him unsatisfied in another one. For example, wealth is a partial or imperfect good, for it cannot buy health or power or respect. It is also imperfect because its power to produces happiness ends at death. (4) Man has a craving to be perfectly happy. He wants to be completely satisfied in every respect and for an unending period. He consciously and unconsciously works toward this goal. (5) God who created man does nothing in vain, for He is infinitely intelligent. For example, God would have acted without a purpose if he had created a tooth to chew food but had not created food, or lungs to inhale air but no air for them to inhale. God created man with a craving to be perfectly happy. Since happiness comes from possessing that which is good, it follows that there must be in existence the Perfect Good that is capable of making man perfectly happy. (6) God Himself is the Perfect Good who alone can make man perfectly happy. He is man's goal in life. "For Thyself, Thou hast created us, O God, and our hearts are not at rest until they rest in Thee."[3] (7) Man advances toward his goal when he practices religion. He cannot satisfy his desire to be perfectly happy unless he reaches his goal. Since man cannot escape the craving to be perfectly happy, neither can he escape the duty to practice religion.

§ 6. *The type of religion that man must practice is dictated by the type of goal that God wants him to reach.*

It is impossible for man legitimately to substitute another ultimate goal in place of God. But God can be seen in one of two ways. He can be seen by the natural light of reason or He can be seen face to face. Religion is the means we use to reach God. If God wants us to see Him by the natural light of reason, then we must practice natural religion. If He wants us to see Him face to face, that is, supernaturally, then the practice of natural religion is completely inadequate to bring it about. We must then practice supernatural religion. The content of supernatural religion is much greater than the content of natural religion, for the happiness that comes from seeing God face to face is much greater than that produced by seeing Him by the natural light of reason.[4] Man is not free to choose between these two goals. He must seek the one that God has assigned to him. If he refuses to seek the one assigned to him, he will reach neither of them.

We cannot presume that God has assigned a supernatural

goal to us. If He has done so, it must be proved by historical inquiry. Our procedure will be to investigate the historical sources of the different religions in existence today. If they can prove that God is speaking to us through them, then we must listen to them. But, they must first present valid credentials proving their divine authorization. The first religion whose credentials we shall examine will be Christianity. If Christianity can prove its divine institution, then we need not search any further, for God would not found two organizations to do the job that one by itself could do more quickly, more completely, and with less confusion.

§ 7. *Apologists have always pointed to the Gospels as documents containing evidence of the origin of Christianity.*

Christianity did not start with the Gospels. We say that the Gospels record the historical beginnings of Christianity. The trustworthiness of the Gospels must be tested with the same canons with which a historical scientist tests the trustworthiness of a seemingly historical document.

The first step in the process of testing is to ascertain the integrity of the text. Can we prove that the text of the Gospels has come down to us in the same condition that it was when it left the hand of its author? The process is long and complicated but there can be no doubt as to its results. Even the bitterest enemies of Christianity admit that the Greek Gospels in existence today are identical with the originals composed nineteen centuries ago. No pagan Latin or Greek classic has nearly the amount of manuscript evidence to support it, as have the Gospels.[5]

The authors of the Gospels did not sign their names to their writings. But this does not mean that we cannot learn their identity. As the original Gospel manuscripts were reproduced, the scribes noted the names of the Evangelists on the transcriptions they made. It was necessary to do this in order to prevent people from being deceived by the many apocryphal writings then in circulation. Papias (+120), St. Justin M. (+160), Clement of Alexandria (+211), St. Irenaeus (+202),[6] Tertullian (+220)[7] and many other very ancient writers are unanimous in testifying that the Evangelists were Matthew, Mark, Luke, and John. The conclusion we set down here in two short paragraphs is based on premises that fill many volumes. These studies are indispensable links in the study of apologetics as is evidenced by the astonishing amount of effort expended by critics of Christianity to destroy them.[8]

§ 8. *There is clear proof that the events which are recorded in the Gospels actually took place.*

The inquiry into the historical trustworthiness of the Gospels is a logical sequence from the inquiries into their integrity and authorship. (1) The Evangelists were in a very favorable position to learn firsthand the truth of the events which they record. Matthew and John were eye-witnesses to these events, for they were Apostles. Mark received his information on them from Peter, an Apostle; Luke received his information from Paul; Paul in turn received it from Apostles. (2) The Evangelists, not only knew the truth of the Gospel events, but suffered rather than change their testimony. No one suffers for a lie when truth will set him free. (3) The events recorded in the Gospels were public events. Hundreds of people saw them and thousands learned of them. If the Evangelists wrote deceptive or even erroneous reports, they would have been exposed, and Christianity would have been discredited. The early enemies of Christianity never challenged the veracity of the Gospels although a successful challenge would have struck most telling blows against it. (4) The early converts to Christianity from Judaism or paganism checked the veracity of the

Gospels and found them to be accurate. The earnestness of their investigation was spurred by the fact that those who became Christians invited imprisonment, exile, and even death. (5) One of the best proofs for the historical reliability of the Gospels is the inability of critics to find errors or discrepancies in the Gospel narrative. Such critics as Reimarus, Strauss, Bauer, Paulus, Ritschl, Renan, and Harnack have not been able to substantiate their denials of the historical value of the Gospels. Many of them have freely admitted the fruitlessness of their efforts in this matter.

§ 9. *The Gospels clearly show that Jesus Christ claimed to be God in the strict literal sense of the term.*

Once we have established the historical trustworthiness of the Gospels, we are warranted to investigate their contents. The striking feature about these writings is that they pay so much attention to the sayings and doing of a Person called Jesus Christ. Why should they give Him such attention? It is because He made most unusual claims. He claimed to be God. On different occasions, He claimed the divine prerogative to forgive sin, to be Lord of the Sabbath, and so forth. He was not content to make His claim in an implicit fashion. He repeatedly stated it as clearly and as explicitly as He could. He made it to the Apostles, to the common folk, and to the learned teachers. Space permits us to cite only one of these instances, but it is one of the most celebrated. The place is the chamber of the Jewish Sanhedrin. The High Priest, Caiphas, is seeking a charge against Christ that will justify the death penalty. The false witnesses who are brought in cannot agree as to what testimony they should give. Caiphas then resorts to that formality in Jewish trials of the day called "adjuration." The presiding officer puts the defendant under oath and then makes him testify for or against himself. Caiphas says to Christ,

"I adjure Thee by the living God that Thou tell us whether Thou are the Christ, the Son of God." Jesus answered "Thou hast said it. Nevertheless, I say to you, hereafter you shall see the Son of Man sitting at the right hand of the Power and coming upon the clouds of heaven." At this the high priest tore his garments and said, "He has blasphemed." (Matt. 26:65) The fact that the Sanhedrin understood Christ's response as blasphemy proves that even they interpreted it as a claim to divinity.

§ 10. *Christ proved His claim to divinity by working miracles and by making prophecies.*

Christ did not work miracles and prophecies merely to impress people or to fill people with awe as a sleight-of-hand artist might try to do. He explicitly stated that these works were to be looked upon as credentials which supported His claim to divinity. "If I do not perform the works of my Father, do not believe me. But if I do perform them, and if you are not willing to believe me, believe the works, that you may know and believe that the Father is in Me and I in the Father." (Jn. 10:38) There are more than thirty-five miracles described in some detail in the Gospels. We are certain that Christ worked a great many more of them. In fact, the Evangelists often cluster many miracles in a single verse. "The chief priest and the Pharisees therefore gathered together a council and said, 'What are we doing? For this Man is working *many signs.*'" (Jn. 11:47)

The theme of all four Gospels is Jesus Christ. The Evangelists did not wish to write a biography of Christ or a systematic compilation of His teachings or sayings. Although all the Evangelists clearly state that Christ worked miracles in proof of His claim to divinity, St. John states it in a particularly clear fashion. In a statement which summarizes the theme of his

Gospel, this Evangelist writes, "Many other signs also Jesus worked in the sight of His disciples, which are not written in this book. But these are written that you may believe that Jesus is the Christ, the Son of God, and that believing you may have life in His Name." (Jn. 20:30) Notice how neatly this passage ties together Christ's claim and the miracles He performed to prove it.

§ 11. *The miracles that Christ worked are acts that only God could perform, for they require infinite power.*

There are many loose meanings attached to the term "miracle." Philosophically speaking, its meaning is clear and precise. As it is used in apologetics, a miracle is a visible act exceeding the powers of all created nature and so possible only to God. It is more than an unusual or superhuman occurrence. It is something that only God can perform, for only a being having infinite power can work it.

There are several types of miracles, for example: miracles of creation and miracles of immediate substantial change. Let us briefly sketch one of them; that is, a miracle of creation. The distance to a star may be so great that it must be measured in light years. Yet the distance to the farthest star is finite and limited, for there are two definite terminals. The "distance" from somethingness to nothingness is unlimited, for there are not two definite terminals which would make measurement possible. The "distance" from nothingness to somethingness is likewise unlimited or infinite. It can only be bridged by a being having unlimited or infinite power, that is, by God alone. This is precisely what takes place in creation, and it is the reason why we say that only God can create. Christ exercized this power when He multiplied the loaves and fishes at Capharnaum.

Miracles of immediate substantial change are in a broad

sense "miracles of creation," and so, can be worked only by one possessing infinite power. Christ worked this kind of miracle when He changed water into wine at Cana, and whenever He raised the dead to life or gave sight to the blind, and so forth.

§ 12. *As it pertains to man, the core of Christ's teaching and activity was built around the fact that God has assigned a supernatural goal to man.*

Christ came to tell us the good news that God has assigned to us the goal of seeing Him face to face. The happiness caused by seeing God in this way is so wonderful that we can only describe it in negatives. "Eye has not seen or ear heard, nor has it entered into the heart of man, what things God has prepared for those who love him" (I Cor. 2:9) This is our supernatural goal. It is so great that even God with His infinite power could not give us a goal greater or more wonderful than this one. It is literally a participation in the love and happiness that is proper to God.

In order to reach our supernatural goal, we must live a supernatural life. Man is born destined to a supernatural end, but at the same time is deprived of supernatural life. He moves on a plane essentially lower than his supernatural goal. This essential disproportion must be bridged. Man must be lifted onto the supernatural plane if he is to reach his new goal. Sanctifying grace or supernatural life must be infused into him. This new life is the life proper to God.

It remains for us to learn what a person must do to acquire supernatural life. He must practice supernatural religion. He must believe and do what God wants him to believe and to do. These doctrines are true because they come from God. Since they are true, they must be immutable, for the truth does not change. Since they are true and immutable they must also be indispensable. We can conclude that they are to be accepted by all men in all ages. To tamper with these doctrines makes it ultimately impossible for one to receive supernatural life. And this in turn makes it impossible for him to reach his supernatural goal.

§ 13. *Christ founded an easily recognizable Church to carry on His work until the end of time.*

The term "church" has often been given a loose meaning. In reality, it has definite elements which set it apart from any other organization. Christ uses this term three times in the Gospels. Any organization is made up of the same *people* directed by the same *officials* in the use of the same *means* to reach the same *goal.* These same elements are to be found in such groups as labor unions, corporations, sovereign states, churches, and so forth. The Gospels show that Christ's Church has these elements, and so it is a definite, easily-recognizable society. The elements permit one to distinguish this Church from profane organizations and even from false churches. The distinguishing feature about Christ's Church is that He personally designed the nature of the four elements referred to above. Christ stated that all *people* would be invited to be members of His Church. He empowered the Church's *officials* to act with His authority. Christ delivered the *means* that His Church would use, namely, the truths it would teach and the channels of grace it would distribute. He finally designated the *goal* of the Church as the salvation of its members, that is, it would lead them to see God face to face in heaven. Any organization which lacks any of the elements that Christ determined cannot legitimately claim to be His Church.

The Catholic Church is a unique society. It is not a loose association of people like a national political party. It is a living organism. When a person becomes a member of the Church he becomes a member of the Mystical Body. He is like a branch that has been grafted onto the vine which is Christ.

§ 14. *Christ identified His Church by stamping fool-proof marks on it.*

Christ saw that, as His Church was launched on its task of teaching, many false churches would spring up to teach doctrines in conflict with His. Unless the True Church was clearly identified, it would not be found by even sincere inquirers. A means would have to be devised to shield the inquirer from confusion. Error in finding the True Church leads to disaster. Christ saw to it that the honest inquirer need never despair of finding supernatural truth and the route to his supernatural goal. He stamped four marks of identification on His Church. To be fool-proof, these marks would have to be visible, permanent, and non-copiable. In other words, the marks could easily be found; they could not be lost; and they could not be stolen. We must not imagine that Christ hung these marks on His Church as auto-workers hang parts on a car going down an assembly line. Each mark grows out of one of the four elements of the Church, namely, people, officers, means, and end. To destroy these marks, one would have to destroy the Church itself, for they cannot be separated from her. It is a comparatively simple task to discover those marks, for they are clearly contained in the Gospels. Having found them there, we must then search which Church of today has them. That Church will be the True Church. Christ purposely avoided giving His Church a name, for names can easily be copied. Instead He gave it marks which cannot be copied. Any organization which lacks these marks, lacks authorization to teach the doctrines of revelation.

It is usurping prerogatives which were given by Christ only to His Church.

§ 15. *The first mark of the True Church is apostolicity; that is, the ability to trace the line of its supreme rulers back in unbroken series to Peter.*

There are two passages in the Gospels which prove that Christ conferred on Peter a primacy of power. The first reads, "Thou are Peter and upon this rock I will build my Church .... and I will give thee the keys to the kingdom of heaven." (Matt. 16:16) The second reads, "Simon, son of John, dost thou love me more than these do?" He said to Him, "Yes, Lord, Thou knowest that I love Thee." He said to him, "Feed my lambs .... Feed my lambs .... Feed my sheep." (Jn. 21:15-18) There is more evidence in the Gospels which corroborates Peter's position of supreme ruler of Christ's Church.

It is a comparatively simple task to trace the line of Peter's successors down to the present day. It can be proved conclusively that Peter eventually set up his See in Rome and that he died in that city.[9] St. Irenaeus then lists the names of the bishops of Rome from Peter down to his own, that is, to about 178 A.D. He names the twelve pontiffs who ruled the Church during that period.[10] St. Optatus names the Roman Pontiffs from Peter to about 366 A.D.[11] St. Augustine lists them down to about 400 A.D.[12] There is a great deal of evidence after the Fourth Century to show the unbroken line of Peter's successors down to the present bishop of Rome.

Paralleling the proof for the unbroken line of Roman Pontiffs is the proof that the whole Christian world recognized this pontiff as having a primacy, not merely of honor, but of jurisdiction.

It is an easy matter to show that none of the non-Catholic sects can lay claim to the mark of apostolicity. Lutheranism was founded by Luther in 1520; Anglicanism by Henry VIII in 1534; Methodism by John Wesley in 1744 and so forth. They were all founded many centuries after Christ.

§ 16. *The second mark of the True Church is that this Church must be found among all races and in all ages.*

There are numerous passages in the Gospels which record that Christ stated that His doctrines would be taught to all nations. "And this gospel of the kingdom shall be preached in the whole world, for a witness to all nations" (Matt. 24:14). "Go into the whole world and preach the gospel to every creature. He who believes and is baptized shall be saved, but he who does not believe shall be condemned" (Mark 16:15). The term worthy of particular attention is "all nations." A nation here is not a sovereign state but a race, an ethnic division. Christ said that His Church would be found among all nations. It is impossible for Christ's Church to teach all nations unless it teaches in all ages, for new nations or generations of men are continuously appearing on the face of the earth.

The Catholic Church has a universality of time and of place. We have already made the inquiry establishing the first, namely, the fact that she has had a continuous line of supreme pontiffs going back to St. Peter. There is much evidence even in ancient history that the Church has always had universality of place. Already in 107 A.D., St. Ignatius of Antioch in his *Epistle to the Smyrneans* (Ch. 8) calls this Church by its most striking feature, namely, its universality. He was the first to call it "The Catholic (meaning universal) Church." Less than a century later, St. Irenaeus lists the geographical regions to which the Church had spread. He lists Italy, Gaul, Spain, Germany, North Africa, Egypt, and the Near East.[13] A check of these regions on a map of the ancient world shows that the Church had already spread to every major quarter of the civilized world. Tertullian, Origen, St. Augustine, and many others give a great deal of evidence on the universality of the Church in early times. Present day non-Catholic churches do not have a universality of time, for they were founded many centuries after Christ.

§ 17. *The third mark of the True Church is that it is one; it has a single government and teaches a single set of doctrines.*

Christ implied that His Church would have a single government when He gave supreme power to only one man and his successors. He implied this unity when He said, "And other sheep I have that are not of this fold. Them also I must bring, and they shall hear my voice, and there shall be one fold and one shepherd." (Jn. 10:16) The unity of doctrine that Christ's Church must teach flows from the fact that the doctrine is true, immutable, and indispensable. Christ referred to the body of doctrine that His Church was to teach as "My Gospel" or "This Gospel" thereby indicating a unified set of truths.

The Catholic Church has always been one in government, for it has always had one supreme ruler on earth, namely, the Roman Pontiff. It has always taught a single set of doctrines. We show this by comparing the doctrines taught by the Church in ancient, medieval, and modern times. Since there is harmony among them, it is evident that the Church has taught and still teaches only one body of truth. A compilation of all the official pronouncements of the Holy See and ecumenical councils proves the Church's unity of doctrine. Many catechisms and creeds drawn up at different places are still extant. A comparative study of them proves beyond doubt the perfect uniformity of the Church's teachings throughout the world and throughout the ages. St. Irenaeus put it this way: "The Church having received this preaching and this faith, although scattered throughout the world carefully preserves it. She also believes these points of doctrine just as if she had but one soul and one and the same heart, and proclaims and teaches them and hands them down with perfect harmony as if she possessed but one mouth."[14]

Non-Catholic sects lack the mark of unity. The Lutheran Church is a sect distinct from the Methodist Church. But the lack of unity does not stop there. There are twenty-two autonomous groups of Methodists. Many more figures could be cited on this score.

§ 18. *The fourth mark of the True Church is that it is holy in its founder, in its doctrines, and in many of its members.*

The fact that Christ proved His divinity warrants the conclusion that the True Church is holy in its Founder. The True Church is also holy in its doctrines. When we say that doctrines are holy, we mean that they produce holiness in a person who believes them and puts them into practice. The doctrines taught by Christ's Church must do this for they are the supernatural means that lead one to one's supernatural goal. A last phase of the mark of sanctity is that it is characteristic of Christ's Church to have many holy members. Christ Himself said that the practice of the heroic virtues, and the willingness to suffer for Him would indicate sanctity.

We saw that the line of supreme rulers of the Catholic Church goes back in unbroken succession to Peter upon whom Christ built His Church. In the last number, we saw that the body of doctrine taught by the Catholic Church today is the very one it received from Christ. It has been characteristic only of the Catholic Church to have the members of its clergy willingly leading lives of celibacy in order to be completely free to carry on Christ's work. This Church alone has had immense numbers of its members practicing the herioc virtues of religion; that is, poverty, chastity, and obedience. This Church alone has suffered so much persecution throughout her history.

Christ did not give His Church a name, but He did give it four marks of identification. The True Church derives its name from its four marks, and so is called the One, Holy, Catholic and Roman Church.

§ 19. *Jesus Christ endowed His Church with infallibility in teaching doctrines of faith and morals.*

We prove the existence of the Church's endowment of infallibility by studying the nature of the commission it received from Christ. Christ said to His Church, "Go into the whole world and preach the gospel to every creature. He who believes and is baptized shall be saved, but he who does not believe shall be condemned." (Mark 16:15) When Our Lord uses the term "gospel," He is referring to the articles of faith and precepts of morals that all are to accept and to live by. But notice that the acceptance of these teachings is a matter of the most serious obligation. It is certainly not an optional affair. If Christ's teachings as transmitted by His Church were or even could be admixed with error, then Christ would be obliging the acceptance of error under the penalty of damnation! This is abolutely impossible, for Christ, being God, is infinitely truthful.

What persons in the Church are endowed with infallibility? They are the successors of those whom Christ authorized to teach in His place. Christ gave Peter a primacy of power over the entire Church. Included in this primacy is the authority to teach. Since the Roman Pontiffs succeed to Peter's power, they by themselves can make infallible pronouncements. Christ also commissioned the Apostles to teach, but he commissioned them as a group. The bishops of the Church are the successors of the Apostles. When the majority of the

bishops dispersed throughout the world or assembled in ecumenical council teach the same doctrine, we can be sure that it is true. Singly, bishops can err. The infallibility of the pope and the bishops does not stem from their native ability, but from the power of God protecting His Church from error.

§ 20. *The Catholic Church has solemnly defined that the truths of revelation are found in Sacred Scripture and in Sacred Tradition.*

Sacred Tradition is the set of truths of revelation delivered by God to the Church in spoken form. We can say that it is the Unwritten Word of God. The Gospels tell us that Christ preached to the people. Nowhere is there evidence that He committed His teachings to writing. In fact, He left no writings. All documents which claim Him as their author are invariably apocryphal. Christ died in about 30 A.D. When the Church began its task of saving souls on Pentecost, it had all the truths and means necessary to do so. That was about twenty years before the first book of the New Testament was written. The conclusion is that God delivered the truths of revelation to His Church in spoken form.

The Church has defined that some of the truths of revelation were also delivered to us in written form.[15] That writing is called Sacred Scripture or the Bible. It was inspired by God, for He was so present to its human authors that only what He ordered them to write, they understood and were moved to write down faithfully in apt words and with infallible truth. The very last verse of the New Testament to be written cautions us that all that we must believe and do is not found in the Bible. But it is found completely in Sacred Tradition. There is no conflict between Scripture and Tradition, for God is ultimately the Author of both of them. The Church taught

Tradition before she received the New Testament writings. With several qualifications, we can say that the Church does not teach us revelation because she first discovered it in the New Testament. It is more accurate to say that it is found in the New Testament because it was being taught by the Church.

§ 21. *In general, it may be said that the Church defines a doctrine when that doctrine is attacked by heresy.*

God's revelation to man ended with the Apostles. That revelation has been transmitted intact through the teaching authority of Holy Mother the Church to all men for the past nineteen centuries. She has not added to or subtracted from the number of truths confided to her by God. But this does not mean that she has not invited gifted theologians to unfold the hidden meaning of individual truths. Our understanding of a doctrine can and should be deepened. A theologian, who unfolds the meaning of revealed truth, certainly does not add foreign ideas to it. Newman likened the deepening of our understanding of a doctrine to the growth of a tree. An oak remains an oak at every stage of its development.

Historically speaking, the Church usually defines that a doctrine has been revealed by God only when that doctrine is attacked by heresy. The reason is obvious. It is to prevent confusion caused by the sudden appearance of the error. For the first fifteen centuries of her existence, the Church made comparatively few definitions on the Sacraments. The reason is that very few heresies attacked the Sacraments during this whole period. But in the Sixteenth Century, the leaders of the Protestant revolt did attack them almost *en masse*. We quote verbatim many of the decrees of the Council of Trent on the sacraments throughout this book. The student should notice their clarity and precision. They leave no room to doubt the meaning of the truth revealed to us by God through His Church.

§ 22. *An act of faith is a firm assent of the intellect to a truth revealed by God, made by the command of the will assisted by divine grace, and motivated by the authority of God, who cannot deceive or be deceived.*[16]

There are four elements in an act of faith. (1) The intellect is man's knowing power. It grasps truth. Apologetics proves that there can be no reasonable doubt that God transmits revealed truth through the medium of His Church. Since God cannot err, His Truths must be accepted firmly and unwaveringly. (2) Even though the evidence for the divine authority of the Church is conclusive, there is nothing about it which prevents a person from deliberately blinding himself to its cogency. Such a person does not want to believe. He has some irrational motive for turning away from the evidence. By making an act of faith, a person freely chooses to accept valid evidence presented to him. (3) Man is born into this world in the natural state. Of himself, he cannot do anything which is above his native powers. He clearly cannot perform a supernatural act, which is precisely what an act of divine faith is. For this, he must receive supernatural help. That help is divine grace. (4) Since God is infinite in every respect, it is absolutely impossible for Him to deceive, for this would be against His attribute of infinite Truthfulness. Faith may be likened to a telescope. A person may have perfect vision, but there are some stars so far away that they cannot be seen with the naked eye. If we look at them through a telescope, they can be seen and studied. The truths of revelation are so profound that they cannot be discovered by our unaided intellects. God offers us the gift of faith so that we can see them, study them, and live according to them. The sacraments we now study are truths revealed by God.

NOTES

1. Alexander, *College Apologetics* (Chicago: Henry Regnery Co., 1954).
2. St. Thomas Aquinas, *Summa Theologica*, Par. 1, Ques. 2, Art. 3.
3. St. Augustine, *Confessions*, Bk. I, 1.
4. Wilhelm-Scannell, *Manual of Catholic Theology* (London: Kegan-Paul Co., Ltd., 1890), Bk. I, p. 6.
5. Chapman, *The Four Gospels* (New York: Sheed and Ward, 1944), p. 5.
6. *Adversus Haereses*, Bk. III, 1, 1.
7. *De Praesciptionem Haereticorum*, Ch. 32.
8. Felder, *Christ and the Critics* (London: Burns, Oates, 1933), pp. 17-117.
9. *H. E.*, Bk. II, 15, 2.
10. *Adversus Haereses*, Bk. III, 3.3.
11. *De Schismate Donatistarum*, Bk. II, 1.
12. *Ep.* 53.
13. *Adversus Haereses*, Bk. I, 10.2.
14. *Adversus Haereses*, Bk. I, 10.2.
15. D-784.
16. Alexander, *College Moral Theology* (Chicago: Henry Regnery Co., 1958), p. 56 ff.

II

Sacraments in General

§ 1. *A sacrament of the new law is defined as a permanent, sensible rite instituted by Christ to confer grace efficaciously.*

The term "sacramentum" had a variety of meanings in ancient times. It was used in both sacred and profane contexts. Among pagans, it was used to refer to a soldier's oath of allegiance. Among early Christians, it was used to designate any religious sign or symbol. The ambiguous term "sacramentum" was used as a translation for St. Paul's term "To Mysterion." (Eph. 5:32) There was little uniformity among the early Fathers and Doctors of the Church on the precise meaning of the term. Its present meaning was fixed in the Twelfth Century. The definition above embodies the distinctive nature of the rite used today. Let us note the elements of a sacrament. (1) The definition quoted here refers to a sacrament of the New Law. It is specifically different from Old Law rites which were sometimes called sacraments. (2) A Sacrament is a permanent rite. It was confided to the Church from the beginning; it has been used in the Church up to the present day; it will be used until the end of time. The Church cannot do away with it. (3) It is a sensible rite; that is, it can be grasped by one or more of the senses, such as sight, hearing, taste, or touch. There is external action

24

connected with its administration and reception. (4) When we say that Christ instituted the sacraments we mean that He determined their essential elements at least in a general way. He may have left it to His Church to lay down regulations and to devise ceremonies surrounding their administration. (5) A sacrament works efficaciously; that is, its effectiveness does not depend on the fitness or sinlessness of the person who administers it. In fact, some effects may result in spite of the moral unworthiness of the one who receives it. All of these elements are indispensable for each sacrament. We shall point them out when we study each one in greater detail.

§ 2. *The Church has solemnly defined that the sacraments of the New Law are exactly seven in number.*

There is reference made to all seven sacraments in ancient Christian literature. The oldest extant, extra-Scriptural writing, namely, The *Didache,* (c. 60-100 A.D.) certainly refers to two and probably three of them. Tertullian (+ 220 A.D.) tells us of five of them in different passages of his writings. Ancient writers composed monographs on individual sacraments. A great many of these are extant today. The distinction of being the first writer or theologian to treat all seven sacraments in a single work seems to belong to Peter Lombard. His work is called *The Book of Sentences* finished in about 1150 A.D. It proved to be one of the most influential writings of the Middle Ages. The Church administered all seven sacraments from the very beginning of her existence.

For centuries there was no need to make any solemn pronouncement as to their exact number. But in the Sixteenth Century, the leaders of the Protestant revolt made the sacraments a prime target for their attacks. In 1523, Luther finally decided to keep only two of the seven sacraments. Melanchthon, Luther's colleague, at first wanted to keep only two sacraments, but in 1530 decided to keep two more. Anglicanism (1534) decided to keep four of the seven. Calvinism (1560 A.D.) discarded five of them. To prevent any confusion as to the number of sacraments confided to the Church, the Council of Trent in 1547 A.D. defined, "If anyone should say that the sacraments of the New Law are more or less than seven; namely, Baptism, Confirmation, Holy Eucharist, Penance, Extreme Unction, Holy Orders, and Matrimony, or even that any of these is not truly and properly a sacrament, let him be anathema." (D-844) The student must not imagine that this was the first time that reference was made to the sacraments in official pronouncements of the Church. We find these pronouncements dating from the first centuries of Christianity.

§ 3. *Jesus Christ immediately instituted all seven sacraments of the New Law.*

The Council of Trent defines, "If anyone should say that the sacraments were not all instituted by Jesus Christ, Our Lord, let him be anathema." (D-844) When we say that Christ *immediately* instituted the sacraments, we mean that He personally fixed all of their essential elements. He substantially designated the matter and form, the purpose, and the properties of each one of them. Christ could have empowered the Church to institute them, but, *de facto,* He did not do so. We have several reasons for our conclusion. (1) The first and clearest is the statement of the Church quoted above. (2) There is evidence in the Gospels of Christ instituting four of the seven sacraments. This fact has led theologians to conclude that immediate institution by Christ was an essential element of each sacrament. The Gospels are not theological treatises, nor biographies of Christ. Therefore, it is not surprising that they do not tell us when He instituted the three besides the four referred to here. This information apparently did not fit into the theme of any of the four Gospels. (3) It is extremely unlikely that Christ would have begun the task of personally instituting the sacraments and then, when it was only half finished, to turn it over to the Apostles for completion. This unlikelihood is heightened when we recall that the Apostles themselves needed instruction even after Christ had ascended into heaven. It took the descent of another Person of the Blessed Trinity to complete it. (4) When the Church was launched on her task of saving souls on Pentecost Sunday, she was fully equipped with all the means necessary to distribute grace. She wanted for nothing. This would not have been true if some of the sacraments had not as yet been instituted or if they were instituted by Apostles — even with Christ's authorization — after Christ had departed from this earth. These same arguments appear in the writings of those ancient Fathers who wrote on the sacraments.

§ 4. *Each sacrament has its own special matter and form which will remain substantially unchanged until the end of time.*

The terms "matter" and "form" were adopted by the Scholastic theologians of the Middle Ages from Aristotelian philosophy. They are used in Scholastic cosmology to explain hylomorphism. Although they are not exactly the same, the roles of matter and form in the sacraments resemble the roles of these two things in the composition of material objects. (1) The matter of a sacrament is the perceptible but yet undetermined element used in the conferring of the rite. By itself, this matter is completely powerless to bring about a sacramental effect. It is not half of a sacrament. It receives determination or precise meaning only when joined with the form. In the case of four of the sacraments, the remote matter is also a material thing as water for Baptism, and chrism for Confirmation. In the case of three sacraments, the matter is perceptible to the senses but is not material; for example, sorrowful confession for Penance. (2) The form of a sacrament is the element which determines or gives precise meaning to the matter. Again, by itself, it is not half a sacrament. It has power to bring about a sacramental effect only when used in conjunction with the matter. The form may be described as the set of words that accompanies the application of the matter. (3) The matter and form of each sacrament were somehow determined by Christ, at least in a general way, for otherwise He could not be said to have instituted them. Since Christ gave the sacraments to the Church as permanent rites, it follows that their matter and form will remain substantially the same until the end of time. This is of considerable practical importance. If the rite of a sacrament, that is, the joining of the matter and form, is essentially different from the way laid down by Christ, then its unity is destroyed and no sacrament is conferred. This remains true even though the disruption of the rite takes place accidentally.

§ 5. *The sacraments are effective means of grace to all who do not place an obstacle in the way of this grace.*

The term in the proposition which must be given special attention is the term "effective." It means more than "successful." In many explanations of this subject, the word "efficacious" is used. In this explanation, the word "effective" means that Christ embedded the power to confer grace in the rite of the sacrament. It does not need to draw power from any other source to fulfill the purpose for which it was instituted. The effectiveness of a sacrament, therefore, does not depend on the sinlessness of the one who administers it. We shall see that some sacraments confer some effects even though their recipients are in the state of mortal sin. If the soil be good and the seed be good, the diseased hand of the sower will not destroy, nor cut down the size of the crop. The only way that a sacrament can be prevented from conferring grace is by the recipient of the sacrament placing a barrier to this grace. But this does not prevent a sacrament as such from being an effective means of grace. It keeps its status so long as the rite is properly performed. It is not even necessary for the one who administers it to believe in its effectiveness. The sacraments can be effectively conferred even by atheists. The efficacy of sacraments, independent of the sinlessness of the one who confers them, was denied by heretics in ages past. In the Fifth Century, the Donatists in North Africa held this error. Luther went a step farther and denied all inherent efficacy in the sacraments. He said they were merely rites that might be used to incite one to be pious. Zwingli said that they were empty symbols of Christian belief.

§ 6. *A sacrament has no effect on a person who refuses to receive it.*

The sacraments are rites instituted by Christ to permit one to receive grace. Along with the many wonderful means that God has given us to advance toward our supernatural goal, He has left us with free will. He offers His love to everyone, but forces it upon no one. If the sacraments could work their salutary effects on persons who refused to receive them, God would be taking away free will. A person who steadfastly refuses to receive a sacrament does not receive its grace, nor even a title to grace even though the rite is properly administered to him.

A person might be still willing to receive a sacrament even though he made his intention to receive it at some time in the past. His intention to receive a sacrament may be actual or virtual. In some cases, it can even be habitual. We shall point out the instances when one can receive the full benefits of a sacrament even though he is, for instance, unconscious at the time of its reception. In the cases referred to in this paragraph, the person willingly receives the sacrament even though he has not renewed the intention he once made.

It sometimes happens that a person steadfastly refuses to receive a sacrament while he is conscious but then lapses into unconsciousness or into a coma. Moral theologians have laid down certain norms approved by the Church as to how these cases are to be handled. The person is to be given the benefit of the doubt. The proper sacraments may be administered to him conditionally. If he has retracted his refusal but is unable to express his retraction, he has at least one prerequisite for valid reception, namely, the desire to receive it.

§ 7. *Christ instituted the sacraments that we might receive supernatural help in every phase of our spiritual development.*

Every phase of the process of justification is supernatural. A person cannot make any progress in advancing toward his goal without the supernatural help that only God can give. That help is called actual grace. The process of justification is completed by the reception of sanctifying grace. A person needs actual grace to receive, to increase, and to keep sanctifying grace. A sacrament receives its specific character from the role it plays in one's supernatural life. Each sacrament has a special role in that life; that is, it has a part that only it can play. All of the sacraments confer actual grace. If the actual grace of each sacrament was not specifically different from that of the other sacraments, there would have been no need to institute seven of them. One would have been quite sufficient, but as it is, they play seven roles in the same drama. For example, a nurseryman who specializes in roses uses a variety of tools in his work. He uses a hoe, a sprayer, a budding knife, shears, and others. Each tool is used for a different purpose but they all concur in the same ultimate goal; namely, the production of beautiful roses. Each sacrament confers a different actual grace, but they are all meant to further one's progress in the spiritual life.

Notice that the proposition says that a sacrament *entitles* one to actual grace needed to fulfill a specific task. It may be necessary to perform that task for a long time — even for a lifetime. The title to actual grace that a sacrament gives lasts as long as the specific task lasts. The actual grace keeps on coming so long as there is sanctifying grace in the soul. As soon as a mortal sin replaces the sanctifying grace, the title to actual grace remains but the person has no right to sacramental grace. Any of it that he would receive would be due to God's liberality. The title is "reactivated" when sanctifying grace again replaces mortal sin. It must be added, however, that a number of theologians hold that one has some congruous rights to actual grace even when one has mortal sin on his soul.

§ 8. *Sacramental actual grace is the transient, supernatural influence of God in the soul moving it to perform salutary acts.*

Sacramental actual grace is actual grace given to enable one to fulfill the purpose of the sacrament. It is a transient help. It strengthens one at a particular time and in a particular way. This help cannot be stored. If it is not used when it is given, its power is lost.

The actual grace one derives from the sacraments is clearly a supernatural influence having a definite place in the process of justification. It enables one to increase or to keep the sanctifying grace he has already received. Only God can give this grace, for it is essentially superior to any created help.

Actual grace influences the two powers of the soul, namely, the intellect and the will. These two powers do not act isolated from each other. They act as a unit. The grace of which we speak suggests salutary thoughts to the intellect. The distinctive feature of these thoughts is that they are geared to action. A person receiving this grace sees that he may not or should not remain indifferent to the suggested course of action. It may be a truth that he must believe, a sin that he must avoid, a motive that should impel him, an opportunity that he must seize, and so forth. A salutary thought is one that invites the action of the will.

Actual grace strengthens the will to choose good. The term "strengthen" here does not mean that grace merely facilitates the effort of a natural will. This is the heresy of Pelagiansim. Grace does not leave the will a natural power. It elevates the will to the status of a supernatural power capable of performing supernatural acts. A person in sanctifying grace is habitually in the supernatural state. But he must still receive new actual grace to perform new supernatural acts.

Even under the influence of grace the will remains perfectly free. It is a choosing power which works in close conjunction with the intellect. Actual grace enables the intellect to see what must be done for one to increase in sanctity. The grace then, enables the will to choose what the intellect sees.

§ 9. *Each sacrament entitles its recipient to a different actual grace called sacramental grace.*

Every phase of our earthly life has its counterpart in our supernatural life. We can distinguish certain phenomena in our natural development. There may even be crises and times of stress. A close study of the sacraments shows that these same phenomena and crises also occur in one's supernatural development. Jesus Christ provided us with powerful means of help at every point on our journey toward the goal that He has assigned to us. A person is born; he takes food to maintain strength; he grows to adulthood; he receives medical attention when sick; he convalesces after a siege of sickness; he has earthly parents; he has a family of his own. Notice now how the sacraments parallel these stages. A person is spiritually born in Baptism; he receives the Holy Eucharist to nourish his spiritual life; he grows to spiritual adulthood by receiving Confirmation; he rids himself of spiritual disease by Penance; if he be in danger of death, he can rid himself of at least some of the remains of sin by the reception of Extreme Unction; Holy Orders provides him with spiritual parents; Matrimony elevates the roles of natural parents so that they can rear their children to be citizens of the kingdom of heaven.

The repeatability of the sacraments also fits in neatly with the parallel set down above. A person can be born and can grow to adulthood only once. Baptism and Confirmation which parallel these can be received only once. He needs food daily; he may receive the Holy Eucharist daily. Sickness and disease can strike him at any time; he can receive Penance as often as he wishes. While he can receive Extreme Unction only once in the same sickness he may receive it at any time of the day or night for he can fall into the danger of death from sickness at any time. The other two are not necessary for each individual. A person can suffer harm at any stage of his natural life. He will suffer harm if he neglects to receive the sacrament instituted to provide care in the corresponding stage of the supernatural life.

§ 10. *Each sacrament gives its recipient the title to the special actual grace he needs to meet a particular crisis is his life when he needs special help from God.*

The Council of Trent teaches that there is a difference among the sacraments. A majority of theologians hold that the difference between the sacraments must be found in the effects of each sacrament;[1] many of them hold that all sacraments confer the same sanctifying grace. This would seem to indicate that the peculiar feature of each sacrament must be sought in the actual grace that each sacrament confers. Each sacrament entitles its recipient to a different kind of actual grace. Theologians have attempted to pin down the specific difference between sacramental grace and actual grace. They have concluded that there must be a reason why sacramental grace rates a different label. Sacramental grace may be actual grace, but not all actual grace is sacramental grace. Some hold that sacramental actual grace has a special perfection or power which ordinary grace lacks. Others hold that it gives a claim to those actual graces which correspond to the particular purpose of the sacrament. They hold that by virtue of this claim, the graces are given out as needed.

What are the needs for which the sacraments supply actual grace? Baptism entitles its recipient to the actual grace he needs throughout life to perform his ordinary duties as a Catholic; Confirmation gives one the actual grace he needs to profess publicly his faith in Christ; Holy Eucharist gives one the grace to grow rapidly in the love of God; Penance entitles one to the grace he needs to keep the resolution not to sin which he has just made in confession; Extreme Unction gives the grace to overcome the temptations and fears that often accompany the danger of death; Holy Orders gives the grace to fulfill well the duties of the clerical state; Matrimony gives the grace to perform well the duties of the married state.

§ 11. *Sanctifying grace infuses supernatural life into the soul. This life is essentially superior to natural life.*

The propostion embodies a truth of stupendous magnitude. Let us see how Christ described it to the people. He spoke to people unaccustomed to abstract ideas. He, therefore, found it necessary to use copious examples and illustrations. In illustrating the greatness of the new life of grace,

Christ used an example familiar to all listening to Him, namely, the difference between life and death.[2] He was speaking to healthy, living people, and yet He said that they were dead. The implication is obvious. Supernatural life is as far superior to the natural life with which one is born, as natural life is superior to death. Why did Christ choose this example? It is because there is nothing farther away from life than death, and nothing farther away from death than life. Supernatural life is as far above natural life as any life can be. It is essentially higher. The superiority is not one of degree but of kind. A thousand degrees of natural life could never add up to one degree of supernatural life. To tell the whole world that God wants us to have this "new" life was the burning passion of St. Paul. It is the theme woven into all of his epistles and sermons. When he tells the Corinthians, Ephesians, Romans, and the others that they must be "reborn," and must become "new creatures," and must "put on Jesus Christ," he is telling them that they must receive supernatural life if they wish to attain their supernatural goal. He repeatedly drives home the truth that in comparison with this new life everything else pales into insignificance, and that they must not allow fire, sword, rejection, imprisonment, or any other danger to separate them from "the love of God which is in Christ Jesus, Our Lord." (Rom. 8:38)

§ 12. *When a person receives sanctifying grace, he receives a share in the life that is proper to God.*

In this number, we consider the root of the greatness of sanctifying grace. Everything else we say about it takes its meaning from this explanation. In the last number, we saw that sanctifying grace gives one a new life, a life that is essentially superior to natural life. All creatural life is natural in itself. This is true of angels as well as men. Even though angels have wonderful intellects, they are natural beings as such. If some of them see God face to face, it is because they have received the sanctifying grace that elevated them onto the supernatural plane. It has been revealed that angels were created in sanctifying grace. There is no intermediary plane between the natural and the supernatural, between life proper to creatures and life proper to the Creator. It follows that sanctifying grace gives us a life essentially superior to natural life, a life which is a share of the life proper to God.

We must not think that sanctifying grace makes a person lose his limitations or finite capacities. It does not make him lose his individuality and cause him to become absorbed in God like drops of rain that fall into a lake. Then too, we must not think that the divine life that one shares by virtue of having sanctifying grace in his soul has been split off from God. God is a pure Spirit, devoid of parts. It is impossible to split off a part of Him. We are evidently confronted with a mystery that must be accepted on faith. But even from the few ideas we have learned from revelation, we can gather some notion of the staggering greatness, importance, and value of grace. We can understand a little better why St. Paul could not find suitable adjectives to express its superlative qualities.

§ 13. *God loves a soul in sanctifying grace with the same love that He loves Himself.*

Love is seeking to confer or to preserve goodness or perfection upon or in another. This is possible if the other person has a capacity to receive the perfection. If that capacity has already been filled, one loves another by seeking to insure that he will not lose the perfection. The greatness of the love that one has for another is measured by the magnitude of the perfection he seeks to confer or to preserve. A spiritual benefit is clearly of greater value than a temporal one. Seeking to preserve another's spiritual health is more important than seeking to preserve his physical health. Let us now apply these ideas to God's relationship to a soul in sanctifying grace. God must love Himself, for He sees Himself to be the infinitely perfect being. He must love a soul in sanctifying grace, for He sees that soul to be a participator in the life proper to Him. It follows that God must love that soul with the same love that He loves Himself. There is, however, a difference in the intensity of these types of love. God loves Himself with an infinite love because He is an infinitely perfect being. His love for a soul in sanctifying grace is not of infinite intensity.

A person can only have a finite amount of sanctifying grace in his soul, but any finite capacity can be enlarged or made greater. This is true of the amount of one's sanctifying grace. While one is living on earth, he receives from God the supernatural help needed to enlarge his store of grace. On the other hand, he can also lose the grace that he has amassed, but God gives him the supernatural help he needs to fight off all temptations that would cause him to lose it. All this is a consequence of God loving a soul with the same love that He loves Himself.

§ 14. *Sanctifying grace entitles one to citizenship in the kingdom of heaven.*

We consider the aspects of sanctifying grace one by one in order to get a clearer notion of this grace. Actually, we are merely unfolding the implications of the truth that a person in sanctifying grace shares in the life proper to God. The very first sentence of the Sermon on the Mount reads, "Blessed are the poor in spirit for theirs is the kingdom of heaven." (Matt. 5:3) In describing the Last Judgment, Christ said that He would say to the just, that is, to those in sanctifying grace, "Come, blessed of my Father, take possession of the kingdom prepared for you from the foundation of the world." (Matt. 25:34) Several other passages containing similar ideas could be quoted here. In ancient times, a king was looked upon as being the source of the prosperity that his kingdom enjoyed. In God's kingdom, it follows that He is looked upon as being the Source of the benefits. Citizenship in a kingdom meant that one was entitled to share in the prosperity of the realm provided by the king. In the present context, a citizen of God's kingdom is entitled to the benefits that God has provided. We are told what those benefits will be in heaven. The citizens of God's kingdom will have the happiness and joy that only God can give. Seeing God face to face is supernatural happiness. This is the happiness that is proper to God. One first receives title to this happiness by his very first reception of sanctifying grace, but he does not begin to enjoy it then. He must wait until after death to have the fruition of grace that he received while still on earth.

§ 15. *A person can receive or increase sanctifying grace only during his life on earth.*

It would be wrong to consider one's life before death and one's life after death as isolated from each other. In fact, life before death makes very little sense unless seen in relationship to life after death. The first is a period of probation; the second is intended to be a period of fruition. The presence or absence of sanctifying grace in the soul decides whether the period of probation has been a success or a failure. A person is worthy of reward only if he chooses good when he could have chosen bad. There is no merit or room for praise where there is no freedom of choice. While one sojourns on earth, he is completely free to chose or to reject. He can choose a thing one day and reject it the next. He can select one of several alternatives. He can even choose not to choose.

At death, a fixity seizes man's will. He can no longer choose and reject. He is still free, but he uses his freedom to perpetuate the selection he had made at death. He can no longer choose good instead of bad or vice versa. Since it is impossible for the soul to change its decision after death, it must keep forever whatever merits or demerits it received up to that point. Our interest in this is that one cannot increase his store of sanctifying grace after death. This teaching is repeated by the Church's doctrine on the finality of one's Particular Judgment. She teaches that this judgment takes place immediately after death, that it covers the deeds of one's whole lifetime, and that it is irrevocable. This teaching is incompatible with any opinion that holds that one can increase or lose his store of sanctifying grace after his period of probation has been terminated. Prayers for the dead, while perhaps very salutary, cannot gain for them a higher place in heaven.

§ 16. *The sacraments confer more grace on persons better prepared to receive them.*

This proposition in no way conflicts with the fact that the sacraments are efficacious signs of grace. If a sacrament does not at times confer grace, the difficulty must be sought, not in the sacrament, but in the dispositions of its recipient. We must then examine the capacity of the soul to receive grace. The presence of mortal sin blocks all sanctifying grace from entering the soul even though one is unconscious of this sin's presence. But there are other things besides mortal sin that can be present in the soul. Perhaps we should not call these other things "obstacles" to grace, for they do not block it out completely. Let us call them "hindrances" to greater grace. They cut down or lessen the amount of grace that a sacrament can infuse into the soul. These hindrances are venial sin and affection for sin. A person who commits venial sin shows that he does not love God as much as he should. He has affection for sin when he neglects to take the necessary means to rid himself of a habit of venial sin. These hindrances cut down the amount of grace that one can receive from a sacrament because they lessen the charity or fervor with which a sacrament can be received. Let us illustrate. When sponges are harvested from the ocean floor, they are filled with bony material, sand, and so forth. They must be treated and cleaned. Their capacity to absorb water is measured by the thoroughness with which they were cleaned. The presence of foreign matter will cut down the sponge's capacity to absorb water. In like manner, a person about to receive a sacrament can enlarge his capacity for the grace by ridding himself as thoroughly as possible of venial sin and affection for sin.

§ 17. *The conditions necessary for the valid reception of a sacrament do not usually coincide with those necessary for its fruitful reception.*

Only in the case of Penance are the conditions for fruitful reception exactly the same as those for valid reception. There is variation in the conditions for valid and for fruitful reception in the cases of the other six. A person receives a sacrament when the rite is properly administered to one capable of receiving it. It is possible to receive a sacrament while not receiving its grace. Some sacraments cannot be administered to a person a second time within a fixed period. For example, Extreme Unction cannot be received validly a second time by one in the same danger of death.

A person receives a sacrament fruitfully when he receives sanctifying grace along with the valid reception of the sacrament. Mortal sin is the only thing that can block the entry of this grace into the soul of a baptized person. Venial sin or affection for venial sin will not prevent the fruitful reception of a sacrament.

The sacraments give both sanctifying and actual grace. Sanctifying grace is the first fruit of all the sacraments. Along with sanctifying grace come actual graces given for the proper end of each sacrament. Then there remains a title or right to further actual grace to be given at the proper time. If no sanctifying grace is given in the reception of a sacrament, the person has no right to any actual graces either. Some hold that some grace may be given to a sinner who has a title to grace, but he does not receive it because he has a strict right to it.

§ 18. *A person who has received a sacrament validly but unfruitfully will receive its grace when all mortal sin has been removed from his soul.*

If a sacrament was received validly but unfruitfully, its grace can be received at a future time provided the person still retains title to this grace. We saw that this is possible with all the sacraments except Penance. Penance cannot be received validly unless it is also received fruitfully. Mortal sin is the obstacle that makes fruitful reception impossible. There are several ways that this mortal sin can be removed, and the "impounded" grace received by the recipient of the sacrament. (1) If one received the sacrament sacrilegiously, that is, he deliberately and freely received it while in mortal sin, he must make an act of perfect contrition or he must receive valid absolution in order to receive the sanctifying grace to reactivate the title to actual grace. (2) It may well happen that a person received a sacrament in mortal sin but he was not conscious of the presence of this mortal sin. Even though he did not realize his state of sin, he is deprived of grace. He received the sacrament unfruitfully, but not sacrilegiously. He receives the graces of the sacrament by making at least an act of imperfect contrition for all his serious sins. (3) What has been said above certainly applies to the sacraments which can not be repeated within a fixed time. Holy Communion is a special case. One receives it when he receives the Sacred Species. If he has received it unfruitfully because he is unconscious of the presence of mortal sin he can receive its grace provided he removes the mortal sin before the Sacred Species dissolve. He removes that sin by making at least an act of attrition. If he received it sacrilegiously, he must make an act of perfect contrition or receive valid absolution.

§ 19. *A person who deliberately receives a sacrament in mortal sin commits a grave sacrilege.*

A sacrilege is the abuse of a person, place, or thing publicly and specially consecrated to the service of God. A sacrament is obviously one of these sacred things, and to receive one sacrilegiously is a sin against the First Commandment of God. A person is guilty of a grave sacrilege in the reception of a sacrament when the sinful reception is deliberate and free. It is deliberate when the agent has clear knowledge of the seriousness of his act or when he is acting on a doubtful conscience, that is, when he has good reason to suspect that the act he is about to perform is forbidden. An act is free when the impediments to the will do not prevent it from being a human act. One is guilty of sacrilege in receiving a sacrament in mortal sin even if he plans to recover the fruits of the sacrament at a future date. Sacrileges can be grave or light, that is, they can be mortal or venial sins. While it is no sacrilege to receive a sacrament in venial sin, it is a venial sacrilege to commit a venial sin in connection with the reception of a sacrament as when a penitent tells a venial lie to the priest in confession. Unless excusing circumstances are present, it is a sacrilege to administer a sacrament to one who will receive it invalidly or unfruitfully. A priest, for example, would be guilty of a sacrilege if he pronounced absolution over a "penitent" who refused to make a firm purpose of amendent. A couple administering Matrimony to each other would thereby commit a serious sacrilege if they plan to practice birth control after the marriage has been contracted.

20. *One who lacks complete certitude as to his freedom from mortal sin may receive a sacrament provided he has a solid reason for holding that he would receive it fruitfully.*

One may never act when the moral value of the act he is about to perform is uncertain or doubtful in his mind. He must resolve this doubt before he may act. He has a doubt when he thinks an act may be permissible but knows that his judgment may be wrong. He is guilty of sin when he "takes a chance" on the moral permissibility of his act. This principle of morality is true, not only regarding the reception of the sacraments, but regarding morality in general. Willingness to act on a doubtful conscience indicates a willingness to sin.

There are times when certitude is impossible regardless of how completely the case is investigated. One may then use probabilism or its equivalent in resolving this impasse. He must take the following steps. The case must be thoroughly investigated by one competent to do so. If certitude is still impossible, one may act provided he has at least one, good, solid reason for judging the act to be permitted. He is then not acting on a doubtful conscience. One has a doubtful conscience when he is uncertain of the moral value of an act before an investigation has taken place. He can have a probable conscience only after the investigation has taken place. The Church never permits one to act in the first case; she does permit him to act in the second.

The application of the above principles to the reception of the sacraments is obviously important. If one has reason to suspect that he has mortal sin on his soul, he may not receive a sacrament deliberately and freely until his doubt is resolved. If he thoroughly investigates the matter and discovers that he has at least one, good, solid reason for thinking that he has the requisites for fruitful reception, then he may receive the sacrament. He has fulfilled the directives of competent theologians for resolving a difficult moral case. One must guard against the reckless use of these principles.

§ 21. *One must be empowered by God to administer a sacrament validly.*

We read that in the Third Century, the Montanists held that there was no real difference between clergy and laity among Christians. The error was resurrected in the Sixteenth Century when Luther interpreted *I Peter 2:9* in a completely arbitrary way. The conclusion that he tried to draw from his erroneous interpretation is that anyone is empowered to administer the sacraments. It was necessary for the Church through the Council of Trent in 1547 to define the official teaching held from the beginning. The Church said, "If anyone shall say that all Christians have power to administer the word and all the sacraments: let him be anathema." (D-853)

It is not difficult to see why Christ could require that one be specially empowered to administer the sacraments. Christ merited the grace that is distributed through the sacraments. It is His property. He, therefore, can lay down conditions under which it is to be distributed. As a matter of fact, He has laid down the indispensible condition that one cannot administer a sacrament unless empowered to do so. For a person to attempt to do so without this authorization is a case of attempted usurpation. In the case of five of the sacraments, the power to administer them validly is transmitted through Holy Orders. Everyone with the use of reason has the power to administer Baptism. Baptized persons can administer Matrimony to other baptized persons. The student must not think that this power is the only requisite necessary to administer a sacrament validly. It is one of the elements necessary for all of the sacraments. Each sacrament may have others added to this one. Those elements together with the conditions necessary for lawful administration will be studied when the sacraments are examined individually.

§ 22. *A person who has God's permission to administer a sacrament validly must also have the Church's permission to do so lawfully.*

The study of apologetics conclusively proves that Christ founded only the Roman Catholic Church to carry on His work of saving souls. On the first Pentecost Day, the Church was equipped with all the means needed to lead people to their supernatural goal. Of paramount importance among these means were the sacraments. They were confided to the Church. She was charged with a two-fold responsibility toward them. She had to distribute them to all who reasonably asked for them. She had to see to it that no abuse grew up around their administration. One cannot fulfill responsibilities without corresponding authority. Since the Church's responsibility is clear, her authority is equally clear. The Church has prescribed that all those empowered by God to administer the sacraments validly must nevertheless be licensed by her to administer them lawfully. Keep in mind that God has authorized the Church to lay down this regulation.

The Church's motive in requiring that all who administer the sacraments receive her permission to do so is not the desire to keep the sacraments away from men, but to prevent abuse, to preclude reckless distribution which eventually would redound to the spiritual harm of the Church's members. We have many parallels of this procedure in civil matters. A person who has successfully finished medical school may not practice medicine without a state license. Even after that license has been issued, it can be revoked if the physician abuses it. The purpose of this procedure is not to deprive people of medical attention, but to make sure that they receive it from competent doctors. The same motive lies behind the licensing of lawyers, engineers, architects, nurses, teachers, and other professional people.

§ 23. *Those who can confer the sacraments validly and lawfully must administer them to all who reasonably ask for them.*

Christ instituted the sacraments for the spiritual benefit of men. He did not give us the opportunities to receive the sacraments without at the same time imposing on us an obligation to make use of them. And when He gave us the right and duty to receive the sacraments, He imposed an obligation on empowered persons to confer them. (1) A parish priest is bound in justice to administer the sacraments. Since he has the right to the support of the laity, so does he have the duty to distribute the means of grace to them. This duty obliges the parish priest when the law obliges people to receive the sacraments, when people need them to overcome sin or temptation, and when people ask for them in order to advance in the spiritual life. A parish priest who refuses a request for the sacraments in these circumstances can easily be guilty of mortal sin. (2) A priest who does not have the care of souls, such as a member of a religious order not working in a parish, is bound in charity, not justice, to administer the sacraments. But this obligation can bind him under penalty of mortal sin. The author wishes to add the observation based on work in several parishes that the willingness of priests to administer the sacraments is far greater than the willingness of the laity to receive them. (3) The sacraments must be administered when reasonably requested. It is perfectly reasonable to call a priest to administer the Last Sacraments during the night or in inclement weather. An unrepentant birthcontroller is unreasonable when he requests to be absolved. Neither is one reasonable when one requests the sacraments when their administration will cause scandal as the administration of Holy

ommunion to a drunken person. In the vast majority of
ases, requests for the sacraments are perfectly reasonable and
riests are happy to administer them even outside of regularly
:heduled hours, as those set for confessions.

NOTES

1. Pohle-Preuss, *Sacraments* (St. Louis: Herder, 1944), Vol. I, p. 71.
2. Jn. 4:15; Jn. 6:47 ff.

III

Baptism

§ 1. *Baptism is the sacrament by which a man is spiritually born by means of washing with water and the invocation of the Three Persons of the Blessed Trinity.*

God wishes us to have a happiness far superior to any that we can experience on earth. Earthly happiness is short and limited because it is produced by possessing limited goods. The happiness of heaven is complete and everlasting because it comes from seeing God face to face. In short, the happiness of heaven is a share of the happiness proper to God. No happiness could be greater, no goal could be higher.

A person cannot reach his supernatural goal in heaven unless he lives a supernatural life on earth. This flows from the fact that the goal to be reached and the life needed to reach it must be on the same plane. Man is born into this world with only natural powers. They are totally inadequate to help him climb onto the higher plane. God alone can furnish the new help in the form of sanctifying grace or actual grace.

All actual grace is given to help us to receive or to preserve sanctifying grace. A soul in sanctifying grace has been elevated to the plane on which it has supernatural life. It now has a life as far above natural life as natural life is above death. The person has become an adopted child of God; he has been

born; he has become a new man; he has become an heir to
he kingdom of heaven; he has received title to the joy of
paradise. All of these flow from the fact that he shares in the
life, beauty, and love proper to God.

A person is first ushered into the incomprehensibly wonderful realm of sanctifying grace by the fruitful reception of the
sacrament of Baptism. The phrases used by sacred orators
to describe it are far from being exaggerations. They are
really feeble attempts to describe effects so wonderful that
a lifetime of contemplation could not grasp.

2. *The Church teaches the absolute necessity of Baptism for
salvation.*

There are several types of necessity. The first is the necessity
of means. A thing is of a necessity of means when it is impossible to bring about a desired effect without it. The cause
admits of no exception or substitution. The need for using
this particular cause is complete and absolute. Even the
greatest difficulty will not dispense one from using this
cause if one wants to secure the desired effect. The second
type of necessity is necessity of precept. A competent authority
commands the use of a particular cause in order to bring
about a desired effect. But in this case, conditions can be so
difficult that a person could be excused from blame if he does
not obey the precept. This cause does admit of exceptions and
substitutions. The need of using a particular cause in this case
is not absolute but relative. There is nothing contradictory
between the two types of necessity we have discussed. A cause
can at once be of a necessity of means and a necessity of precept.

The Church teaches that Baptism has both of the types of
necessity mentioned above. It is in this way that we must interpret the canon of the Council of Trent regarding this sacrament. It reads, "If anyone shall say that Baptism is optional,

that is, not necessary for salvation: let him be anathema.
(D-861) The Church was impelled to make this definition be
cause of the different ways that the leaders of the Protestan
revolt were interpreting the term "necessary." Very few c
them held that it was of necessity of means for salvatior
Many of them said that the reception of Baptism was bindin
only by a necessity of precept. This is surprising in the fac
of the loose meaning Protestants attached to the term "sacra
ment." The Quakers, founded by George Fox in 1624 A.r
followed the Protestant view on the necessity of Baptism as
sacrament to its logical conclusion. They held that even ar
adult could go to heaven without being baptized.

§ 3. That Baptism is necessary of means and of precept *
clearly stated in both Scripture and Tradition.

In Sacred Scripture we read that Christ said "Amen, amen
I say to thee, unless a man be born again of water and th
Spirit, he cannot enter into the kingdom of God.."(Jn. 3:5) I
this passage, the term "man" means any human being regard
less of age or race. Christ eliminates all restrictions as to wh
must be baptized in order to be reborn. He offers no substi
tute for Baptism; He excuses no one from receiving it. Thi
is an indication that the reception of Baptism is of necessity o
means of salvation.

When Christ was about to ascend into heaven, He commis
sioned the Apostles with the words, "Go, therefore, and mak
disciples of all nations, baptizing them in the name of th
Father, and of the Son, and of the Holy Spirit."(Matt. 28:18
The parallel passage in St. Mark's Gospel, while slightly differ
ent in wording, says the same thing. It reads, "Go into th
whole world and preach the gospel to every creature. He wh
believes and is baptized shall be saved, but he who does not be
lieve shall be condemned."(Mark 16:15) These latter passage
at least prove that the reception of Baptism is of necessity o

recept. Christ imposes on the Apostles and through them
n the Church the obligation to teach and to baptize; He
kewise imposes on "all nations" the correlative duty to be-
eve and to be baptized. Here again Christ in no way restricts
ho must believe and who must receive Baptism.

St. Augustine is evidently summarizing the teaching of the
Church from the beginning of its existence when he writes,
Whoever says that even infants are vivified in Christ when
they depart this life without the participation of His Sacrament (Baptism) both opposes the apostolic preaching and con-
emns the whole Church which hastens to baptize infants, be-
ause it unhesitatingly believes that otherwise they cannot pos-
ibly be vivified in Christ."[1] It would be difficult to match the
larity of this passage with other passages found in Patristic
ritings.

4. *A child can be validly and lawfully baptized even before
e has reached the use of reason.*

The proposition refers primarily to the Baptism of infants.
As early as the Fifth Century, there were heretics who denied
he need for infant Baptism because they denied the existence
f original sin. Their denial was refurbished in the Sixteenth
Century. The Second Council of Milevis in 416 A.D. con-
emned the first group; the Council of Trent condemned the
econd with the words: "If anyone should say that infants . . . .
fter having received Baptism are not to be numbered among
he faithful, and, therefore, when they have reached the years
f discretion are to be rebaptized, or that it is better that their
Baptism be omitted . . . . let him be anathema." (D-869) We
ave already quoted the Gospel passages referring to Baptism.
t was noted that no one is excused from the reception of Bap-
ism. This clearly includes infants and children.

There are a number of very clear quotations from the writ-
ngs of the early Fathers that could be made here. In the

Second Century, St. Irenaeus of Lyons wrote (+202) "Chri
came to save all men through Himself; all, I repeat wh
through Him are born again (baptized) unto God; infant
youth, men, and the old aged."[2] In the Third Century, Or
gen of Alexandria (255 A.D.) wrote, "The Church has recei
ed from the Apostles the tradition to confer Baptism als
upon little children."[3] In 415 A.D. St. Jerome rhetorical
has a Pelagian ask why *infants* are baptized by the Churc
He then answers, "That sins may be forgiven them in Ba
tism."[4]

The necessity of baptizing infants is obvious from the do
trine of the universality of original sin. While one is in or
ginal sin, he is an enemy of God and totally incapable c
reaching his supernatural goal. We have seen that the nece
sity requiring the use of Baptism to have this sin removed
one of means. The conclusion is that Baptism is to be admir
istered to infants as well as to persons of other age levels.

§ 5. *Baptism is the only sacrament that can remove origin*
sin from the soul.

God endowed our First Parents with sanctifying grace, tha
is, the new life necessary for them to reach their assigne
goal. They lost this new life for themselves and for the
children by committing original sin. Every human bein
except the Blessed Virgin, was conceived with this sin on h
soul. This state of fallen nature is more than human natur
stripped of sanctifying grace. Original sin is a real sin, for
is an effective barrier to supernatural life. By His death o
the Cross, Our Divine Lord won for us a new opportunity t
reach the supernatural goal that God has assigned to us. Th
indispensable gateway to all of these spiritual riches is th
sacrament of Baptism.

By a fruitful reception of Baptism, the process of initi
justification is completed. A person becomes a friend of Go

nd an heir to heaven. But even a fruitful reception of Baptism does not mean that a person will infallibly reach the goal ssigned to him. He can subsequently commit mortal sin, nd thereby lose justification. "If anyone shall say that a man nce justified can sin no more, nor lose grace, and that therefore, he who falls and sins was never truly justified . . . . let him e anathema. (D-833) The Council of Trent was compelled to nake this definition in the face of heresies teaching the exact pposite. Our Divine Lord could have instituted several ways y which a person could receive initial justification. There s great prudence in instituting only one way, namely, reception of Baptism. Not only would more than one way be superuous, but having only one would avoid any confusion that vould inevitably arise if there were more than one. It is atently easier to teach and to learn the essentials of one than o teach and learn the essentials of many.

6. *It is possible to receive Baptism validly but unfruitfully.*

The conditions necessary for valid and for fruitful Baptism re not the same. It is possible, therefore, to receive Baptism vithout receiving the sanctifying grace that Christ intended t to confer on the occasion of one's being baptized. There s a variation in the conditions for valid reception of Baptism lepending on the age of the subject to be baptized. If the ubject is an infant, the only condition necessary for valid Baptism is that he was not previously baptized. Unwillingness on the part of parents does not prevent the sacrament rom being validly conferred or received. If the subject has eached the use of reason, two conditions are necessary for valid reception, namely, the subject was not previously baptized and he has at least a habitual intention to receive the acrament. A person who refuses to receive this sacrament annot receive it validly. He may be baptized conditionally when he has lapsed into unconsciousness.

An infant, that is, one who has not as yet reached the us
of reason receives Baptism fruitfully when he receives i
validly. All who have not as yet reached the use of reason ar
classified as infants regardless of their chronological age. Thi
obviously includes persons who are habitually feeble-minded
If a subject has reached the use of reason and has fallen int
mortal sin, he must make either an act of perfect or imperfec
contrition in order to receive Baptism fruitfully. There i
no need to make these acts if one has fallen into only venia
sin, for sanctifying grace can coexist in the soul with venia
sin. But one must remember that these venial sins are not r
moved without proper sorrow even when one receives th
sacrament fruitfully.

§ 7. *Circumstances dictate what one who received Baptisn
unfruitfully must do to receive its grace.*

The Church officially teaches that not only original sin bu
also all actual sins are removed by a fruitful reception o
Baptism. The Council of Florence in 1439 A.D. taught, "Th
effect of this sacrament (Baptism) is the remission of ever
sin, original and actual, also of every punishment which is du
to the sin itself." (D-696) The Council of Trent in 155
taught, "By putting on Christ in Baptism, we are made an en
tirely new creature in Him, obtaining a full and complete re
mission of all sins." (D-895)

We have seen that an adult can receive Baptism validly bu
at the same time can lack the requisites for fruitful reception
He receives it unfruitfully if he fails to make the prescribed
act of contrition for any unforgiven mortal sin. If a person
received Baptism unfruitfully because he unwittingly failed
to make the prescribed act of contrition for mortal sin, he can
receive the grace of the sacrament by making at least an act
of attrition for this sin. If he received Baptism sacrilegiously
that is, if he freely and deliberately did not make an act o

orrow for his mortal sins, he must make an act of perfect con-
rition or receive absolution in order to receive the grace of
Baptism. It is possible for one to commit new mortal sins
after he has received Baptism unfruitfully. He must then
make an act of perfect contrition or receive absolution to receive the grace of Baptism. When a person makes his confession, he must not confess the mortal sins he committed before
he was baptized. Those sins are not matter for absolution.
He must, however, have proper sorrow for them.

By committing mortal or venial sin, a person incurs a debt
of guilt for sin and a debt of temporal punishment due to the
sin. The Council of Trent teaches that Baptism effects complete remission of all sins. This sacrament has the power to
remit even temporal punishment due to sins committed before its reception.

§ 8. *Baptism imprints a mark on the soul that cannot be
erased.*

The reality of the indelible mark conferred on the soul in
Baptism is proved by the explicit teaching of the Council of
Trent. It defined, "If anyone say that in . . . . Baptism . . .
there is not imprinted on the soul a character, that is, a kind
of spiritual and indelible sign, by reason of which (Baptism)
cannot be repeated: let him be anathema." (D-852) There
are several things to be said concerning this mark. (1) It has
a reality or existence of its own. It is more than an idea. It
can and does exist outside the mind of one looking at the soul.
This mark is not like the power with which a person elected
president is invested. The power that a president receives
or loses does not change him physically. His title to power is
not stamped on his person. But the mark of Baptism is stamped
on the soul. It exists independently of another's gaze. We
may liken it to a brand on livestock. (2) The character or
mark of Baptism is spiritual and supernatural. All things

that are spiritual are not also supernatural. The mark mus
be spiritual, for the soul on which it is imprinted is a spiritua
substance. Keep in mind that there are both material an
non-material substances. A substance as opposed to an acci
dent is anything that can exist by itself. The mark must b
supernatural, for it transfigures me to Christ the Priest. Thi
is a deed and gift beyond my deserts and my nature. It car
only be imprinted by God. (3) The definition of the Churcl
does not qualify or limit the period when the mark of Baptisn
remains. It remains on the soul for all eternity. (4) The onl
requirement necessary to receive this mark is to receive th
sacrament validly. It is not necessary to receive it fruitfully
We must add, however, that this mark is "deactivated," tha
is, one does not have the right to the sacramental grace a
long as one is in the state of mortal sin.

§ 9. *Since Baptism confers its own indelible mark; it can b
received only once.*

The indelible characters which certain sacraments confe
entitle one to some share in the priesthood of Jesus Christ
This statement must not be interpreted in the heretical fash
ion that Luther did. He tried to erase the distinction betweer
clergy and laity. The participation that we refer to here i
different from the one conferred by Holy Orders. In St
Paul's *Epistle to the Galatians,* he bids the people "to put or
Christ." The Council of Trent uses this very passage in saying
that we "put on Christ by Baptism." Our Lord's Incarnation
His public ministry, His passion and death were parts of one
over-all mission. He was the Mediator between God and man
This is precisely what a priest is, namely, a mediator. The
Latin term "pontifex" meaning "priest" nicely expresses this
When we "put on Christ" in Baptism, we must put on or mus
share in His priesthood. That priesthood has an active and a
passive phase. Baptism confers principally the passive one

hat is, the baptized person receives title to the fruits of
Christ's priesthood. In themselves, these fruits are infinite.
Any limitation comes, not from God's power to give, but
from the soul's capacity to receive. The mark of Baptism is
person's title to those fruits. These truths form the basis for
he conclusion that Baptism can be validly received only once.
There is no room for it to work its effects a second time in the
soul of a recipient. The original sin it removes cannot revive.
The mark entitling one to a share in the fruits of Christ's
priesthood cannot be lost. The reservoir containing those
fruits is limitless. If Baptism could be received several times,
he several receptions could confer more spiritual benefits on
he soul of the recipient than if he received it only once.
These are the reasons why we conclude that this sacrament
can be received only once.

10. *The mark of Baptism entitles one to the special actual
grace he needs to avail himself of the fruits of Christ's Priesthood.*

When Christ commissioned His Apostles to carry on His
work, He said, "Go into the whole world and preach the
gospel to every creature. He who believes and is baptized shall
be saved, but he who does not believe shall be condemned."
Mark 16:15) We call attention to the use of the term "be-
ieve." Since a person's salvation depends on believing, the
erm must be interpreted in the light of all of Christ's teach-
ng and activity. The truths that Christ taught fall into
wo categories, namely, articles of faith and precepts of
morals. When Christ says that all must "believe" in Him, He
means a great deal more than giving intellectual assent to His
doctrines. This term means that one must accept Christ completely. He must put Christ's teachings into practice. He
must act like Christ. In short, he must lead a supernatural
life. A twofold duty is imposed on one who has decided to

lead a supernatural life. He binds himself to increase in the
love of God, and he binds himself to avoid anything that will
force the loss of this love. When a person assumes a duty, he
is also entitled to a right. In Baptism, one assumes the duty
to live a Christ-like life until death. In Baptism, he must also
receive the right to all the helps he needs to fulfill this duty.
The indelible mark of Baptism is his permanent title to these
supernatural helps, that is, to the actual graces. Many hold
that mortal sin makes one lose the right to the grace even
though it does not destroy the mark. New grace will again
flow from it by right as soon as the person recovers sanctifying
grace.

§ 11. *Baptism begins the work of one's configuration to
Christ; it prepares one to receive the other sacraments which
complete this configuration.*

The mark of Baptism prepares one to participate in the
fruits of Christ's redemption. If there is no obstacle to grace
in the soul, the mark calls forth from God the sanctifying
grace necessary for salvation. Baptism does not prepare one
for justification. It produces justification. This is why it is
the only absolutely indispensable sacrament.

Baptism makes one capable of receiving the remaining six
sacraments which complete one's configuration to Christ. It
can prepare a person to use the other means of grace which
intensify this configuration. Prayer, sacraments, and good
works are the means instituted to transmit sanctifying grace.
All three remain completely ineffective channels of grace for
one who has not received Baptism of water or its equivalent.
By prayer, an unbaptized person can receive actual grace but
never sanctifying grace unless he first makes an act of perfect
charity. Good works in the sense of meritorious works are
deeds from which one receives an increase of sanctifying grace.
A person obviously cannot perform meritorious works before

Baptism or its equivalent, for such a person still has original sin and this sin blocks sanctifying grace from entering the soul. These are some of the reasons why we hold that Baptism ultimately gives title to all the benefits that Christ wanted the members of the human race to have.

§ 12. *Baptism confers on one the right to the actual grace he needs to perform all of his duties as a Catholic.*

So long as the mark of Baptism coexists in the soul with sanctifying grace, it can call forth some grace from God. The latter type of grace is a special kind of actual grace called sacramental grace. In fact, this sacramental grace can only come from Baptism. Actual grace suggests salutary thoughts to the intellect; it strengthens the will to choose a salutary course of action. The sacramental grace of Baptism suggests those salutary courses of action that one must take to increase or to preserve his supernatural life. These thoughts can influence action. On the positive side, they can impel one to prayer at different times throughout the day. They can point out the wisdom of frequent reception of the sacraments and strengthen one to overcome obstacles to frequent reception; they can enlighten the mind to the value of performing the spiritual and corporal works of mercy; they can urge the practice of mortification and the observance of the Commandments.

The sacramental graces of Baptism can strengthen the will to avoid any and all mortal sins; they can suggest methods to root out a habit of sin; they can brace one against even the most violent temptation. These actual graces can flow in a never-ending stream into the soul of a baptized person. Let us illustrate the constant flow of sacramental grace of Baptism. Few people appreciate the importance of water more than a desert nomad. He is careful not to waste a single drop of it. Imagine his reaction if he were suddenly transported from the Sahara to the foot of Niagara Falls. Here he sees the precious fluid tumbling over the brink in incredible abundance. He thinks that surely this flow is too valuable to go on for a long time. He waits to see the flow end. It keeps on coming. This parallel can be used to give us a better idea of the constant flow of sacramental grace that pours into the soul of a baptized person. Many Catholics look upon Baptism as a sacrament they received long ago. They forget that it is an inexhaustible gusher of spiritual benefits.

§ 13. *The remote matter of Baptism is natural water.*

For almost fifteen centuries, the whole Christian world understood the water prescribed by Christ for Baptism to be water in the commonly accepted sense of the term. The *Didache* (60-100 A.D.) leaves no doubt as to its meaning. It remained for certain "reformers" to say — without the slightest proof — that when Christ said "water," He meant "any liquid suitable for bathing." The Council of Trent said, "If anyone shall say that real and natural water is not necessary for Baptism, and on that account those words of Our Lord Jesus Christ: 'unless a man be born again of water and the Holy Spirit' are distorted into some sort of metaphor; let him be anathema." (D-858)

The remote matter of a sacrament is the material that is to be used in the performance of the rite. The natural water used in Baptism is that found in rivers, lakes, springs, rain, and so forth. It remains natural water even after small amounts of chemicals have been added to it to kill bacteria. Liquids that are almost entirely water but are usually not labeled water may not be used in Baptism. These would include such liquids as tea, milk, coffee, thin soup, and the like. To use these would constitute matter for a sacrilege and the Baptism would be invalid.

When Baptism is solemnly administered, the water used

must be properly blessed for Baptism. Small quantities of holy oil are used in the blessing. It is usually blessed on Holy Saturday. Solemn Baptism usually takes place in a Church or baptistry. The sacrament is administered with all the ceremonies prescribed by the Church. Unblessed natural water may be used for private Baptism. In this case, only the essential rite of Baptism is performed. Private Baptism is often administered in cases of emergencies in such places as accident rooms or maternity wards of hospitals. It can, of course, be administered anywhere and at any time.

§ 14. *The proximate matter of Baptism is washing with water.*

The proximate matter of a sacrament is the manner that the material is actually used in the administration of the sacrament. The proximate matter for valid Baptism is a true washing with water, that is, the water must actually flow over a major member of the body such as the head. There are three ways to apply the water in Baptism. (1) Baptism can be conferred by infusion, that is, the water is poured on the person being baptized. The Church anathematizes those who say that this is an invalid way to baptize. (D-856) When St. Peter baptized the several thousand converts of Pentecost, he most likely used infusion. The *Didache* (60-100 A.D.) explicity instructs the reader to "pour water on the head thrice in the name of the Father, and of the Son, and of the Holy Ghost."[5] (2) For about the first twelve centuries of the Christian era, Baptism was conferred by immersion as well as by infusion. As the name indicates, immersion is conferred by dipping or plunging the person into water. Although it is a valid way to baptize, the Latin Church has not used it for some centuries. An aborted fetus must be baptized. This is done by opening the membraneous envelope enclosing the fetus under water while pronouncing the form of Baptism. (3) Aspersion is Baptism by sprinkling. This was never widely used probably because it was too difficult to secure the washing necessary for the valid administration of the sacrament. It is not enough that water merely rest on the hair or skin. There must be a flowing. Any amount of water that truly flows over the head or major member of the body fulfills the washing prescribed for valid Baptism.

§ 15. *The form of Baptism must express the act of baptizing and must contain an explicit invocation of the Three Persons of the Blessed Trinity.*

The form of Baptism is the precise set of words that must be pronounced while the water is being poured on the person being baptized. The proposition says that it must express two things. The form of Baptism must express the action of the person administering this sacrament. The words, "I baptize thee" clearly do this. The phrase "to baptize" is derived from a Greek verb meaning "to wash" or "to plunge into water." It recalls the proximate matter of this sacrament. The form of Baptism must contain an explicit invocation of the Three Persons of the Blessed Trinity. As early as 382 A.D., the Church was called upon to emphasize this point in the face of certain heresies (D-82). The Gospels make it quite definite that Baptism must be administered with this invocation in its form. St. Augustine said that in his day it was easier to find heretics who did not baptize than it was to find heretics who did not invoke the Three Persons of the Blessed Trinity when they did. In the Latin rite, the form is "I baptize thee in the name of the Father, and of the Son, and of the Holy Ghost." In the Oriental rite, it is, "The servant of God is baptized in the name of the Father and of the Son and of the Holy Ghost." Both forms express the action of baptizing and the invocation of the Blessed Trinity.

The person who pours the water must also pronounce the form. The Baptism is invalid if one person pours the water while another pronounces the form. The pronouncing of the form must be simultaneous with the pouring of the water. The two things must form one unit. If the form is pronounced after the water is poured or vice versa, the unity of the rite is destroyed and Baptism is invalidly conferred. It is strongly urged that all Catholics learn how to baptize. It would seem that nurses and doctors are bound under pain of sin to learn how to confer this sacrament.

§ 16. *The Church prescribes under pain of mortal sin that whenever possible the ceremonies of solemn Baptism accompany the administration of this sacrament.*[6]

The ceremonies of solemn Baptism have been authorized and prescribed by the Church. These non-essential rites do not affect the validity of the sacrament. They can be changed or modified. In fact, the Church in recent years has permitted the vernacular to be the language used in the ceremonies of Baptism. These are the principal ceremonies of solemn Baptism: the pinch of salt symbolizes the wisdom of having embraced the true faith; the sign of the cross on the senses indicates the opening of these channels of knowledge to the pursuit of supernatural truth; the anointing with oils symbolizes the strength of the sacramental grace of Baptism; the breathing on the person being baptized shows that he becomes a temple of the Holy Ghost; the lighted candle represents the light of faith; the white cloth indicates the innocence which this sacrament produces; the meaning of the profession of faith and the renunciation of the devil are obvious.

The solemn ceremonies may be postponed when Baptism is administered by a layman, or when it must be administered in an emergency by a priest. But they must be supplied under penalty of mortal sin at a later date. There is no time limit within which they must be supplied, but this matter should be attended to as soon as it is convenient. It is a fact of pastoral experience that many infants who were baptized in emergency never have the ceremonies supplied to them due to the neglect of their parents. The ceremonies of solemn Baptism must be supplied even in the case of a person being conditionally re-baptized. This is the case when converts to Catholicism from a non-Catholic sect are received into the Church. The profession of faith and absolution from censure in the case of some converts are distinct from the ceremonies of Baptism even though they immediately precede the ceremonies.

§ 17. *A child of Catholic parents is to be baptized in the rite of his father.*[7]

The Church today authorizes a Latin rite and four principal Uniate rites, namely, Antiochean, Alexandrine, Byzantine, and Armenian. All the Oriental rites are very old and very beautiful. The Church does not want them lost. The Oriental rites must not be confused with the schismatic and heretical Orthodox sects. The Holy See exercises its jurisdiction over clergy and laity through the ordinaries of the different rites. She has laid down clear norms pointing out to laymen who their ordinary is, and to ordinaries who their subjects are. The rite of Baptism plays a major role in this determination. If his parents are of the same rite, a child is to be baptized in the rite of his parents.

If his parents belong to different rites, a child is to be baptized in the rite of his father. If this regulation is not observed, the child belongs to the rite in which he should have been baptized. We should notice that this is true even in cases where the parents belong to different Oriental rites. For example, if the father is an Oriental but the child is baptized as a Latin, the child still belongs to the Oriental rite even though there was no Oriental church in the place were they lived. He remains an Oriental even though the Oriental pastor gave permission for the Baptism to take place in the Latin rite.

It sometimes happens that a person of one rite wishes to transfer to another rite. The fact that he has attended Mass in the latter rite for a long time or has even gone to its parochial school or received his First Communion there does not transfer him to that rite. He must make application to the Holy See for permission to transfer his rite. If the Holy See judges that he has valid reasons to transfer, it will grant his request. When persons of different rites marry, the bride may elect to transfer to the rite of her husband, but a husband may not elect on his own to transfer to the rite of his wife. He must obtain permission to transfer to her rite.

§ 18. *An infant, not in danger of death, may not be baptized unless there is a well-founded indication that he will be raised as a practical Catholic.*

Baptism confers on a person the rights and privileges of being a Catholic. At the same time, it imposes on him the duty to obey the Church's commands directing him to his supernatural goal. An infant cannot express the desire to accept the rights and duties that come with Baptism. His parents and godparents do it for him. The priest who baptizes has the duty to see to it that parents and godparents are sincere when they promise that the child will be raised as a practical Catholic.

Where parents and godparents are practicing Catholics, the priest may presume that the child will also be raised as a practical Catholic. If the parents are not practical Catholics, the priest is required to have concrete proof that the child's religious upbringing will not be neglected. In many cases the only basis for hoping that the child will be raised as a Catholic is that lax parents begin to practice their faith and that other children of the family begin to receive a Catholic training, or that the godparents be sincere and trustworthy of their charge.

It sometimes happens that a non-Catholic parent vehemently objects to his or her child being baptized in the Catholic Church. The Catholic parent should then consult the pastor as to what can be done in these circumstances. A dying child is to be baptized even against the wishes of its parents.[8] Bigoted parents have no right to rob their child of the reward and happiness that God wishes all souls to have. These parents seriously abuse their authority as parents when they refuse to have their children baptized. They are easily guilty of sins of multiple malice.

§ 19. *Catholics are to have their infant children baptized as soon as the children can leave the house with safety.*[9]

The Church's solicitude for the speedy baptism of infants stems from the fact that salvation is impossible without this sacrament. Due to the great variety of circumstances that can surround individual cases, it is difficult to lay down a hard and fast time limit within which an infant is to be baptized. (1) An infant who is seriously ill and in danger of death must be baptized without delay. This emergency is a true sick call and the priest must be summoned immediately, that is, any time of the day or night. Prudence will dictate whether or not Baptism by a layman should be administered. Blameworthy delay in baptizing this dangerously sick infant can easily constitute matter for mortal sin. (2) Unless circumstances indicate otherwise, it is usually considered matter for venial sin to postpone the solemn Baptism of a child beyond three weeks after birth. It is held by all theologians that notable culpable delay in this matter is a mortal sin.[10] How long is "notable delay?" It is generally considered matter for a mortal sin to postpone needlessly the solemn Baptism of an infant beyond two or three months after birth. Some hold that it may not be postponed beyond one month without it being matter for serious sin. (3) There are a number of valid reasons that can be urged for postponing solemn Baptism. They are prolonged inclement weather, non-grave sickness, or poor transportation needed to take the child to the church. In mission areas of the country or of the world, the fact that a priest comes once a month or so is certainly a valid reason. Parish priests are familiar with a number of foolish excuses by which people attempt to cover up their neglect. Some "excuses" are the inability to select a name for the child, or to find godparents. It must be remembered that culpable delay in having infant children baptized also constitutes matter for scandal.

§ 20. *Catholic parents who offer their child to be baptized in a non-Catholic sect are guilty of mortal sin and are excommunicated.*[11]

The serious penalty inflicted on Catholics who have their children baptized in a non-Catholic sect is an indication of the seriousness of this crime. (1) The mortal sin and the excommunication reserved to the Ordinary is incurred by these Catholic parents even though the child is illegitimate or born to parents living in an invalid marriage. The Church condemns with the same excommunication the practice in some countries of baptizing the boys born of a mixed marriage in the religion of the father and the girls in the religion of the mother. The law explicitly states that all children born of a mixed marriage are to be baptized and raised only as Catholics. The Catholic party may not concede on this point even under pressure or "to keep peace in the family." (2) A Catholic guilty of the sin being discussed is suspect of heresy. He gives good indication that he holds that "one religion is as good as another." If he does not remove the cause for suspicion within six months after having been warned, he incurs the penalty for heresy which is a new excommunication.

(3) The offering of a child to a non-Catholic clergyman is forbidden even though the child will be validly baptized. The clergymen referred to can belong to either Protestant or Orthodox sects.[11] (4) It is difficult to see how a Catholic who offers his or her child to be baptized in a non-Catholic sect can escape committing an added mortal sin against charity, for he or she very likely causes great spiritual harm to the child. In many cases, the child remains unbaptized, for the non-Catholic clergyman does not properly perform the rite. Very often, the Catholic parties take no steps to correct the spiritual harm for which they are responsible.

§ 21. *To be baptized validly and fruitfully, an adult must consent to it, be properly instructed, give assurance to live as a Catholic, and have sorrow for mortal sin.*[12]

These conditions are laid down to determine whether or not one has really decided to make God his supernatural goal in life. (1) An adult in the sense used in the proposition is not necessarily one who has reached his majority. It is anyone who has reached the use of reason; that is, one who knows right from wrong. A person reaches this stage when he is about seven years old. (2) An adult must consent to be baptized, for otherwise the administration of this sacrament is invalid.   (3) A person cannot sincerely choose God unless he also intends to learn what he must do to reach Him. He must, therefore, learn at least the basic truths of Catholic doctrine. If he is in danger of death, he may be baptized if he knows the truths that must be known by a necessity of means. If he is not in danger of death, he must know the truths that must be known by a necessity of precept, namely, at least the substance of the Lord's Prayer, Creed, Commandments, and the Sacraments he receives.   (4) The priest who baptizes an adult may rightly ask for external evidence of sincerity on the part of the person who requests Baptism. He may inquire into the catechumen's attendance at Mass and observance of the Commandments of God. (5) It is a sacrilege to receive or to administer deliberately and freely the sacrament of Baptism when the conditions for both valid and fruitful reception are lacking. An unrepented mortal sin prevents Baptism from being received fruitfully. An adult in mortal sin must make at least an act of imperfect contrition before being baptized. We have already pointed out how one who receives Baptism unfruitfully may later on receive the graces that God intended to confer through this sacrament.

§ 22. *Converts to Catholicism from a non-Catholic sect are sometimes conditionally re-baptized.*

Anyone with the use of reason can validly baptize provided he performs the rite properly. He can confer a true sacrament even though he confers it unlawfully. This becomes a matter of prime importance when we consider the validity of persons baptized in non-Catholic sects. The validity of their Baptism must be investigated before the proper steps can be taken to receive them into the Church. It is impossible to lay down a general rule that will resolve all doubts in this matter. The Orthodox sects have fairly definite beliefs on the nature and necessity of Baptism and on the manner in which it must be administered. But there is no uniformity among Protestants on this subject. We have seen that some of these sects do not even hold that Baptism is necessary for salvation. It does not follow that a person's adherence to a particular Protestant sect indicates that he was baptized in that sect. The priest receiving the person into the Church will be far more inclined to question the validity of the Baptism of Protestants than validity of the Baptism of those belonging to an Orthodox sect. If he has even one solid doubt as to the validity of the person's Baptism, he will re-baptize the person at least conditionally. The condition is that he intends to confer Baptism only if the "baptism" by the non-Catholic clergyman was invalid. Immediately, preceding the ceremony of conditional Baptism, the convert makes a public renunciation of past errors and makes a profession of faith in the teachings of the Church. The general practice is to have the convert make his first confession and receive conditional absolution immediately after having been conditionally re-baptized. He is usually required to make his First Communion within several days after having been received into the Church.

§ 23. *The priest is the ordinary minister of solemn Baptism; any person with the use of reason can validly and, at times, lawfully baptize.*

In solemn Baptism, the rite whereby the sacrament is actually conferred is accompanied by ceremonies and prayers prescribed by the Church. It usually takes place in the baptistry of a parish church. While any priest is the ordinary minister of solemn Baptism,[13] only a parish priest may lawfully baptize his parishioners. Proper permission must be obtained for a priest to baptize persons of another parish. A person belongs to the parish where he now lives even though he has not registered there. If he does not belong to a national parish, he must belong to a territorial parish. A deacon is the extraordinary minister of solemn Baptism.[14]

Anyone with the use of reason can validly baptize. He need not be a Catholic. He can be a heretic, infidel, or even an atheist who does not believe that the rite he performs has any supernatural effects. He must, of course, properly and seriously perform the rite of Baptism. It is important that he at least have the implicit intention to do what the Church wants done in administering this sacrament. As early as the Third Century, the Church explicitly taught that even heretics can validly baptize. This was brought out during the well known controversy between Pope St. Stephen and St. Cyprian.[15] The

Roman Pontiff reminded the bishop of Carthage that the received teaching was that anyone, even heretics, could validly
baptize and that baptized converts from heretical sects were
not to be re-baptized.

Laymen must have the Church's permission to baptize law·
fully in an emergency. The reason for this regulation is not
to deprive people of Baptism, but to prevent abuse from
creeping into the administration of this most important sacrament. Everyone already has this blanket permission to baptize when the person to be baptized is in danger of death and
a priest cannot be called in time to administer even private
Baptism.

§ 24. *It is a serious precept to have at least one qualified godparent in solemn Baptism; there should be at least one in
private Baptism.*[16]

The rights and duties of godparents resemble the rights
and duties of natural parents. Those possessing authority
must guide their subjects to their proper goal. And those subject to authority must accept the guidance of their superiors.
The Church wants us to have godparents so that the important duty of guiding a person toward his supernatural goal
will receive the attention that it should receive. The Church
directs under penalty of mortal sin that in solemn Baptism,
there be at least one, but not more than two godparents. If
there be only one, the godparent must be of the same sex as
the godchild. The father or mother of the child cannot also
be its godparents. Persons who have lost their right to act as
godparents because of, for example, being excommunicated,
cannot validly accept this office. Grandparents can act as godparents.

To assume the office of godparent *validly,* a person must
fulfill these conditions: he or she must have the use of reason,
be baptized, have the intention to assume the office, touch the

child while it is being baptized, and be free from invalidating impediment such as excommunication.[17]

To assume the office of godparent *lawfully,* a person must fulfill these conditions: he or she must have all the qualifications for valid godparenthood, be at least fourteen years old, and know the essentials of Catholic doctrine. When the office of godparent is assumed by proxy, the godparent must designate the person who is to act in his place during the actual Baptism.[18] A child, who is baptized in an emergency without godparents receives them when he is brought to church to receive the ceremonies of solemn Baptism.

§ 25. *Godparents in Baptism assume the duty binding under pain of mortal sin to see to it that the godchild is raised as a practical Catholic.*

In recent years, there has been a tendency on the part of certain Catholics to look upon the office of godparent as merely being one of honor. In reality, it imposes heavy responsibilities. Unless persons intend to fulfill these duties they have no business accepting the office. (1) There are three principal phases to the work of raising a child as a practical Catholic. The child is to be properly instructed in Catholic doctrine. Godparents will see to it that the child either attends a Catholic school or regularly attends catechism classes. The child must receive the sacraments when prescribed by law and then frequently thereafter. The frequency must be such so that the child will form a good habit. The child must observe the Commandments of God and of the Church. Regular assistance at Sunday Mass is a fairly good indication of whether or not the child is practicing his religion. (2) Godparents must begin to perform their duties as soon as the natural parents begin to fail to raise the child as a practical Catholic. The duties that godparents assume are lifelong duties. They are never outgrown and they may not be rejected. (3) The duty of godparents binds under pain of sin. Serious neglect, a common occurrence today, is matter for mortal sin. Slight neglect is matter for venial sin. Godparents are to check periodically to ascertain whether or not the godchild is living as a practical Catholic. Failure to do this results in culpable ignorance. Godparents are not guilty of sin if their sincere efforts have proved fruitless. (4) Just as godparents are bound under pain of sin to guide their godchild, so does the godchild have the duty binding under penalty of sin to follow the guidance of his godparents. One of the great causes of leakage in the Church is the lack of adequate religious training of children attending non-Catholic schools. A great deal of this harm could be prevented if godparents would attend to the duties they assumed at the time of the Baptism.

§ 26. *The custom of giving a child being baptized the name of a canonized saint dates back to the Fourth Century.*[19]

The Church solemnly teaches that the saints who reign in heaven can intercede with God in behalf of those on earth. Any honor that we pay them redounds to the greater honor and glory of God. One way that we can honor the saints is to imitate their virtues. The name of a canonized saint is given to a child in Baptism so that the child will have a special heavenly patron and may have a particular model of virtue to imitate. In keeping with this, we should familiarize ourselves with the biography of our heavenly patron. It is perfectly permissible to give variations of the saint's name. This is, in fact, a very common practice. Examples of these variations are too many to list here. Pamphlets are available listing suggested Christian names and their variations.

The duty to impose a Christian name does not bind parents under pain of sin. But if the parents fail to do this, the Church directs the priest who baptizes to do it. The priest gives the child a saint's name as a second name; and this second name is also entered into the baptismal register of the parish. In practice, this matter causes very little difficulty.

At the time of the Baptism, parents should ask the priest to issue a certificate proving that the child has received the sacrament. This document must be produced when the person receives First Communion, Confirmation, and Matrimony. It is wise to keep this record, in view of the fact that vast numbers of people move from parish to parish and from city to city. Another reason is that, due to the constant shifting of population, some parishes are eventually suppressed and their records transferred to another parish. It may then be more difficult to secure a copy of the baptismal record quickly.

§ 27. *In extraordinary circumstances, perfect charity has some of the effects of Baptism of water.*

The perfect charity referred to in the proposition is often called Baptism of desire. The student must not be confused by the similar sound of words and imagine that Baptism of desire means only a desire for Baptism. It implies a great deal more than this latter desire. The essential note of Baptism of desire is perfect charity, that is, loving God above all things because He is infinitely worthy of our love. It implies the rejection of all serious sin and a desire to do all that God wants one to do to save his soul. This act constitutes at least an implicit desire to receive Baptism of water. To refuse to receive Baptism of water is in itself matter for mortal sin.

There were several ocassions when the reality of Baptism of desire is mentioned in the documents of the Holy See. (cf. D 388, 413, and 796) The passage in Sacred Scripture which is quoted as pointing to the existence of Baptism of desire is John 14:21. It reads, "But he that loves me shall be loved by my Father, and I will love him and manifest myself to him." This passage says that a person who loves God will be loved

by God. The bond of love existing between God and this
person indicates the presence of sanctifying grace. This grace
coming into the soul destroys sin, even original sin. St. Bonaventure wrote, "God obliges no one to do the impossible —
and therefore it must be admitted that Baptism of desire
without Baptism of water is sufficient, provided the person in
question has the desire to receive baptism of water, but is
prevented from doing so before he dies."[20]

There are several important differences between Baptism
of desire and Baptism of water. The most notable is that Baptism of desire does not imprint an indelible mark on the soul
entitling it to sacramental grace and the right to receive the
other sacraments, nor does it make one a member of the
Mystical Body of Christ.

NOTES

1. *Ep.*, 28.
2. *Adv. Haer.*, Bk. II, 22-4.
3. *Com. in Rom.*, 5-9.
4. *Dial. Contra Pelg.*, 3-13.
5. Ch. 7.
6. Canon 755.
7. Canon 756.
8. Canon 750.
9. Canon 770.
10. Davis, *Moral and Pastoral Theology* (London: Sheed and Ward, 1945), Vol. III, p. 65.
11. Canon 2319, No. 1.
12. Canon 752.
13. Canon 738.
14. Canon 741.
15. Pourrat, *Theology of the Sacraments*, 4th Ed. (St. Louis: B. Herder, 1930), pp. 116-130.
16. Canon 762.
17. Canon 765.
18. Canon 766.
19. Canon 761.
20. *Com. in Sent.*, IV, 4-2.

IV

Confirmation

§ 1. *Confirmation is defined as the sacrament by which we receive the Holy Ghost so that we may be enabled to profess publicly our faith in Jesus Christ.*

Confirmation has all the essentials of a true sacrament, but it also has specific elements whereby it retains its distinct nature. In common with all the other sacraments, Confirmation was instituted by Christ; it has its own special matter and form; it confers grace efficaciously.

Confirmation has several elements that other sacraments do not have. The first of these is that by this sacrament a person receives the Holy Ghost in a special way. This is an indwelling of the Holy Ghost which is different from His indwelling in the soul of a person who has received sanctifying grace in Baptism. The second is that Confirmation imprints a special indelible mark on the soul that only this sacrament can imprint. Its purpose is different from the one conferred in Baptism. It fits its recipient to participate in a special way in the priesthood of Christ.

This sacrament has a part in the supernatural development of a person that parallels a phase in one's natural growth. By Confirmation, a person, who was spiritually born in Baptism, becomes a spiritual adult. The fourth is that Confirmation entitles its recipient to a special actual grace that can be received from no other sacrament. This is the sacramental grace one needs to profess publicly his faith in Christ. We shall see that this grace is a help to perform a positive task. It would be wrong to think, as many do, that a person is given the special actual grace of this sacrament only to remain firm in the faith during time of persecution. A comparison of these elements with those of Baptism shows that Confirmation is indeed a maturing of the life infused by Baptism.

§ 2. *The Church solemnly teaches that Confirmation is a true sacrament.*

The Council of Trent, in the face of Protestant denials, defined, "If anyone says that the Confirmation of those who have been baptized is an idle ceremony, and not rather a true and proper sacrament; let him be anathema" (D-871). The same truth was stated on several occasions in history before this council defined it.

The existence of Confirmation is proved from Sacred Scripture. Before revealing several truths, Christ prepared the people beforehand for the revelation by promising to reveal it. We recall His promise to confer the primacy on Peter. He also promised to institute Confirmation sometime before He actually did so. These are the words of this promise: " 'He who believes in me, as the Scripture says, From within him there there shall flow rivers of living water.' He said this, however, of the Spirit whom they who believed in him were to receive; for the Spirit had not yet been given" (John 7:38). Notice how this passage refers to a continuous source of grace due to a special indwelling of the Holy Ghost in persons who already believed.

The time and the place of the actual institution of Confirmation are not recorded in the New Testament. We know that it was instituted, for we read in the *Acts of the Apostles* that St. Peter and St. John administered it. "Then they laid their hands upon them and they received the Holy Spirit. But when Simon saw that the Holy Spirt was given through the laying on of the apostles' hands, he offered them money" (Acts 8:16). These details supplement the information that was given in the promise of the institution. The passage in the *Acts of the Apostles* indicates that this sacrament can be administered only by especially empowered persons and that it is administered by a precise external rite, namely, the imposition of hands. It repeats that a striking feature of Confirmation is that by it there is caused a special indwelling of God the Holy Ghost. There is much evidence of Confirmation in the writings of the Fathers. St. Cyprian wrote that what was lacking to the baptized Samaritans "was supplied by Peter and John — and we do the same today so that the baptized are presented to the bishops of the Church and by (their) prayer and imposition of hands they receive the Holy Ghost and are made perfect with the Lord's seal.[1]"

§ 3. *Confirmation imprints an indelible mark on the soul that is different from the one received in Baptism.*

The existence of the mark of Confirmation was defined by the Council of Trent with the words, "If anyone shall say that in . . . . Confirmation there is not imprinted on the soul a sign, that is, a certain and indelible mark, on account of which (it) cannot be repeated; let him be anathema"(D-852). Since the Church defines the existence of this mark alongside her definition of the mark of Baptism, it shows that she speaks of two different and distinct marks conferred by these sacraments. Although the marks of Baptism and Confirmation are different, they do have several points of similarity. They are both supernatural and everlasting. The existence of the mark in the soul is a person's title to the sanctifying and sacramental graces that Christ intends this sacrament to confer.

It is important for an understanding of the mark of Confirmation that we notice that it entitles one to a new share of a fuller participation in the priesthood of Jesus Christ. Again, we must keep in mind that this in no way implies erasing the distinction between clergy and laity. A layman's participation in Christ's priesthood can be active or passive or both. The mark of Baptism entitled one to a participation that was principally passive. It fitted one to receive the fruits of that priesthood. Confirmation entitles one to participate actively in the priesthood. But there are degrees of active participation. The one that Confirmation confers is the one of lower grade. It builds on or enlarges the share given in Baptism. It is another indication that Confirmation can best be understood when seen in its relationship to Baptism, and that Confirmation makes a spiritual adult out of a person spiritually born in Baptism.

§ 4. *Confirmation authorizes one to proclaim publicly the divinity of Christ.*

Confirmation gives us an active share in the priesthood of Christ. To understand the nature of this share, it is necessary for us to study the phases of Christ's life. Two-thirds of the Gospels are devoted to Christ's public ministry. During this time, His principal concern was to teach. The Evangelists call Christ "Master" in the sense of a teacher. They give Him the title no less than fifty-three times.

A careful examination of the Gospels reveals that Christ usually worked miracles before, during, or after a teaching session. "And Jesus was going about all the towns and villages, *teaching* in their synagogues, and *preaching* the gospel of the kingdom, and curing every kind of disease and infirmity" (Matt. 9:35). Many passages could be quoted showing that teaching and miracles were firmly tied together. The occurrence of teaching and miracles in the Gospels is too frequent for it to be merely a coincidence. There is a relationship between the two. There is no doubt that the purpose of miracles was to instill faith in the minds of those who listened to Christ. Miracles were worked to convince the people that what Christ said was true.

The principal truth that Christ wanted His listeners to accept was the truth that He is God. "Many other signs also Jesus worked in the sight of his disciples, which are not written in this book. But these are written that you may believe that Jesus is the Christ, the Son of God, and that believing you may have life in his name" (Jn. 20:30). Christianity is built around the divinity of Christ. It is implied in the authority of the Church, in the institution of the sacraments, in the value of the Redemptive Act. Faith is the basis of justification. Confirmation entitles one to an active share in the priesthood of Christ. It authorizes one, for instance, to proclaim to others that salvation is impossible unless they accept the fact that Christ is God.

§ 5. *The mark of Confirmation entitles one to the sacramental grace necessary to proclaim publicly the divinity of Christ.*

The sacrament of Confirmation is geared to positive action. We have seen that it entitles one to an active participation in Christ's priesthood. This participation implies authorization and obligation for instance to proclaim Christ's divinity publicly. This means a great deal more than preaching this one doctrine. It includes proclaiming by word or example all the truths built around this central article of faith.[2] It implies telling everyone the meaning and privileges of belonging to Christ's kingdom. The privilege of being a participator in Christ's priesthood implies the duty not to neglect the obligations it imposes. The reward that one receives for proclaiming Christ is the sanctifying grace through the channel labeled "good works." It may be well here to review the stupendous greatness of sanctifying grace. The punishment for neglecting the duty imposed by Confirmation is that one does not receive the grace he could otherwise receive. The only misfortune worse than not receiving the grace that one could receive is losing it by mortal sin.

The duty to proclaim Christ publicly is only one of the duties imposed by Confirmation. All these duties imply the right to the help one needs to fulfill them. This help is sacramental grace. Confirmation imprints an indelible mark on the soul. It is one's permanent title to God's supernatural help. It is an active source of grace so long as the soul is in the state of sanctifying grace. Should the person fall into mortal sin, the title remains, for the mark is indelible, but is as it were "de-activated," but it is now only at best a congruous right. No grace of any kind flows from it in justice until the soul recovers the grace that it had lost. The mark of Confirmation behaves in exactly the same way as the mark of Baptism except that the kinds of sacramental grace that flow from them are different due to the different purposes of the sacraments.

§ 6. *The special actual grace of Confirmation enables one to work in the lay apostolate.*

The lay apostolate may be described as using as many means as possible to prepare as many persons as possible to receive as much grace as possible. It is having a genuine love of neighbor. The work that must be done in Christ's vineyard is long and difficult. The harvest is great but the laborers are few. Confirmation gives a layman the actual grace to do splendid work in this field.

A layman can effectively spread the kingdom of God by working in the instruction program of the Church. He can labor as a catechist motivated by the realization that the greatest enemy of Christ is ignorance of Christ. This same motive may lead him to organize and to lead study groups and information classes and to promote the diffusion of Catholic literature.

Pope Pius XI labeled help given to the missions as one of the greatest forms of charity. Lay apostles can work to spread Christ's kingdom on earth quite literally by helping those heroic men and women working in mission fields. There are a thousand different ways by which zealous laymen can lend badly needed assistance to missionaries. He can make the work of the missionaries known; he can be active in mission circles; he can sponsor catechists in foreign lands.

Every parish priest is conscious of the good work that laymen can do in preparing others to return to a life of grace. There are numerous opportunities to urge the wayward to return to the sacraments; they can be instrumental in helping those sorely tempted by alcohol; they can unite with those who combat immorality in literature and entertainment; they can be active in groups such as the Sodality and the Legion of Mary. Work in these fields is work in the lay apostolate. Confirmation entitles one to the actual grace he needs to participate fully and fervently in them.

§ 7. *Confirmation entitles one to the sacramental grace he needs to profess his faith in Christ in spite of ridicule, hatred, and even death.*

Christ said, "Everyone who acknowledges Me before men, I also will acknowledge him before my Father in heaven. But whoever disowns Me before men, I in turn will disown him before my Father in Heaven" (Matt. 10:32). There are many passages in the Gospels in which Christ forewarns His followers of persecutions aimed at making them deny their faith in Him. Throughout history there have been two types of persecution leveled against the Church. They may be called the red and white persecutions.

In a red persecution, Catholics are called upon to shed their blood rather than deny Christ. Every age and practically every country has had its red martyrs. We are familiar with the ten general persecutions which pagan Rome decreed against the Church. The motive behind these attacks was to weaken the Church by trying to force Christians to deny Christ. The pattern of those early persecutions has been adopted in numerous other places. An almost diabolical hatred of Catholic faith has inspired fantastic variations of inflicting pain and death. The red persecutions of the past nineteen centuries have erupted in spectacular fashion leaving a lasting mark on history.

In a white persecution, Catholics are not called upon to shed their blood. New, subtle, refined methods are used to try to make them abandon their faith in Christ. One method is ridicule of Catholic doctrines and practices such as confession, abstinence from meat on Friday, and others. Other methods of such persecution have been the refusing of employment to Catholics, keeping them out of desirable positions in government and industry, penalizing them for sending their children to parochial schools and the like. White persecutions never erupt in spectacular fashion, but they do take their toll. Confirmation gives one all the necessary actual grace he needs to stand firm in the faith in the face of red persecution which he may never face and white persecution which he can never escape.

§ 8. *The remote matter of Confirmation is Holy Chrism; its proximate matter is the actual anointing of the forehead with this Chrism together with a special imposition of hands.*[3]

The Council of Lyons I in 1245 A.D. made this very clear statement on the topic we consider: "All bishops individually in their own churches on the day of the Lord's Supper can, according to the form of the Church, prepare chrism from balsam and olive oil. For the gift of the Holy Spirit is given by the anointing with chrism." (D-450) The Church has repeated her teaching on the matter used in Confirmation whenever the occasion demanded it.

The remote matter of any sacrament is the very material used in administering it. For Confirmation, it is holy chrism, that is, a mixture of olive oil and balsam blessed by the bishop on Holy Thursday. Balsam is a sweet smelling resin secreted by the balsam tree. Writers are undecided whether or not balsam must be added to the olive oil to be valid matter for Confirmation. They also discuss whether or not a priest can be empowered to consecrate holy chrism.

The proximate matter of a sacrament is the material in the very act of being applied in the administration of the sacrament. There is considerable discussion as to the proximate matter of Confirmation. Some hold that anointing the forehead with chrism in the form of a cross is sufficient to confer the sacrament validly. Others hold that both the anointing with chrism and the imposition of the bishop's hands is necessary. Most modern theologians hold that the one and the same gesture of anointing is considered both an anointing and an imposition of hands at the same time. We leave this largely theoretical discussion to learned theologians for solution. In practice, the Church prescribes under penalty of mortal sin that neither the anointing, nor the imposition of hands may be omitted. If either of these is even accidentally omitted, there is some doubt as to the validity of the sacrament.

§ 9. *The Church has defined that the form used in Confirmation today is valid for the administration of this sacrament.*

The form of a sacrament is the set of words which gives definiteness or meaning to the application of the matter, thus producing a sacrament. (1) The form used to administer Confirmation in the Latin rite was explicitly set down in the

Decree for the Armenians drawn up at the Council of Florence between 1438-1445. It reads, "I sign thee with the sign of the cross and I confirm thee with the chrism of salvation, in the name of the Father, and of the Son, and of the Holy Ghost." (2) A person who administers Confirmation in the Oriental rite pronounces a form worded somewhat differently when he anoints with chrism. It reads, "The sign (meaning seal) of the gift of the Holy Ghost." The wording of the form used in the Oriental rite can be traced to the Council of Constantinople in 381 A.D. In spite of the difference of wording of the forms used in the Latin and Oriental rites they both express the two necessary elements, namely, the act of sealing and the grace of the Holy Ghost. The forms used in both rites are the ones received by the Church. The Council of Trent pronounced anathema against anyone who said that they are not the ones to be used for the valid administration of Confirmation. (cf. D-856) (3) Since the Twelfth Century, it has been the custom in the Latin rite for the person being confirmed to receive a slight blow on the cheek. This blow is not the special imposition of hands which is part of the proximate matter. It is, in fact, a reminder to the person being confirmed that he should be ready to undergo ridicule, hatred, and even death in performing his duty to profess publicly the divinity of Christ and all that this means. Since this blow was added to the ceremony of Confirmation by the Church, it is not essential for the valid reception of this sacrament.

§ 10. *A person must be baptized in order to be confirmed validly; he must be in the state of grace to receive it fruitfully.*[4]

A person can be validly confirmed anytime after he has been baptized. It is not necessary that he should first reach a certain age.[5] In ages past, even Catholics of the Latin rite were confirmed before they reached the use of reason. In those times, it was the custom to administer this sacrament before the child had reached the age of discretion or about seven years old. The law in force today states that in the Latin rite children are to be confirmed after they have reached the use of reason except in cases where an infant is in danger of death or when there are other weighty reasons.[6] There is variation in the customs of the Oriental rite Catholics. In some rites, a person is confirmed on the day he is baptized. In others, the custom is the same as the one observed by the Latins.

Confirmation is a sacrament of the living, meaning that one must already be in the state of sanctifying grace in order to receive the grace that God wants this sacrament to confer. Like any other sacrament, Confirmation confers more grace on persons better prepared to receive it. One is urged to cleanse himself of venial sin and the affection for sin as completely as possible before presenting himself to be confirmed.

The code of Canon Law states that a person with the use of reason is to be properly instructed before being confirmed. How much instruction must he receive? It depends on how ignorant that person is of the truths of religion. All with the use of reason must know at least in substance those truths that must be known by a necessity of precept. These are the Lord's Prayer, Creed, Commandments, and the Sacraments they receive. Just as the Church has the duty to teach the truths of revelation, so do people have the duty to learn them. The duties bind under penalty of mortal sin. Those persons who once knew the truths referred to but who have now forgotten them are bound in conscience to relearn them, for it is impossible to lead a Christian life without them.

§ 11. *A person who receives Confirmation validly but unfruitfully can receive its grace at a future time.*

Mortal sin, not only completely strips the soul of sanctifying grace, but it also effectively blocks its re-entry. It remains an obstacle to grace even though the person is not conscious of its presence in his soul. The sanctifying grace that a confirmed person should have received but did not receive is not irretrievably lost. Confirmation imprints on the soul an indelible mark or title to this grace. (1) If the person deliberately and freely received Confirmation in mortal sin, he committed a grave sacrilege. He must make an act of perfect contrition or must receive the sacrament of Penance in order to receive the sanctifying grace that he should have received when he was confirmed. (2) If he was not conscious of the mortal sin on his soul when he was confirmed, he is not guilty of sacrilege. The forgotten sin nevertheless blocks grace from entering the soul. To receive the grace of Confirmation, he must make at least an act of imperfect contrition. We presume that he has not committed new mortal sins after having been confirmed. If new mortal sins were committed, he must make an act of perfect contrition or receive Penance. (3) A person approaching Confirmation in mortal sin need not go to Confession to recover the sanctifying grace needed for fruitful reception. He may make an act of perfect contrition before receiving the Sacrament. A person who received Confirmation unfruitfully and who received its graces by making an act of perfect or imperfect contrition after being confirmed, is still obliged to confess those mortal sins when he next receives the sacrament of Penance.

§ 12. *It is a venial sin to neglect to receive Confirmation out of sloth; it is a mortal sin to neglect to receive it out of contempt or when neglect will lead to serious spiritual harm.*

In itself, Confirmation is not absolutely necessary for salvation, for one can receive or recover sanctifying grace without it. But the Council of Trent has defined that none of the sacraments are superfluous. When God gives us privileges, He expects us to use them and He will hold us responsible for neglecting them. We could here review with profit the parable of the talents as found in the Gospels. (cf. Luke 19:11 ff) Then too, the law of the Church cautions that no one may neglect to receive Confirmation when the opportunity presents itself. The question at hand is this: What is the penalty for disobeying this law? While it binds under penalty of sin, it cannot be proved that this law binds under penalty of mortal sin. It is a venial sin to neglect out of sloth the opportunity to be confirmed. This sin is repeated as often as fresh opportunities present themselves and are neglected.

Circumstances can oblige one to receive Confirmation under penalty of mortal sin. These are some of them. A person would be seriously bound to receive it if the lack of its sacramental grace would cause him to deny or abandon the faith or if he foresaw that he would need the grace to help his neighbor in extreme spiritual need. A person is clearly guilty of mortal sin, if hatred or contempt for the sacrament causes him not to be confirmed. We believe that mortal sins due to the causes listed here are not common. But we do believe that many people are guilty of mortal sins of neglect in this matter due to a false conscience. They are under the mistaken notion that it is always a serious sin to neglect to receive Confirmation. Then, too, we must not discount the possibility of scandal aggravating the malice of neglect.

§ 13. *A bishop is the ordinary minister of Confirmation; any priest can be empowered to be the extraordinary minister of this sacrament.*

Papal documents from ancient times have spoken on the minister of Confirmation. The Council of Trent stated it explicitly. It said, "If anyone shall say that the ordinary minister of holy Confirmation is not the bishop alone, but any simple priest: let him be anathema" (D-873). In the administration of Confirmation recorded in the New Testament, it was bishops, namely Peter and John, who conferred it even though deacons in Holy Orders were present. Passages could be quoted from the writings of a number of early Christian writers witnessing the fact that bishops administered Confirmation.

The legislation embodied in the Code of Canon Law is covered by the Church's endowment of infallibility. Canon 782 states that an ordinary priest can be given the faculty to confirm. Those who have this faculty are extraordinary ministers of Confirmation. Without this faculty, they confirm invalidly. There is proof many centuries old to the effect that priests could be empowered to confirm. In 1947, the Holy See granted faculties to all pastors of the Latin rite to confirm infants, children, and adults when three conditions obtained. These are the conditions: a bishop must not be available; the pastor is empowered to confirm only within the limits of his parish; and the subject must be in danger of death.

Priests of Uniate rites who have faculties to confirm do so as extraordinary ministers of this sacrament. They may validly and lawfully confirm only the members of their rites. It is valid but unlawful for them to confirm persons of the Latin rite. Uniate priests confirm a person immediately after they baptize him. Converts to Catholicism from the Orthodox Church are usually reconfirmed conditionally. The reason is that there is often serious doubt as to the validity of the matter used in Confirmation by the Orthodox priest.

§ 14. *There are six requisites for valid sponsorship in Confirmation.*[7]

In accordance with a most ancient custom, the Church desires that all candidates for Confirmation have sponsors. The obligation to have this sponsor is a grave one. The office of sponsor carries with it weighty obligations. And the Church knows from experience that only persons of quality will fulfill them. She lays down certain conditions to test the quality of persons selected to be sponsors. In this number we list only the requisites for valid sponsorship. (1) The designated sponsor must be validly baptized and have the use of reason. Children usually reach the use of reason when they are about seven years old. (2) He must himself have been confirmed and intend to assume the duties of this office. (3) He may not be a heretic or schismatic or guilty of any act which carries with it the penalty of excluding him from validly acting as sponsor. (4) The sponsor may not be the father or mother or spouse of the candidate to be confirmed. (5) He must have been selected by the candidate to be confirmed, or by his parents, or by the pastor. (6) He must physically touch the candidate while the sacrament is being administered. The duties of the office of sponsor in Confirmation can be validly assumed by proxy, but the sponsor is to designate the person who is to stand in for him when the sacrament is being conferred. If this procedure regarding the selection of a proxy is not observed, the intended sponsor doubtfully assumes the duties of the office. A person who presumes to act as a sponsor in Confirmation while knowing that he cannot validly assume this office is guilty of mortal sin. This flows from the fact that there is a grave obligation to have this sponsor. Of course, the fact that one's sponsor lacked the requisites for valid sponsorship does not affect the validity of the sacrament.

§ 15. *There are six requisites for lawful sponsorship in Confirmation.*[8]

The requisites for lawful sponsorship are over and above those laid down for valid sponsorship. (1) The sponsor must be at least fourteen years old unless the bishop who administers the sacrament admits a younger person for a good reason. (2) He must not be the same person who was the candidate's godparent in Baptism unless the minister allows it or unless Confirmation takes place immediately after Baptism as in some Oriental rites. (3) The sponsor must be of the same sex as the candidate unless the minister thinks that there is a reasonable cause to allow an exception to this rule. (4) He must be free from any act whose penalty is exclusion from the office of sponsorship. Canon Law clearly states a public criminal may not act as a sponsor in Confirmation. The Holy See has said that Catholics whose lives are unchristian and scandalous may not be sponsors. We believe that it can be argued that persons who regularly neglect Sunday Mass fall into this category. Missing Mass is a symptom as well as a sin. Those who habitually neglect Sunday Mass rarely receive the sacraments; they are a real source of scandal to their children; they usually are ignorant of those truths that must be known by necessity of precept; the religious sense and conscience is evidently not a great force in their lives. (5) He must know the rudiments of faith. (6) A novice or a professed member of a religious community or cleric may not act as sponsor unless his proper superiors permit it. The person selected to be sponsor must have the qualifications for both valid and lawful sponsorship. In most cases there is very little difficulty except on the question of the sponsor knowing the truths of faith and leading a Christian life. Candidates can avoid a great deal of embarrassment and resentment if they carefully investigate the quality of their desired sponsor before asking him to assume the office.

§ 16. *A Confirmation sponsor is to see to it that the person he sponsors receives the training he needs to profess publicly his faith in Christ.*[9]

When we say that Confirmation entitles one to the grace to profess Christ publicly, we do not necessarily mean that it then and there wipes out all deficiencies. It means that Confirmation confers the grace that will enable one to prepare himself to profess Christ in the future. If this were not true there would be no need to have Confirmation sponsors. The whole tenor of Confirmation is that it completes the work commenced by Baptism. In Confirmation, one who was spiritually born in Baptism now becomes a spiritual adult. The duties of a sponsor begin where the duties of a godparent leave off. A sponsor builds on the work of the baptismal godparent. By his own reception of Confirmation, he receives the grace he needs to fulfill the duties of a sponsor.

A godparent in Baptism must see to it that the godchild learns and retains the truths to be known by a necessity of precept. The sponsor in Confirmation must see to it that this person is able to explain and to defend those truths. The child can hardly learn this if he does not attend a Catholic high school, or at least instruction classes for children in public high schools. By word or by example, a sponsor will urge active participation in work whose end is the spread of Christ's kingdom on earth. He can be active in Catholic action groups, mission circles, study clubs, Catholic Charities endeavors, parish societies, and the like.

Sponsorship imposes life-long duties. It is a mortal sin to neglect them completely. The reason why a candidate may choose his own sponsor is because it is presumed that he will be inclined to accept this person's coaching and guidance more than another's. The office of sponsor is far from being merely a position or office of honor. It imposes heavy duties but it also promises rich supernatural rewards.

NOTES

1. Ep. 73, n. 9.
2. McAuliffe, *Sacramental Theology* (Herder: St. Louis, 1958), p. 100.
3. Canon 780.
4. Canon 786.
5. Canon 788.
6. *Ibid.*
7. Canon 795.
8. Canon 797.
9. Canon 797.

V

Holy Eucharist

§ 1. *Holy Eucharist is the sacrament in which Jesus Christ is really, truly, and substantially present under the appearances of bread and wine.*

A veritable flood of passages from the works of early Christian writers could be quoted proving that the Church has always taught a perfectly uniform doctrine on the Holy Eucharist. It is indeed surprising that the first notable heresy to attack the Church's teaching on the Real Presence appeared more than a thousand years after Christ. It was the error of Berengarius, who lived in the Eleventh Century. Even he recanted his error in 1079 A.D.

The great attack on the Holy Eucharist in history was leveled by the leaders of the Protestant revolt in the Sixteenth Century. It was not surprising, therefore, to find special attention paid to this dogma by the Council of Trent. That Council defined, "If anyone denies that in the Sacrament of the Most Holy Eucharist are contained really, truly, and substantially the Body and Blood together with the Soul and Divinity of Our Lord, Jesus Christ, and consequently the whole Christ: let him be anathema."(D-883) The student will notice that three adverbs are used in the definition. Each is aimed at a variation of the Protestant denial.[1] The word "really" is aimed at Luther's error which said that Christ is not permanently present in the Holy Eucharist, but that He is there only "as fire is present in hot metal." The word "truly" prevents the misunderstanding inherent in Zwingli's error which held that Christ is only figuratively present in this sacrament. According to Zwingli, Christ is present in the Holy Eucharist much as a person is present in a photograph of himself. The word "substantially' is in answer to Calvin's error which seemed to say that those who receive the Holy Eucharist do not receive Christ's Body and Blood, but a special benefit or grace that could only come from this "sacrament." In the decree of the Council of Trent, we have a good example of how the Church words a definition to meet a heresy opposed to a revealed doctrine.

§ 2. *Christ promised to institute the Holy Eucharist a long time before He actually did so.*[2]

There was a definite pattern in the method that Christ used in instructing. There are many passages in the Gospels that can be cited showing that Christ usually worked miracles in conjunction with His lessons. The purpose of those miracles was not merely to impress or to inspire awe in people but to drive home to them that what Christ taught was true. In the sixth chapter of St. John's Gospel there is recorded the promise of the institution of the Holy Eucharist. Christ sets the stage for the promise by working the miracle of the multiplication of the loaves and fishes. It sharpened the people's attention and heightened their interest in what He was about to say.

The promise of the institution of the Holy Eucharist is contained in verses 52, 54, and 56 of the sixth chapter. Verse 52 reads, "The bread that I will give is my flesh for the life of the world." Verse 54 reads, "Unless you eat the flesh of the Son of Man and drink his blood, you shall not have life in you." Verse 56 reads, "For my flesh is food indeed, and my blood is drink indeed." We shall see that non-Catholic exegetes have not been able to build a single sound philological argument against the literal interpretation of these verses.

The Evangelist records the reaction of the Jews and Apostles to the words just quoted. They understood Christ in the literal sense on other occasions. When listeners understood Christ in a sense that He did not want to be understood, He stopped and corrected their mistaken notions. In the episode we examine, the people understood Christ literally and then some "walked with Him no more" because they looked upon the truth as being incomprehensible. On the other hand, if they had misunderstood Christ, He would have stopped and re-explained His point. But Christ did nothing of the kind. In fact, He re-emphasized His original statements, thus proving that the people had understood Him as He wanted to be understood, namely, as speaking literally.

§ 3. *The literal interpretation of the promise of the institution makes it imperative that the words used in the actual institution also be interpreted literally.*

St. John was the last Evangelist to write a Gospel. The Synoptic Gospels, composed by Matthew, Mark, and Luke, were written about 50-70 A.D. John wrote his Gospel sometime between 80-100 A.D. Not only did John write his Gospel after the Synoptics, but he was well acquainted with these writings. His Gospel supplements the information found in the Synoptics. For example, the first three Evangelists dwelt on Christ's Galilean ministry; John dwelt on Christ's Judean ministry. John records miracles not recorded in the Synoptics.

John wrote his Gospel to combat the Docetist heresy that had shown its head at Ephesus. This error held that Christ did not have a real body composed of flesh, blood, and bone, and sinew but a phantom body, that is, one that had the appearance of a real one but really was not. We notice that John is careful to include those episodes in Christ's life which demonstrate that Christ had a real body.

When preparing to write his Gospel, St. John noticed that all three Synoptic Evangelists had recorded the actual institution of the Holy Eucharist. In fact, they had quoted the very words that Christ had used at the Last Supper. When he did write his Gospel, he avoided repeating this episode for the fourth time. Instead, he recorded that Christ had promised to institute the Holy Eucharist a long time before He actually did so. In promising to institute the Holy Eucharist, Christ wanted to be understood as speaking literally. When He said "body" he meant "body"; when He said "blood," He meant "blood." The circumstances of the writing of St. John's Gospel and its relationship to the Synoptics show that the words of the actual institution of the Holy Eucharist must be taken literally, and not figuratively. We cannot resist the urge to point out that at the Last Supper, St. John was in a better position than any other Apostle to hear the actual words of institution uttered by Christ.

§ 4. *The words that Christ pronounced over the bread at the Last Supper meant that He changed this bread into His Body.*

Matthew writes, "Jesus took bread . . . . and said, 'Take and eat; this is my body' " (Matt. 26:26). Mark writes, "Jesus took bread . . . . and said, 'Take; this is my body' " (Mk. 14:22). Luke writes, "And having taken bread, he (Jesus) . . . . gave it to them saying, 'This is my body, which is being given for you' " (Lk. 22:19). In spite of a slight variation of wording, the ideas are identical in all three passages.

All three Evangelists explicitly state that Christ took bread and was referring to this bread when He began to speak. It will not do to separate the reference to bread from the rest of what Christ says. The two things are tightly bound together. Notice how carefully Christ uses the demonstrative term "this." He does not say, "this bread is my body." That would be a contradiction, for the object could not have been bread and Christ's body at the same time. He says "this" and then tells what it refers to, namely, "my body." He is clearly imply-ing that this object is no longer bread, but is now His Body.

In his account of the institution, St. Luke adds the ex-tremely significant clause "which is being given for you." In this clause, Christ is reminding the Apostles of what he had already told them, namely, that at Jerusalem He would be de-livered into the hands of sinners to be nailed to a cross and thereby be the ransom paid to free men from the slavery of sin. (Matt. 20:17) He now uses the present tense to indicate the great proximity of the fulfillment of the prophecy. What was "being given" to be nailed to the Cross? It was Christ's physical body. The chain of ideas is now complete. Christ's physical body is being given as a ransom. The object that Christ is holding in His hand is His physical body; the object which is now Christ's body at one time was bread. What has happened? Christ has changed bread into His body. He has instituted the Holy Eucharist.

One must not fail to notice that a long time before the Last Supper Christ had promised to give His body and blood to be our food and drink. We saw that He wanted these words to be taken literally. In instituting the Holy Eucharist He said, "Take and eat" and "All of you drink of this." The parallel between the promise and the institution is unmistakable.

§ 5. *The words that Christ pronounced over the wine at the Last Supper mean that He changed this wine into His blood.*

Matthew writes, "And taking a cup, he (Jesus) gave thanks .... saying 'All of you drink of this; for this is my blood of the new covenant, which is being shed for many unto the forgive-ness of sin. But .... I will not drink henceforth of this fruit of the vine' " (Matt. 26:27). Mark writes, "And taking a cup .... he said to them, 'This is my blood of the new covenant, which is being shed for many .... I will drink no more of the fruit of the vine.' " (Mark 14:23) Luke writes, "In like man-ner he took also the cup after the supper, saying, 'This cup is

the new covenant in my blood, which shall be shed for you' "
(Lk. 22:20).

All three Evangelists say that Christ took a cup of wine
and was referring to it when He began to speak. It is obvious
that Christ's action toward the wine perfectly parallels His
action toward the bread. He had just changed bread into His
body; He is now changing wine into His blood. He explicitly
states what He has done. As in the case of the changing of the
bread, Christ did not say "This wine is my blood." This would
be a contradiction or figurative language. When He says,
"This is my blood," He can only mean that the contents of the
cup and His blood are identically the same.

All three Evangelists add that the contents of the cup is the
same blood that was later to be shed by Christ on the cross.
Now the blood shed by Christ was certainly not blood in the
figurative or imaginary sense. It was blood in the strict literal
sense. Again, we have a chain of thoughts. At the beginning,
Christ holds a cup of wine; He then says that the cup contains
His blood; He emphasizes that it is the blood He will shed on
the Cross. Matthew and Mark picture the shedding as being
in the present. Luke pictures it in the future. These tenses do
not change the fact that Christ is saying that the contents of
the cup are literally His blood. The force of the words of institution is fully brought out by the original Greek text.[3] The
first reads, "This is my body, the very one which is being given
for you." The second reads, "This is my blood, the very blood
which is being shed for you."

§ 6. *St. Paul's epistle to the Corinthians repeats that in instituting the Holy Eucharist, Christ really changed bread and
wine into His body and blood.*

St. John records the institution of the Holy Eucharist as an
event of the future; the Synoptics record it as an event of the

present; St. Paul refers to it as an event of the past. We will now see that St. Paul's account is in perfect harmony with the accounts of the Evangelists. His account appears in the 11th chapter of his first epistle to the Corinthians.[4] The harmony between St. Paul's account and that found in the Synoptics could hardly be greater than it is, for St. Paul's words and St. Luke's words telling of the institution are the same verbatim. Since the words of the Synoptics must be interpreted literally, the words of St. Paul must also be interpreted literally.

In *I Corinthians,* St. Paul writes, "Whoever eats this bread or drinks the cup of the Lord unworthily, will be guilty of the body and the blood of the Lord" (I Cor. 11:27). He says that anyone who eats or drinks unworthily commits an act against the body and blood of Christ. This would be clearly impossible if Christ's body and blood were not really, truly, and substantially present in the Holy Eucharist.

In verse 29 of the same chapter St. Paul writes, "For he who eats and drinks unworthily, without distinguishing the body, eats and drinks judgment to himself." The key here is the term "distinguishing." St. Paul says that a distinction must be made between what this object seems to be and what it really is. If he wanted to say that this object that had the appearance of bread and wine was really bread and wine then he would be underscoring the obvious. But he is cautioning that this object is *not what it appears to be*. It is the body and blood of Christ under the appearances of bread and wine. He tells the people that they will be penalized if they did not penetrate external appearances and grasp the true nature of the Eucharist.

St. John records that people would in the future receive Christ's body and blood as their food and drink; the Synoptics quote Christ as giving His body and blood as food and drink. St. Paul states that the reception of Christ's body and blood as food and drink is an established practice among Christians.

§ 7. There is no philological basis for a figurative interpretation of the Scripture passages pertaining to the Holy Eucharist.

The circumstances that occasioned the many figurative interpretations of the Eucharistic passages are indeed enlightening. Almost all of them came into being in the Sixteenth Century. They were propounded by men who first broke with the Church and then began a wholesale denial of her doctrines. These men put forth their figurative interpretations of the Scripture passages we have examined in an attempt to give plausibility to their denials. Figurative interpretation means that although Christ said one thing, He really meant something else. The heretics of the Sixteenth Century put forth their opinions to destroy belief in the Real Presence of Christ in the Holy Eucharist. Let us examine several of them. (1) Heretics have tried to say that when Christ said, "Unless you eat the flesh of the Son of Man, you shall not have life in you." He really meant "Unless you have *faith* in the Son of Man, you shall not have life in you." This interpretation is absurd. There is no language justification for it whatsoever.[5] In the Aramaic language which Christ spoke, the eating of another's flesh and drinking his blood meant to hate and persecute him. It never meant to have faith in him. The absurdity is apparent at once. Imagine! Unless one hates and persecutes Christ, he shall not find salvation! (2) In no lexicon of the Aramaic language can it be shown that bread and wine are figurative synonyms for flesh and blood. Any attempt to say that they are such synonyms is intellectual dishonesty. (3) Critics have tried to say that the Aramaic language was poor in verbs. They have said that some verbs in this language had to do double duty, and as a result "is" sometimes meant "represents." These critics are trying to force a simply wild interpretation onto the Eucharistic text. They are trying to make "This is my body" mean "This represents my body," thus destroying Scriptural justification for the Real Presence. Cardinal Wiseman crushed their attempt by showing that if Christ really wanted to say "This represents my body," He would have had forty ways to say "represents" in the Aramaic language which He spoke.[6] Practically all the attempts at figurative interpretation besides those listed here are variations of these refuted here.

§ 8. *Early Greek writers of the Christian era attest to the correctness of the literal interpretation of the Eucharistic passages and therefore, of the real presence of Christ in the Blessed Sacrament.*

We call attention to the cities where the writers we quote lived. It brings out the fact that the literal interpretation of the Eucharistic passages was the only one held throughout the Greek-speaking world. (1) The *Didache,* written probably in Corinth before 100 A.D., reads "On the Lord's Day, come together, break bread and hold Eucharist, after confessing your transgressions that your offering may be pure." (Ch. 14) Notice how this passage parallels St. Paul's admonition to the Corinthians. (2) St. Ignatius of Antioch in Syria was a disciple of St. John the Evangelist. He died in 107 A.D. He writes, "Heretics abstain from the Eucharist because they do not believe that the Eucharist is the flesh of our Savior, who suffered for our sins."[7] (3) In about 150 A.D. St. Justin, born in Palestine but martyred in Rome, wrote, "And this food is called by us the Eucharist .... we do not receive it as ordinary food or ordinary drink .... but it is the flesh and blood of that Jesus who was made flesh."[8] (4) In the Fourth Century, St. Cyril of Jerusalem (+386) wrote, "Since Christ declared and said of the bread, 'This is my body,' who shall dare to doubt any longer? And since He Himself affirmed and said, 'This is my blood,' who shall ever hesitate, saying that it is not His blood?"[9] (5) St. John Chrysostom, Patriarch of Constantinople (+407) first interprets literally the words of the promise found in John VI:51-56 and then adds, "Jesus has given to those who desire Him, not only to see Him, but even to touch and eat Him, and fix their teeth in His flesh, and to embrace Him and satisfy all their love."[10] (6) Theodore of Mopsuestia in Cilicia (+428) wrote, "Christ did not say: This is the symbol of my body, and this is the symbol of my blood, but He said, 'This is my body and This is my blood.' "[11] He anticipates and refutes Protestant figurative interpretations of the Eucharistic passages by twelve centuries. Scores of other Patristic citations could be made from the works of the Greek Fathers but these are sufficient to indicate how widely held was the literal interpretation of the Eucharistic passages of the New Testament.

§ 9. *Early Latin writers of the Christian era also attest to the correctness of the literal interpretation of the Eucharistic passages of the New Testament.*

Latin Christian literature is not as old as Greek Christian literature. All extant Christian literature composed before 175 A.D. is in Greek, even though it was composed in Rome itself. Even the oldest extant graffiti and inscriptions found in the Roman Catacombs are in Greek.[12] (1) The first important Christian author to write in Latin was Tertullian (c.160-c.220 A.D.) of Carthage in North Africa. He does not attempt a speculative explanation of the Holy Eucharist, but he does affirm the Real Presence. (2) St. Cyprian also of Carthage (+258) explicitly states that the Holy Eucharist is the Body and Blood of Christ. He says that Christ empowered priests to re-enact the Sacrifice of Calvary.[13] (3) St. Hilary of Poitiers (+366), the western champion of Catholic doctrines against Arianism wrote, "Christ says, 'My Flesh is truly meat, and My Blood is truly drink; he that eats My Flesh and drinks My Blood, abides in Me, and I in him.' There is no room to doubt the objective reality of the Flesh and Blood. For now both by the declaration of the Lord Himself, and by our faith, it is truly Flesh and it is truly Blood: and these, when eaten and drunk, effect that we are in Christ and Christ is in us."[14] (4) St. Ambrose of Milan (+397) wrote "What we effect by consecration is the Body taken from the Virgin. Why do you here seek the order of nature, since the Lord Jesus, born of a Virgin, is Himself above nature? Truly, therefore, this is the Flesh of Christ, which was crucified and buried; truly, therefore, it is the Sacrament of His flesh."[15] Anyone who studies the Latin tradition of the Fourth Century cannot but notice the distinctness with which that tradition affirms the reality of the Body and Blood of Jesus Christ in the Holy Eucharist. In this point as in many others, the mind of the West is fixed and settled.

§ 10. *Archeological discoveries of recent decades attest to the belief of the laity of ancient times in the real presence of Christ in the Holy Eucharist.*

Paintings are rare in both Christian and profane archeological discoveries. The fragility of the materials used accounts for this. And yet the most ancient archeological discoveries of Christianity are paintings or murals dealing with the Holy Eucharist. The first is the famous *Fractio panis* discovered in the crypt of Lucina in the catacombs of Priscilla at Rome, and dating from the Third Century. The discovery was made by Wilpert. "The mural consists of two symmetrical representations of a fish, placed on a background colored green, and carrying on its back a basket of wine and bread. A better method of showing the compenetration of the Eucharistic elements with the Body of the Redeemer could not have been found; one cannot doubt that this treats of the Eucharist."[16]

In the catacombs of Callixtus, there was discovered the mural called *Mensa Domini* dating from about 200 A.D. It depicts a large fish resting on a tripod. The tripod was the most common form of altar used in primitive times. In the picture a man is extending his hand over the fish as if to bless it. Another person, in the form of an icon or praying person, assists at the ceremony. That this mural represents the Mass is denied by few; that it represents a Eucharistic scene is denied by no one.

In the same catacombs of Callixtus and also dating from about 200 A.D. is a mural depicting a Eucharistic banquet.[17] Seven persons are reclining around a table. On the table, there is a fish so large that it is within easy reach of all seven persons. There are seven baskets on the table next to the fish. This scene represents more than the Mass, for it depicts seven persons around a banquet table. It certainly represents Holy Communion. Many other ancient Eucharistic scenes and murals found in the catacombs could be discussed here.[18] We have selected these three because of their great antiquity and because the first shows belief in the Real Presence, the second shows belief in the Holy Mass, and the third attests to the existence of Holy Communion among the earliest Catholics of Rome.

§ 11. *The Holy Eucharist has all the notes necessary for a true sacrament of the New Law.*

The Council of Trent has defined that the Holy Eucharist is truly and properly a sacrament. It remains for us to point out how the elements of a sacrament are verified in the Holy Eucharist. (1) It was immediately instituted by Christ Himself. This is clearly indicated in the Scripture passages proving the promise, actual institution, and St. Paul's reference to the Holy Eucharist. (2) The Holy Eucharist has a remote matter and a form. These elements are explicitly contained in the Synoptic Gospels recording Christ's action at the Last Supper. This matter is bread and wine. The form is the set of words pronounced by Christ over the matter. The remote matter and the form of this sacrament have remained un-

changed throughout history. (3) Holy Eucharist is a permanent means of grace. This Sacrament is permanent in two
ways. It is permanent in the sense that Christ is really and
truly present as long as the appearances of bread and wine
remain. It is also permanent in the sense that Christ intended
that the Church should possess this Sacrament until the end
of time. Christ was not speaking to a limited group when He
said that unless people ate His flesh and drank His blood, they
would not have life in them. He was speaking to everyone
coming after Him regardless of the place or age in which they
found themselves. (4) Christ instituted the Holy Eucharist as
an effective means to confer grace. We have seen in the past
that Christ's expression for sanctifying grace is "life." A person
with this grace is supernaturally alive; a person devoid of it is
supernaturally dead. We shall see how directly Christ ties the
reception of the "new life" with the reception of the Holy
Eucharist. (5) This sacrament was confided to the Church and
the Church is authorized to lay down regulations governing
Its lawful reception.

§ 12. *For an understanding of the Holy Eucharist, it is important to grasp the distinction between the substance and
accidents of material things.*

Scholastic philosophy proves that every material object has
substance and accidents regardless of its external appearance.
These are different things and even separable things even
though they accompany each other. The substance of an object is that which makes it exist by itself. This substance embodies the essence of a thing and gives it its physical nature.
Substance gives a material object its individuality; it sets it
apart from other things. For example: a tree is different from
a stone because it has a different substance, not because it has
a different size, shape, and so forth.

    Aristotle showed that there are nine different accidents or

external modifications that can accompany substance. Size, shape, color, taste, weight, qualities, and the like are examples of these accidents. They can change and even be replaced while the substance remains the same. For example, a man's substance remains the same even while his size, shape, weight, and other accidents change.

We can not see an object's substance even with the most powerful microscope. All we can see are the accidents of color, shape, size, and so forth that accompany substance. Accidents cannot ordinarily exist by themselves. They must be supported by substance. For example, we never see motion by itself. We only see something which moves. Thought cannot exist by itself; it is always something which thinks. On the other hand, substance by itself does not occupy space. It is only when substance is accompanied with the accident of size that it occupies space. The conclusion to our brief discussion here is that an object's substance must never be confounded with its accidents. They are not the same even though they usually accompany each other.

§ 13. *In the Holy Eucharist, the substance of the bread and wine is changed into the substance of Christ's body and blood, but the accidents of bread and wine remain.*

We have just seen that it is not only possible but that it is, in fact, necessary to draw a clear distinction between the substance and the accidents of a material object. They must not be confounded. Let us now apply these principles of philosophy to the doctrine of the Holy Eucharist. We have already examined the New Testament passages touching on this sacrament. The conclusion was that Christ's words must be taken literally when He said that He changed bread and wine into His body and blood. We also saw that the substance of an object makes it what it really is; it gives it its physical nature. If, then, only the substance of the bread and wine is changed

nto the substance of Christ's body and blood, it must be said
hat Christ is really, truly, and substantially there. For Christ
o be there, it is not imperative that He "bring along" all the
ccidents of His physical body, that is, His size, weight, color,
nd so forth. In the Holy Eucharist, Christ's body has all its
ccidents except one, namely, quantified extension.

The Council of Trent defines and the New Testament texts
clearly state that in the Holy Eucharist the accidents of bread
nd wine remain after the substance has been changed into
Christ's body and blood. This is most clearly shown in St.
Paul's *First Epistle to the Corinthians*. (I Cor. 11:29) After
having repeated the words by which transubstantiation is ef-
fected, St. Paul cautions the people to make a distinction between the substance of this Object and the visible accidents.
He tells them to avoid making the serious mistake of thinking
that although the object still has the appearances of bread and
wine, that it is what it appears to be. He tells that It now is
the substance of the Body and Blood of Christ. St. John Chrysostom, the Doctor of the Eucharist, is a witness of Sacred
Tradition when he writes, "His (Christ's) word cannot deceive, but our senses are easily beguiled . . . since the Word
says, 'This is my body;' let us be persuaded and believe, and
look at It with the eyes of the mind. Christ has given us things
that cannot be grasped by the senses, but though they are embodied in sensible things, they all are to be perceived by the
mind."[19]

§ 14. *In the Holy Eucharist, Christ is entirely present under
accidents of bread and He is entirely present under the accidents of wine.*

The proposition embodies a definition of the Council of
Trent. The decree reads, "If anyone denies that in the venerable Sacrament of the Eucharist the whole Christ is contained
under each species, and under every part of each species when

separated: let him be anathema." (D-885) We have already seen that when Christ becomes present in the Holy Eucharist, it is His substance that becomes present. It is not necessary for Him to be present there with all His accidents.

When Christ becomes present in the Holy Eucharist, He becomes present as He now is in heaven, but without the one accident of dimensive quantity.[20] At the Incarnation, the Divine Nature of God the Son was united to His human nature. From that moment forward and for all eternity, those two natures will never be separated. They were not even separated when Christ died on the cross. At the Resurrection, the elements of Christ's physical body, that is, His body and blood, became reunited with His human soul once more. When bread is changed into the substance of Christ, the whole Christ becomes present, that is, Christ's Body and Blood, His Soul and Divine Nature become present. The same is repeated when the wine is changed. It is therefore wrong to think that only Christ's Body is present under the accidents of bread and only His Blood is present under the accidents of wine.

For a material object to be divisible, its substance must be accompanied by the accident of dimensive quantity. In the Holy Eucharist, Christ's substance is not accompanied by the accident of dimension. This body therefore is not divided when the Sacred Host is broken. The definition of the Church quoted above makes it very clear that Christ is entirely present under the accidents of bread and wine regardless how small the fragments or drops of the Sacred Species may be.

§ 15. *The Holy Eucharist is a permanent sacrament, for Christ remains present as long as the accidents of bread and wine remain.*

The permanency of Christ's presence in the Holy Eucharist was attacked by Luther, who held that Christ is present only for the instant that it takes one to receive Holy Communion.

The Council of Trent was constrained to restate the Church's teaching on this subject in the face of the non-Catholic heresies. It said, "If anyone says that after the completion of the consecration that the body and blood of our Lord, Jesus Christ, is not in the marvelous sacrament of the Eucharist, but only in use, while it is taken, not however before or after, and that in hosts or consecrated particles, which are reserved or remain after Communion, the true body of the Lord does not remain: let him be anathema." (D-886) This definition of the Church needs little explanation. Its meaning is perfectly clear. Even without this decree, the truth can be learned from Sacred Scripture. If one carefully analyzes the institution of the Holy Eucharist at the Last Supper, he sees that Christ first changed bread and wine into His body and blood and then handed It to the Apostles to receive. He was present under the Sacred Species throughout the period that it took for Him to hand out the Sacred Species and for all of the Apostles to receive It. He did not limit the period during which He would be present in the Holy Eucharist. It follows that He is present after consecration has taken place and as long as the appearances of bread and wine remain. All those who believed in the Real Presence had no difficulty in also accepting Its permanence. St. Basil the Great (+369) testifies to the belief in the permanence of Christ's presence in the Holy Eucharist.[21] He recalls that the Sacred Species was brought to those in prison from the outside, so that they might receive Holy Communion.

NOTES

1. McAuliffe, *Op. Cit.,* p. 115.
2. For a complete discussion of the Holy Eucharist as found in Sacred Scripture read Wiseman, *The Real Presence* (London: Burns, Oates, 1936).
3. *Cf.* Prat., *The Theology of St. Paul* (London: Burns, Oates and Washbourne, 1942), Vol. II, p. 264.
4. Prat. *Op. Cit.,* p. 263 ff.
5. Ricciotti, *The Life of Christ* (Milwaukee: Bruce, 1954), p. 565 ff.
6. Wiseman, *The Real Presence* (London: Burns, Oates, 1934), p. 257.

7. *Ad. Smyr.*, N. 7.

8. *I Apologia*, ch. 67.

9. *Catech. XXII.*

10. *Homilia in Joannem*, 46-3.

11. *Com. in Matt.*, 26-26.

12. It is extremely interesting to notice that of the 341 papyrus scrolls found buried in Pompei, only eighteen are in Latin. All the rest are in Greek.

13. Ep. 63, 2-9.

14. *De Trinitate* VIII, 13.

15. *De Mysterius* 50, 54.

16. Marucchi-Vecchierello, *Manual of Christian Archeology* (Paterson, St Anthony Guild Press, 1935), p. 288 ff.

17. Grossi-Gondi: *I Monumenti Cristiani* (Rome: Gregorian Univ. Press 1923), p. 271.

18. For a discussion of the Eucharistic allusions in the fragment of Abercius confer Cayre *Manual of Patrology* (Tournai, Declee and Co., 1936), Vol. I p. 154.

19. *Homilia in Joannem*, 82-4.

20. St. Thomas Aquinas, *Summa Theologica* III, Ques. 76, Art. 4.

21. *Ep.* 113.

VI

Holy Mass

§ 1. *A true sacrifice has four elements, namely, a gift, a priest, a sacrificial action, and a purpose.*

The term "sacrifice" is often used loosely to denote voluntary suffering endured to further a cause. In this chapter, it has a more precise meaning. Sacrifice was an integral part of the religions of pagan Rome, Greece, Egypt, Assyria, America, and many other places. The Jews of the Old Testament did not offer sacrifice in imitation of their pagan neighbors, but because God Himself revealed to them how they were to offer sacrifice. A study of pagan, Judaic, and Christian sacrifices shows that this act must have four elements to merit this label. (1) There must be a gift or victim. In pre-Christian times both pagans and Jews used gifts such as animals and fruits of the harvest in their sacrifice. In some pagan religions, the victim was often a human being. (2) Every sacrifice must have a priest who offers the gift in the name of the people. Religions that have no sacrifice have no group called "priests." A person is called a priest primarily because he is empowered to offer sacrifice. Priests formed a distinct group among pagans, Jews, and Christians. (3) The sacrificial action consists of a real or equivalent destruction of the gift offered to God. The gift represents the people offering it; its destruction symbolizes that they give themselves to God; the action is performed by the priest in the name of the people. (4) The purpose of sacrifice is to recognize God's supreme Lordship over the universe. Those who offer sacrifice give practical, external expression to their internal conviction that all things must be oriented toward God the Creator. They profess their faith in the truth that He is the goal of their lives and that without Him their lives would not make sense. This is the reason why sacrifice may be offered only to God.

§ 2. *The Church solemnly teaches that the Mass is a true sacrifice offered to God.*

From the very beginning of her existence, the Church has offered the Mass. We shall quote passages from very early Christian writers that the Mass was looked upon as a true sacrifice. It was not merely a commemoration or drama re-enacting the action of the Last Supper as the Bavarian Passion Plays re-enact the action of Good Friday. A passion play has power to excite devotion, but it does not have power to redeem mankind. Regardless of their motives, the leaders of the Protestant Revolt had the opportunity to confuse millions. The Council of Trent was obliged to repeat the truth received from God on the Mass. It defined, "If anyone says that in the Mass a true and real sacrifice is not offered to God, or that the act of offering is nothing else than Christ being given to us to eat: let him be anathema." (D-948)

The same Council quotes the prophecy of Malachias in the Old Testament as foretelling the universal celebration of the Mass. The prophecy reads, "From the rising of the sun even to the going down, my name is great among the Gentiles, and in every place there is sacrifice, and there is offered to my name a clean oblation: for my name is great among the Gentiles, saith the Lord of Hosts." (Mal. 1:11) Many hold that this passage in Malachias does not apply to Old Testament sacrifices.

first, it refers to a sacrifice offered everywhere, that is, among all peoples and all ages. Second, it is offered among Gentiles. Third, the prophecy seems to imply that one sacrifice will supplant the multiplicity of sacrifices of the Old Law. The superiority of this new sacrifice over the old ones is brought out by the fact that it would be "a clean oblation." The adjective "clean" is not to be taken as being physically clean. It is to be taken in the sense of being a sacrifice of superlative quality. It would have the elements that all sacrifices must have, for the prophecy explicitly refers to the oblation as being a sacrifice.

3. *There is clear evidence in Ante-Nicene writings that the Eucharist service was regarded as a true sacrifice by early Christians.*

Ante-Nicene writings were those composed before the Council of Nicea in 325 A.D. We quote these particular authors to show that the belief in the Eucharist as a sacrifice was held throughout the Christian world, and not in some isolated part of it. (1) *Greece or Antioch: The Didache* (60-100 A.D.) says "On the Lord's Day come together, break bread and hold Eucharist, after confessing your sins that your offering may be pure . . . . for this is that which was spoken by the Lord, 'In every place and time offer me a pure sacrifice, for I am a great King' saith the Lord, 'and my name is wonderful among the heathen.' "[1] Notice the clear allusion to Malachias' prophecy. (2) *Syria:* St. Ignatius of Antioch, who died in 107 A.D., wrote "Let it be your endeavor to partake of one Eucharist, for there is but one flesh of our Lord Jesus Christ, and one chalice in the unity of His blood, one altar, as also there is one bishop with the presbyters and the deacons."[2] Notice how neatly St. Ignatius refers to the elements of a sacrifice. (3) *Rome:* St. Justin Martyr (100-165 A.D.) has one of the clearest references to the Mass in all Ante-Nicene literature. In his *First Apology* he writes,

"When he who presides has celebrated the Eucharist .... they whom we call deacons give to those present a portion of the Eucharist species of bread and wine .... we do not receive them as ordinary food, or ordinary drink .... but as both the flesh and blood of that Jesus who was made Flesh."[3] Justin notes that the assembly of all Christians takes place on Sunday. In his *Dialogue with Tryphon* Justin quotes the prophecy of Malachias and explicitly states that the Eucharist offered by Christians is a true sacrifice.[4] *Asia Minor & Gaul:* St. Irenaeus, who died in 202 A.D., has this splendid reference to the Mass, "In the New Dispensation, Christ gave a new sacrifice which the Church received through the Apostles and now offers It to God throughout the world."[5] In another passage of the same work, St. Iranaeus tells us that the Church in his day had spread to Spain, Gaul, Germany, Asia Minor, Egypt, North Africa, and Italy. Notice that this is every major part of the then-known world. (5) That the Eucharistic service was regarded as a true sacrifice is also witnessed by Tertullian (+220) and St. Cyprian (+256 A.D.) from North Africa and Origen (+255 A.D.) from Egypt.

§ 4. *The Mass offered today has the four elements of a true sacrifice.*

We have already quoted the definition of the Council of Trent saying that the Mass is a true sacrifice offered to God. All we need do now is to point out how these four elements are verified in the Mass. But even on this score, the Church has left no room for confusion for she has pointed out these elements for us. "And since in this divine sacrifice, which is celebrated in the Mass, that same Christ is contained (oblation) and immolated in an unbloody manner (sacrificial action) who on the altar of the Cross once offered Himself (priest) in a bloody manner." (D-940)[6] There can be no doubt that Christ's action on the Cross constituted a true sacrifice as St. Paul notes, "Christ also loved us and delivered Himself up for us an offering and a sacrifice to God to ascend in fragrant odor." (Eph. 5:2) This single passage contains all four elements necessary for a true sacrifice. (1) Every sacrifice must have an oblation or gift to be offered. In the Mass the oblation is Jesus Christ. (2) The oblation or gift must be offered by a priest. The very meaning of a priest is a person who offers sacrifice. In the Mass, the priest who offers the oblation is Christ offering Himself to His heavenly Father through the ministry of human priests. (3) In the Mass, there is sacrificial action or immolation of the gift. Christ having died once can die no more. The equivalent immolation necessary for the Mass to be labeled a sacrifice is in the separate consecration of the bread and wine. (4) There should be no difficulty in grasping the fact that Mass is offered only to God. Notice how the Council of Trent refers to the four elements of a sacrifice. In defining that the Mass was a sacrifice, it stated that this sacrifice was offered only to God.

§ 5. *The Sacrifice of the Mass celebrated by Christ at the Last Supper was essentially the same as the Sacrifice of the Cross.*

The essential identity of the Sacrifice of the Last Supper and the Sacrifice of the Cross was officially taught by the Church at the Council of Trent. (D-938) In order to show identity between the two sacrifices, that is, the one of the Last Supper and the one of the Cross, it is necessary that we examine the elements of their composition. (1) In both of them the victim was the same, namely, Jesus Christ. In both of them, the priest offering It was the same. Again it was Jesus Christ, the great high priest. In both of them, Christ offered Himself to His Eternal Father.

An examination of Christ's own words reveals that the sacrificial action or the immolation of the victim is the same. In Matthew 26:28 Christ says, "All of you drink of this; for this is my blood of the new covenant, *which is being shed for many unto the forgiveness of sins.*" In Luke 22:19 Christ says, "This is my body, *which is being given for you* . . . . this cup is the new covenant in my blood, which shall be shed for you." By these words, Christ is tying together the action of the Last Supper and the action of the Cross. Both actions are the same in one respect and different in another respect. They are different for the actions took place on two different days, in two different places, and in two different ways. They are the same for Christ refers to His body and blood as He is holding It in His hand as an object being sacrificed. He does not only say, "This is my Body" and "This is my blood," He says, "This is my body which is being given (i.e., sacrificed) for you." And "This is my blood which is being shed (i.e., sacrificed) for you."

§ 6. *The Mass celebrated in the Church throughout the world today is essentially the same as the Mass celebrated at the Last Supper.*

The Mass celebrated at the Last Supper was a true sacrifice in Itself. It was not an empty prefiguring of a sacrifice. Then too, it was a special sacrifice. Unlike the sacrifices celebrated in the Old Dispensation, the Mass of the Last Supper was essentially the same as the one made on the Cross. Christ's action at the Last Supper had the four elements necessary for a true sacrifice. Immediately after Christ had completed the action, He enjoined, "Do this in remembrance of me." (Luke 22:20 and I Cor. 11:24) Let us analyze these words. In the original Greek, the word "Do" used by Christ is in the second person plural imperative, meaning "I command you to do." The word "this" is a demonstrative which points to the action that Christ had just completed. He had just completed a sacrifice identical with the one on the Cross. Christ never gave a command without also giving the power to fulfill that command. By these words, Christ was empowering certain persons to re-enact exactly the sacrifice that He had just completed.

The Sacrifice of the Mass is clearly a means of grace. In apologetics, we prove that Christ confided to His Church the authority to teach, to rule, and to sanctify. At the Last Supper Christ was confiding to His Church the power to repeat the Sacrifice He had performed. He did not put a time limit on the use of the power He had just given. It would be found in the Church until the end of time. Since Christ predicted that His Church would be spread among all nations, it follows that the Mass would also be celebrated among all nations.

§ 7. *The Sacrifice of the Cross was an absolute sacrifice; the Sacrifice of the Mass is a relative sacrifice.*

It is important that we first consider the precise meaning of the terms "absolute" and "relative." When we consider an object "absolutely," we consider it as it is in itself, irrespective of how it may relate to other things or how it may influence them. For example, the term "man" is an absolute term, for it implies nothing over and above a human being. We need not study anything else in order to get an adequate idea of man. When we consider an object relatively, we examine it in its relationship to other objects. We notice how it influences other objects or how other objects influence it. For example, the term "king" is a relative term, for it implies a person empowered to rule subjects. He would not be a king if he did not have subjects.

The Sacrifice of the Cross was an absolute sacrifice. It fulfilled its role independently of any other sacrifice. Its purpose was to win infinite merit or grace for men. By It Christ filled a reservoir with enough grace to enable all men to reach their supernatural goal. The Sacrifice of the Mass is the divinely instituted means by which the grace that Christ won on the

Cross is channelled to men. The relative character of the Mass does not make It a Sacrifice inferior to the one of the Cross. The two are essentially the same. As Almighty God ordained it, the role of the Sacrifice of the Cross could not have been played by the Sacrifice of the Mass. The role of the Sacrifice of the Mass could not be played by the Sacrifice of the Cross. The Mass channels to man the grace that Christ won on the Cross.

§ 8. *The Sacrifice of the Mass is accidentally different from the Sacrifice of the Cross.*

Two things are essentially different when they have different natures. For example, a tree is essentially different from an animal, for the first has a vegitative nature while the second has a sensitive nature. Two things are accidentally different when their natures are the same but their externals are different. A black leopard and a spotted leopard are essentially the same, but accidentally different. We have already seen that the Sacrifice of the Cross and that of the Mass are essentially the same. But we can readily name several points in which they are accidentally different. (1) The Sacrifice of the Cross could take place only once, whereas the Mass can be repeated many times. (2) On the Cross, Christ offered Himself to His Eternal Father without the ministry of a human priest. In the Mass, Christ does indeed offer Himself to His Eternal Father but only through the ministry of a human priest. (3) On the Cross, Christ offered Himself in His own physical appearance of man. In the Mass, Christ offers Himself under the appearances of bread and wine. (4) On the Cross there was a real slaying of the Victim. Death resulted from the actual shedding of blood. In the Mass, there is a real and mystical slaying. It is accomplished by the separate consecration of the bread and the wine. None of these four points changes any of the elements which justifies the conclusion that the two Sacrifices are essentially the same. The Church anathematizes anyone who holds that any of the above points of accidental difference indicate an essential difference.

§ 9. *By Divine Precept, the matter of the Mass must be wheaten bread and grape wine.*

In 1439, the Council of Florence in its Decree for the Armenians, stated that "the matter of the Sacrament of the Eucharist is wheat bread and wine of grapes, with which before consecration a very slight amount of water should be mixed." (D-698) The Code of Canon Law repeats this.[7] (1) If the bread used, as matter for Holy Eucharist is not made from wheat flour, there is no conversion of the substance into that of Christ's body. (D-692) The Church has laid it down as a matter of discipline that in the Latin rite unleavened bread must be used; while in most of the Oriental rites leavened bread is used. The consecrations by a priest who disregarded these regulations would be valid but unlawful. In the Latin rite, the bread is disc shaped; in the Oriental rites, the bread used at Mass is square shaped and triangular shaped for Holy Communion of the people. (2) The Gospels themselves state that the wine used by Our Divine Lord at the Last Supper was made from grapes. "But I say to you, I will not drink henceforth of this fruit of the vine. (Matt. 26:29) The wine used at Mass must be pure wine made of grapes. It must not be mixed with foreign substances such as sugar or water. Wine made from fruits other than grapes such as berries, currants, and so forth is invalid matter. (3) The Church prescribes that when the priest pours wine into the Chalice at Mass, he must add a drop or two of water. This custom goes back to ancient times. The Council of Trent prescribes it for three reasons. Namely, Christ most probably did it at the Last Supper, blood and water flowed from Christ's side on the Cross, the mixture of the water with the wine is a symbol of the union of the faithful with Christ their head. (D-945) If the small quantity of water was omitted, the consecration of the wine would still be valid.

§ 10. *The chief offerer of the Mass is Christ Himself; the Church is the general offerer; the priest is the specially deputized offerer; all others are participating offerers.*

Jesus Christ is the chief offerer of the Mass. This flows from the fact that the Mass is essentially the same as the sacrifice of Calvary, where Christ was the only offerer. If Christ is not the chief offerer of the Mass, It would be different from the Cross. We would be forced to say that the two sacrifices were only accidentally the same—an opinion condemned by the Church.

The Church is the general offerer of the Mass. Christ confided all the means of grace and worship to His Church. His purpose was not to keep people from It, but to make sure that they received the maximum benefit from It. As the general offerer of the Mass, the Church can authorize or forbid a priest from celebrating Mass; she can lay down regulations touching upon the ceremonies, time, place, prayers, vestments, and other things connected with the celebration of Mass.

At the Last Supper, Christ made it very clear that the Mass in the future would be offered through the ministry of human priests. He conferred the special power these human priests would need to act in His place when He said, "Do this in remembrance of Me." (D-949)

There are many ways in which a person can offer the Mass besides the three listed above. Those who employ any of these other ways are called participating offerers. They can facilitate the celebration of Mass by acting as a server, organist, donor of stipend, and so forth. A person who assists at Mass is indeed a participating offerer, for he joins himself with the priest in offering. He retains this role even though, for example, he assists at Sunday Mass to avoid committing serious sin.

§ 11. *The ceremonies and prayers of the Mass up to the offertory comprise what is called the Mass of the Catechumens.*

While there are older references to the Mass, in Christian literature, the oldest extant description of the Eucharistic service is contained in the *First Apology* of St. Justin Martyr written in the middle of the Second Century.[8] The ceremonies and prayers in the Mass today are a shortened version of the ceremonies and prayers of the Mass in ancient times. (1) The prayers at the foot of the altar stress purification and the contrition for sin. They are a preparation for the solemn moments that follow. Notice the reference to this in the *Didache,* written before 100 A.D. "On the Lord's Day come together, break bread and hold Eucharist, after confessing your transgressions."[9] (2) The priest kissing the altar stone with its relics recalls that in ancient times Mass was often celebrated on a sarcophagus containing the relics of martyrs. (3) The *Introit* sets the theme of the Mass according to the cycle of the liturgical year. It is a remnant of the prayers and the litany recited as the priest and people entered the Church to celebrate Mass. The *Kyrie* is all that remains of the long litany. (4) The most striking feature of the Mass of the Catechumens is the time devoted to instruction of those preparing for Baptism. The lectors read and explained portions of the Bible to the catechumens. These portions are the *Epistle* and *Gospel* of today's Mass. The bishop or priest, who presided at the services, would then preach a homily, which was a discourse or exhortation to the people. "Then the reader (lector) concludes; and the president verbally instructs and exhorts us, to the imitation of these excellent things."[10] (5) The last step of the Mass of the Catechumens showed the fruit of instruction, for the people made a profession of faith in what they had been taught. They recited the Creed. The Creed recited at Mass is the Nicene Creed, formulated about 325 A.D. We do not know the exact date of composition of the Apostles' Creed. It was in existence within two generations after the Apostles. It derives its name, not because it was composed by the Apostles, but because it was formulated in Apostolic times.

§ 12. *The first principal part of the Mass is the Offertory.*

St. Justin's narrative of the Offertory in his *I Apology* (Ch. 66) reads as follows: "And, as I said before, when we have concluded our prayer, bread is brought and wine and water; and the president (i.e., bishop or priest) in like manner, offers up prayers and thanksgiving with all his strength; and the people give their assent by saying 'Amen.' " In conjunction with the Sunday services of ancient times, the faithful offered gifts of food and money to be used for the support of the clergy, the poor, the sick, and the widowed. It was from these gifts that the bread and wine used for the Eucharistic service were set aside. The people would advance toward the presiding cleric to present their gifts. After receiving the gifts, the president, that is, bishop or priest, would wash his hands soiled from handling objects of various kinds. The relic of this act still remains in the Mass today when the priest washes his hands while reciting the psalm beginning with the appropriate words "I will wash my hands among the innocent." (Ps. 25:6) We have mural paintings in the catacombs depicting the priest before the altar. Sometimes Mass was celebrated on the sarcophagus of a martyr, but often It was not. The altar shown in some catacomb murals was not nearly as long as altars are today. It was just wide enough to hold the sacred vessels. It is not difficult to surmise why it was eventually lengthened. The Epistle and Gospel in early times were recited from lecturns away from the very table of sacrifice as is done today at a solemn Mass. In time, it was noticed that it was more convenient for a priest to read the Epistle and Gospel while standing near the altar of sacrifice. In order to make room for the Missal at the altar, the altar was lengthened at both ends, thus accounting for its present rectangular shape.

§ 13. *The essence of the Mass consists of the separate consecration of the bread and wine.*

The third element of a true sacrifice is the immolation of the gift that was offered. In the Mass, the gift is Christ. On the Cross, there was a physical immolation or destruction. The Mass is essentially the same as the Sacrifice of the Cross but Christ, having died once, can die no more. But there must be at least a symbolic immolation of the Victim.

By what act of the Mass is this mystical slaying accomplished? The Church has solemnly defined that the immolation is found in the Mass today, but most theologians have not been able to pinpoint it to the satisfaction of all other theologians. It must be said, however, that the vast majority of them hold that it is in the separate consecration of the bread and the wine. St. Gregory of Nazianzen, one of the greatest of the Greek doctors of the Church, wrote, "Do not hesitate to pray for me . . . . when with a bloodless stroke you separate the Body and Blood of the Lord using speech (words of consecration) as a sword."[11] The form pronounced over the bread is, "For this is my Body." Over the chalice, the priest says, "This is the chalice of my blood of the new and eternal testament . . . . mystery of faith . . . . which shall be shed for you and for many unto the remission of sins."

Although it is generally agreed that the symbolic immolation necessary for the Mass to be a true sacrifice is in the separate consecration of bread and wine, theologians put forth various opinions as to how the separate consecration does effect a mystic slaying. Some of the great theologians of the last five centuries have expended their best efforts in trying to answer this extremely difficult question. The student has infallible assurance that the immolation does take place at Mass. He should leave to theologians the problem of solving how it takes place.

§ 14. *The Communion pertains to the integrity and not to the essence of the Mass.*

The Sacrifice to God is complete when the Body and the Blood of Jesus Christ are made present on the altar as the result of the double consecration. The Communion is not necessary for the essence of the Mass. But when we say that the Communion pertains to the integrity of the Mass, we mean that there is a most serious obligation that it accompany the Consecration. At the Last Supper, Christ pronounced the words of consecration and then added a command. He said, "Take and eat" and "All of you drink of this." The words "take," "eat," and "drink" are in the imperative mood in Greek. There can be no doubt that Christ is demanding that He be obeyed. At the Last Supper, Christ celebrated the first Mass. He then issued the command "Do this in remembrance of me." (Luke 22:20) He thereby ordered that those who would celebrate Mass in the future must do exactly what was done at the Mass of the Last Supper.

A priest saying Mass today must receive Holy Communion under the appearances of both bread and wine simply because Christ enjoined it on all saying Mass. The obligation is so serious that, if after the Consecration, it is impossible for the priest to consume the Sacred Species, another priest must take his place and do so. The Church solemnly teaches that the command issued by Christ at the Last Supper is obeyed even if only the priest receives Holy Communion at Mass. It is not necessary for the laity to do as well. She defined this saying,

"If anyone says that Masses in which the priest alone communicates sacramentally are illicit and are therefore to be abrogated: let him be anathema." (D-955) She also anathematizes those who hold that it is unlawful to receive Holy Communion outside of Mass. (D-889)

§ 15. *The Holy Sacrifice of the Mass pays infinite honor to God.*

Honor is described as the external recognition of excellence. It is legitimate when it is commensurate with the excellence and redounds to the honor of the true source of the perfection. It is right and proper that we recognize excellence, for it is the recognition of truth. Plato once said that the abuse of a good thing soon casts a shadow of suspicion even on its legitimate use. Flattery is not honor but is the disgusting practice of giving honor where there is no legitimate basis for it. The fact that "honor" is paid to many undeserving persons does not prevent it from being good and proper in itself. There can never be baseless honor paid to God, for He is infinitely perfect. In fact, any honor that we, as mere humans, can give to Him falls infinitely short of the amount for which there is basis. The fourth element of a sacrifice is that it is an act recognizing that He is the Creator and Lord of all things.

Sacrifice is basically an act of honor or praise of God. All sacrifices are not on a par. In the Old Dispensation, true sacrifices were offered to God. They indeed paid true honor and praise to God, but they could be superseded by other sacrifices. That they would be superseded was foretold in the prophecy of Malachias which told of "a clean oblation" that would be offered to God. The Mass is that clean oblation. The fact that the Victim in the Mass and the High Priest who offers It is Jesus Christ is clear proof that the Mass has the power to give infinite honor to God. It cannot be improved upon as an act of praise and recognition of God's infinite excellence. The Mass retains this character regardless of the human priest who offers It or the solemnity that may accompany It.

§ 16. *The Mass is the most fruitful means of grace that God has given to us.*

The value of anything is measured by its effectiveness in helping one to reach a goal. The value of a means of grace is measured by its effectiveness in enabling us to reach the goal that God has assigned to us. We know that a person can increase the amount of grace he has in his soul. Apart from the subjective requirements involved, one means of grace is more fruitful than another if it transmits more grace than the other. In its power to transmit grace, the Holy Sacrifice of the Mass is in a unique position among the means of grace. We have already seen that It channels to man the grace that Christ won by His death on the Cross. And being essentially the same as the Sacrifice of the Cross, the Mass is capable of releasing an infinite torrent of grace.

The amount of grace that one receives from assisting at Mass depends generally on his capacity to receive it. He can enlarge his capacity in one of two ways. He can rid himself of venial sin and affection for sin; he can take positive means to increase the charity with which he assist at Mass. Although a person who assists at Mass with mortal sin on his soul cannot receive sanctifying grace from It, he may receive actual grace from It. The fact that he is at Mass indicates that God has already given him some actual grace.

§ 17. *The four ends of the Mass are adoration, contrition, thanksgiving, and supplication.*

God has assigned to us the stupendous goal of seeing Him face to face. In order to reach this goal, a person must have sanctifying grace in his soul at death. All of God's dealings with man are stamped with the mark of love. Nothing happens to man by chance. Everything is designed to draw him toward his goal. This is true of what people call "misfortune" such as sickness, disgrace, disappointment, and death.

God is infinitely happy. Nothing that we can do can increase His happiness. The application of this principle to the ends of the Mass is indeed revealing. (1) Adoration means subjecting ourselves to God's will. God does not need us, nor does He need what we can do for Him. He wants us to adore Him because we are the ones who benefit from this act. (2) Contrition means that one repairs the harm that sin has caused. What is the particular harm of sin? It makes us veer away from our assigned goal. Man is the beneficiary of an act of contrition, for he gets back on the track that leads to his goal. (3) Supplication is the act of asking God for what we need to make progress toward heaven. This request is clearly meant to benefit man. (4) Thanksgiving is the act of gratitude to God for benefits He has already given. So unsearchable are God's ways that He gives us new gifts when we make the very act of thanking Him for those already received. These four ends of the Mass are the same four ends of prayer in general. All of them are offered to God and all of them benefit man. Since the Mass is the greatest act of worship that can be offered to God, it follows that the adoration, contrition, thanksgiving, and supplication expressed in the Mass are far superior to these acts expressed in any other way.

§ 18. *Mass may be offered in behalf of anyone who can profit from it, that is, for the living on earth and for the souls in Purgatory.*

Mass can be offered only in behalf of those who can still be helped to reach their supernatural goal.[12] (1) Mass cannot be offered for Saints, the Blessed in Heaven, and baptized infants who have died before reaching the use of reason. Masses offered in their honor are offered implicitly in honor of God, the Source of their greatness. (2) Mass may be said publicly for the spiritual or temporal benefit of any of the faithful. Needless to say, that person's temporal benefit must be in harmony with his spiritual benefit. A Mass is called public when the intention is publicly announced via the parish bulletin, pulpit announcements, or proclaimed to those assisting at It. It is called private when the intention is kept secret. (3) Private Masses may be said at the request of heretics, schismatics and even pagans provided there is no scandal given and there is no evil, error, or superstition in the requests. (4) The Church teaches (D-983) that the Poor Souls in Purgatory can benefit from Masses said for them. While these souls cannot receive sanctifying grace from the Masses, the duration of their suffering there may be shortened. (5) Public Masses can be said for the dead who were entitled to a Christian burial or for heretics and schismatics who showed evidence of conversion or sorrow for sin. Catechumens about to be converted from a non-Catholic sect fall into this category. (6) In general, only private Masses may be offered for the dead who were not entitled to a Christian burial, but scandal must be precluded. Suicides, creamationists, those living in concubinage, such as in an invalid marriage, fall into this latter category. The possible scandal referred to here lies in the fact that the public Masses may be interpreted as a minimizing of the seriousness of the sin or giving the false impression that one religion is a good as another.

§ 19. *A stipend is an offering made for the priest's support on the occasion of his applying the fruits of the Mass according to the stipend donor's request.*[13]

The practice of accepting stipends for the application of the fruits of the Mass can be traced back to ancient times. The Scriptural passage quoted to justify it reads as follows: "So also the Lord directed that those who preach the Gospel should have their living from the Gospel." (I Cor. 9:14) Pope Pius VI in condemning the errors put forth by the false Council of Pistoria in 1794 stated that it is perfectly permissible to accept Mass stipends. Since the Code of Canon Law allows priests to accept them and since this code is covered by the endowment of infallibility, the acceptance of Mass stipends is not a simoniacal contract. A stipend is not the "price" of the Mass, nor is the amount of a stipend a gauge of the value of a Mass. Church law empowers the local ordinary to fix the amount of stipends.

A person who receives a Mass stipend is bound under pain of mortal sin to say the Mass or to have It said.[14] Each stipend represents a separate and serious obligation.[15] They may not be divided or combined. Let us say that in a given diocese the stipend for a sung Mass is $5.00 and that for a low Mass it is $1.00. Those receiving stipends may not combine five low Mass stipends into one sung Mass stipend, nor divide one sung Mass stipend into five low Mass stipends. This is a practical point today for laymen as well as priests. It is the custom today for friends of a deceased person to leave Mass stipends with the family. That family is bound under penalty of mortal sin not to tamper with those stipends. Those receiving the stipends are merely the stewards of those obligations.[16] They may not divide or combine the obligations they are burdened with. They are to transfer the obligations to the priest without notable delay. They must make good any culpable or inculpable loss that befell the stipends while in their possession.

§ 20. *All Catholics over seven years of age, having the habitual use of reason and not legitimately excused are bound under penalty of mortal sin to assist at Mass on Sundays and Holy Days of Obligation.*

Man is a creature, a contingent being completely dependent on God for his existence and his continuance in existence.

God is his supernatural goal. The Mass is the greatest help man has to reach his goal. It should be the center of his spiritual life. But he also has other duties such as making a living for himself and his family. There is a great danger that he may lose sight of the greatness of the Mass. The Church has legislated that the minimum attention that he can pay to the Mass and still avoid mortal sin is to assist at It once every seven days.

The law binds all Catholics over seven years old who have the habitual use of reason.[17] Children who are under seven years old are not bound by this law even though they have reached the use of reason. Persons over seven who lack the use of reason, such as feeble-minded and so forth, need not assist at Mass even though they are physically able to get to Church.

The law binds Catholics to assist at Mass on all Sundays and Holy Days of Obligation. In Judaism, that is, in the religion of anticipation, the prescribed day of worship was the Sabbath. When the Messias came and there was no more need for a religion of anticipation, the ritual regulations of Judaism lost their binding force. God no longer prescribed worship on the Sabbath. It was then that the Roman Catholic Church legislating with divine authority prescribed Sunday as the day when her members must assist at Mass. Canon Law lists ten Holy Days of Obligation besides Sunday.[18] All of them do not bind in every country. In the United States, they are Circumcision (Jan. 1), Ascension (40 days after Easter), Assumption (August 15), All Saints (Nov. 1), Immaculate Conception (Dec. 8), and Christmas (Dec. 25).[19]

§ 21. *The duty to assist at Mass on Sundays and Holy Days is fulfilled by continuous bodily presence in the designated place.*[20]

The obligation to assist at Mass is fufilled by assisting at It as It is celebrated in any of the rites authorized by the Church, whether it be Latin or Oriental. It is not necessary that one assist at It in the rite into which he was baptized. They are forbidden to assist at Mass in a schismatic Church even when no Catholic Church is available.

In order to fulfill the duty prescribed by the Church, a Catholic must be inside the church building, or if he is outside of it because of the crowd, he must be united to the others who assist at Mass. He would not be united to this crowd if he is more than forty paces clear of them. To follow Mass via radio or televsion is insufficient.

A person's presence must be continuous from the prayers at the foot of the altar to the last blessing. For a just reason, it is permissible to fit together parts of different Masses said on the same day but the Consecration and Communion must be in the same Mass. For example, a person comes into Church at the Offertory. He fully fulfills his duty if he remains for the rest of this Mass and then stays from the beginning up to the Offertory of a later Mass. One may not piece together different parts of several Masses celebrated simultaneously on different altars in the same Church.

The duty may be fulfilled in any Catholic church, chapel, public or semi-public oratory or at Mass celebrated in the open. The duty to assist at Mass in such places as prisons, barracks, hospitals, and ship-board depends on whether or not there is a fixed altar there. One must have the proper intention and attention to fulfill the obligation. He has the first even if he assists at Mass in order to avoid mortal sin. He has the second if he realizes that he is assisting at Mass. He clearly does not realize it if he sleeps throughout the time when Mass is celebrated.

§ 22. *It is a mortal sin to omit without excuse a notable part of the Sunday Mass; it is a venial sin to omit without excuse a small part of this Mass.*

A part of the Mass is notable on one of two scores, namely, dignity or duration. It is notable in dignity to omit the Canon up to the Consecration, even though one is present for the Consecration; from the Consecration up to and including the Pater Noster; only the Consecration together with only the Communion of the priest; the Consecration alone; probably the Consecration of only one Species.

A part of the Mass is notable in duration if it amounts to about one-third of the Mass regardless of the comparative dignity of the parts. It is matter for serious sin if one misses everything from the beginning to the Offertory prayers, or from the beginning up to the Gospel together with all that follows the Communion of the people. It is clear that a part of the beginning and a part of the end of the Mass can be pieced together to form a notable portion.

It is easily possible for those coming in late without excuse to be guilty of an added sin of scandal. Children are very quick to notice the laxity of adults in the matter of punctuality. And every parish priest can attest that they are swift to follow the example of their parents and elders in this matter.

The Church enjoins that a sermon be preached to the people on Sunday unless a good reason excuses the priest. Just as the priest has the duty to preach, so the people have a duty to listen to that sermon. It is wrong to omit it without good reason even though it is not part of the Sunday Mass as such. The practice of omitting the sermon can also very easily be matter for scandal.

§ 23. *Any moderately grave reason or hardship to oneself or to another excuses one from the duty to assist at Mass on a Sunday or a Holy Day.*

Objectively grave sickness excuses one from the duty to assist at Sunday Mass. It is difficult to lay down a rule that could cover all cases. If the sickness is not serious enough to prevent a child from going to school, or an adult from going to work, a woman from doing ordinary household duties, then we find it difficult to see how it could be serious enough to excuse them from Sunday Mass. Parents do great spiritual harm to their children when they permit trifling ailments to keep them from Sunday Mass.

Those who must attend infants, the sick, or the aged, and who cannot find a suitable substitute to perform these duties are excused from Sunday Mass. In these cases, the infant or ailing person could easily suffer notable harm if left unattended. It is the experience of parish priests that persons who sincerely desire to assist at Mass rarely use these excuses.

One is excused from Sunday Mass if his employer requires him to work at the hour when he could be fulfilling this duty. In our highly industrialized economy, a great many factories and furnaces must be kept in continuous operation. There are cases where Sunday work is not urgent from the employee's standpoint, yet if he refused to do so, he would lose his job. This is a valid reason to omit Sunday Mass.

A pastor is empowered to dispense from the duty to assist at Sunday Mass. He may use this power only under several definite conditions. There must be a just reason for using it; it can be given only in a particular instance or case; he can dispense his parishioners sojourning within the parish limits or outside the parish limits; he can dispense others; while they sojourn within the limits of his parish.

NOTES

1. Ch. 14.
2. *Ad Phila.* 4.
3. *I Apol.* 66.
4. *Dial. Cum Tryphonem* 41.
5. *Adv. Haer.* 4-17-5.
6. *Cf.* also D-938.
7. Canons 814-815.
8. Ch. 66 and 67
9. Ch. 14.
10. St. Just., *I Apology*, Ch. 66.

11. *Ep. 71 Ad Amphil.*

12. Canon 809.

13. Canon 824.

14. Canon 829.

15. Canon 830.

16. Canon 839.

17. Davis, *Moral and Pastoral Theology* (London: Sheed and Ward, 1945), Vol. II, p. 59 ff.

18. Canon 1247.

19. This number was requested by the Third Plenary Council of Baltimore and approved by the Holy Office in 1885.

20. Canon 1249.

VII

Holy Communion

§ 1. *Christ's instruction that all receive Holy Communion is at least at matter of counsel.*

The Gospels tell us that Christ issued both commands and counsels. If a person seriously breaks a commandment, he deprives himself of sanctifying grace. If he neglects a counsel, he deprives himself of an added measure of grace. Was Christ's instruction that we receive Holy Communion a command or a counsel? He explicitly stated that it was both. Read carefully the promise of the institution of the Holy Eucharist in St. John's Gospel. (Jn. 6:50-60) With varying degrees of earnestness, Christ tells His listeners no less than seven times in those ten verses that His flesh is to be eaten and His blood is to be drunk.

In the verses cited, Christ utters a counsel. He says, "He who eats my flesh and drinks my blood has life everlasting." (v.55) Again, "He who eats my flesh and drinks my blood, abides in me and I in him." (v.57) Notice that Christ uses the present tense. He says, "He who eats." By this usage, Christ shows that the eating of His flesh and the drinking of His blood is to be a continuous practice. It can be repeated. The second point to notice is the effect that the reception of Christ's Body and Blood has on a person. It gives him super-

135

natural life which is precisely what sanctifying grace is. The grace is annexed to the reception of Holy Communion so that each worthy reception entitles one to an increase of this new life. The third point to notice is who is instructed to receive Holy Communion. Only a person who knows right from wrong can understand why it is profitable to live according to counsel. This excludes infants and irrational persons. We can say that Christ issued His counsel to receive Holy Communion repeatedly to all who have reached the use of reason. Christ in effect said that by neglecting an opportunity to receive Holy Communion one neglects the opportunity to increase in grace.

§ 2. Christ's instruction that all receive Holy Communion is a command.[1]

Even in our relationship with our fellow men, we know that at times we can insult a person by refusing his gift. Any mortal sin is an insult to God, for it is the rejection of one of His gifts, namely, His guidance to heaven. Christ clearly stated that the rejection of Holy Communion is the rejection of supernatural life and heaven. It is an implicit insult to God. It is a mortal sin. We must make a clear distinction between neglecting Holy Communion and rejecting It. They are by no means the same. In John 6:54 Christ said, "Amen, amen, I say to you, unless you eat the flesh of the Son of Man, and drink his blood, you shall not have life in you." Christ spells out the consequences that would befall a person who rejects the reception of Holy Communion. It would entail the loss of supernatural life or sanctifying grace. This effect can be produced only by the commission of a mortal sin. St. John wrote his Eucharistic passage after having read the content of the Eucharistic passages in the Synoptic Gospels. His Gospel clarifies several points of the Synoptics. When Matthew, Mark, and Luke wrote their *Gospels* and St. Paul wrote his *First Epistle to the*

Corinthians, they stated that at the Last Supper Christ said, "Take and eat; this is my body" and "All of you drink of this; for this is my blood." The verbs "take" and "drink" are in the second person plural, imperative. The Greek clearly shows that Christ is issuing a command, but they do not state the binding force of that command. When John noticed this measure of indefiniteness in the previous writings, he felt obliged to clarify it. We have seen that he left no doubt in the minds of his readers on this point. He records the episode where Christ Himself states that anyone who rejected the reception of Holy Communion was guilty of mortal sin.

§ 3. *The Church has the right and the duty to legislate on the frequency with which Catholics are to receive Holy Communion.*

The study of apologetics proves that Christ endowed the Roman Catholic Church with the fullness of power to teach, to rule, and to sanctify. The Church's laws could not have more binding force if they had been made in heaven. "Whatever thou shalt bind on earth shall be bound in heaven, and whatever thou shalt loose on earth shall be loosed in heaven." (Matt. 16:19) On a previous page, we saw that Christ confided to His Church the means of grace and ordered her to distribute them to the maximum spiritual benefit of mankind. Every duty implies a right. The duty to distribute Holy Communion implies the right to enact legislation binding on all Catholics touching upon the reception of this Sacrament. The Church may not abolish the duty to receive Holy Communion, for it was imposed by Jesus Christ Himself.

The Church may legislate with what frequency Catholics must receive Holy Communion and assign the sanction for refusal to obey it. Her authority also extends to the frequency with which Catholics may receive It, the preparations that must be made, the instructions that must be given, the place where Holy Communion may be received, the person who may administer It, and so forth. Anyone who is acquainted with the regulations that *de facto* have been laid down will agree that they are all appropriate and prudent laws. Their purpose is to preclude abuse from creeping into this most sacred act and at the same time to make available this most powerful means of grace to as many people as possible and as frequently as possible. Needless to say, these regulations are covered by the Church's endowment of infallibility.

§ 4. *The Church obliges under the penalty of mortal sin that all Catholics having the use of reason receive Holy Communion at least once a year during the Easter season.*

Our Divine Lord did not say how frequently a Catholic must receive Holy Communion under penalty af sin. The Church does. The legislation on this point was first enacted by the Fourth Council of the Lateran held in 1215 A.D. It is repeated in the Code of Canon Law in force today.[2] (1) In the United States, the Easter season extends from the first Sunday in Lent to Trinity Sunday—a period of roughly one hundred days. Notice that it does not begin on Ash Wednesday as some laity think. (2) All who have reached the use of reason and are not legitimately excused are bound by the precept. A person can reach the use of reason even before he is seven years old. Persons who cannot swallow or who cannot retain the Blessed Sacrament are not obliged by this law. But persons who are confined to their homes due to sickness or old age are obliged to notify the priest so that they can make their Easter duty at home. (3) The duty binds one under penalty of mortal sin. Those who have lost the right to receive Holy Communion because of, for example, excommunication or an invalid marriage are obliged to recover the right in time to make their Easter duty. One commits a mortal sin each time the duty is neglected. The duty is clearly not fulfilled by a sacrilegious Communion.[3] (4) Parents commit a serious sin if because of their neglect their children are not adequately prepared in time to fulfill this duty. There is a certain amount of instruction necessary before a child may be admitted to the reception of this Sacrament. Parents sin each year their neglect prevents their child from making his First Communion. (5) The fulfillment of one's Easter duty may not be anticipated or postponed. A person who does not or cannot fulfill it before Trinity Sunday must fulfill it as soon as possible after this date.

§ 5. *A Catholic who has reached the use of reason and is in danger of death is obliged under penalty of mortal sin to receive Viaticum.*[4]

Each sacrament was given to enable us to meet a special crisis or need. There is no greater crisis for the soul than its transit from this life into the next one. The greatest Sacrament was given to meet the greatest crisis. It is of divine precept that one receive Holy Communion when in danger of death. Unless a person is legitimately excused, he is bound under penalty of mortal sin to receive Holy Communion when he is in danger of death. Physical impossibility, the inability to swallow, irrationality are legitimate excuses. A person spiritually unprepared to receive Holy Communion because of the presence of a mortal sin is bound to make the necessary preparations by recovering sanctifying grace. The duty begins to bind one as soon as there is a prudent reason for thinking that death will probably take place. Notice that death need not be a certainty. The probable cause of death is internal if it has already attacked the body. Examples are a grave wound, serious sickness, or even advanced age. It is external if the person is already or will soon find himself in very dangerous circumstances. Examples would be soldiers going into battle, rescue workers going on an extremely dangerous mission, and so forth. In cases where Viaticum is to be received, the regulations of Eucharistic fast are waived. There is a duty in justice or in charity imposed on those who attend the dying to see to it that the person has an opportunity to receive Viaticum.

It is not strictly obligatory for one to receive Viaticum if he received Holy Communion within the last three days. He is, of course, urged to do so. It is permissible to receive Holy Communion a second time in the same day if the second reception is Viaticum.

§ 6. *One receives the full spiritual benefit of Holy Communion even when he communicates only under one Species.*

There is evidence dating from the Third Century that Holy Communion was sometimes received under only one Species. It was sometimes received only under the appearances of wine. The Council of Constance in 1415 A.D. defined that the laity could receive the full spiritual benefit of the Sacrament by receiving under one Species. A century and a half later, the Council of Trent in 1562 A.D. repeated the same doctrine in the face of Protestant errors. It defined, "If anyone denies that Christ whole and entire, who is the fountain and author of all graces, is received under the one species of bread, because as some falsely assert, He is not received according to the institution of Christ Himself under both species; let him be anathema."(D-936) We have already seen that Christ is entirely present under the appearances of bread. A person who receives Holy Communion only under the appearances of bread really and truly obeys Christ's command to eat His flesh and to drink His blood. The increase of grace is an effect of receiving Christ, regardless of the Species under which He is received. A person who has been given a broken Host in Holy Communion receives as much grace as he would have received if he had communicated under the Species of bread and wine.

The priest at Mass does not communicate under both

species as a necessary condition for receiving the full Sacrament. He does so in order to reproduce exactly the action as It took place at the Last Supper.[5] On that occasion, Holy Communion was received under the appearances of both bread and wine. We must distinguish the Holy Eucharist as a Sacrament and the Holy Eucharist as a Sacrifice.

§ 7. *The Church prescribes that in the Latin rite Holy Communion is to be distributed to laymen only under the appearance of bread.*[6]

In the last number, we saw that it was perfectly justifiable on dogmatic grounds to distribute and to receive the Sacrament of Holy Eucharist only under the Species of bread. In this number, we see that in the Latin rite It must be distributed in this way. The Council of Trent has stated, "If anyone says that the Holy Catholic Church has not been influenced by just causes and reasons to give Communion under the form of bread only to laymen and even to clerics when not consecrating, or that she has erred in this: let him be anathema." (D-935) The Council speaks of "just causes and reasons." It is not difficult to guess what those reasons were. While it is a very simple matter to preserve the Holy Eucharist under the appearances of bread from corrupting, it is a difficult task to preserve It under the Species of wine. Then too, the danger of spilling in the course of distributing It to many hundreds and even thousands would be very great cause of concern.

Notice that the propostion refers only to the distribution of Holy Communion in the Latin rite. Catholics of the Latin rite may receive Holy Communion under both Species at an Oriental rite Mass. Catholics of an Oriental rite may receive Holy Communion only under the appearances of bread from a Latin rite priest. Canon Law urges a person to make his Easter duty by receiving Holy Communion in the rite into which he was baptized, but he can make it by receiving Holy

Communion in any rite. He would, of course, be forbidden to make his Easter duty by receiving Holy Communion in a schismatic church even though the priest was validly ordained and he validly celebrated Mass.

§ 8. *Catholics are urged to receive Holy Communion frequently, and if possible, even daily.*

Holy Mother the Church has always urged her members to make frequent use of the Holy Eucharist as a powerful means of grace.[7] It is erroneous to think that the practice of daily Communion is an innovation of modern times. There is explicit evidence that St. Basil the Great encouraged it in the Fourth Century. In 1691 A.D. the Church condemned the error of Jansenius who held that only those who had reached a high degree of sanctity were entitled to receive Holy Communion frequently. This opinion drew the Church's condemnation, for it contradicted her desire that people look upon Holy Communion as a help to be better rather than a reward for having been good. The preparations of body and soul required for daily reception of Holy Communion are exactly the same as those required for receiving It at other times. The Church wants us to receive Holy Communion as often as we assist at Mass. We are to look upon receiving Holy Communion as being part of the Mass. A person who goes to Mass but neglects to receive Holy Communion should feel a great loss and should bitterly regret having defrauded himself of grace. The frequency with which one receives Holy Communion is a good barometer for measuring fervor in the practice of religion. A fervent Catholic never neglects an opportunity to receive Holy Communion; he goes as often as possible. A practical Catholic receives It at least once a month; a mediocre Catholic only makes his Easter duty; a bad Catholic neglects even to make his Easter duty. There is no valid reason why most Catholics could not receive Holy Communion at least every Sunday. A great many students in our Catholic colleges could easily receive It every day.

§ 9. *Persons confined to their homes have a right to receive Holy Communion frequently there.*

It has been estimated that in an average parish there are about three persons per every one hundred families who are confined to their homes. The causes for confinement are such factors as blindness, old age, sickness, and so forth. It is not necessary that the person be bed-ridden to be labeled as confined. These people have a perfect right to receive Holy Communion at home at frequent intervals and at least once a month.

The room where Holy Communion is to be given is to be properly prepared for the occasion. While it need not be richly adorned, it must be clean and neat. The table where the priest is to rest the Blessed Sacrament is to be properly arranged. All profane and even sacred articles such as pictures, rosaries, vigil lights, and the like must be removed. A large clean napkin is to be spread out; two blessed candles must flank a crucifix; a bottle of holy water, a glass of plain water and a spoon are also to be on the table. A person is to meet the priest at the door with a lighted candle and escort him to the sick room. He is to leave the room if the sick person is to go to confession; otherwise, he is to kneel. If the priest is to make other Communion calls, he is to be escorted to the door with a lighted candle. One should speak only in answer to the priest's questions.

It often happens that the sick person is reluctant to inform the priest of his desire to receive Holy Communion at home or in the hospital. Some are positively frightened by the prospect. The friends, relatives, or neighbors of such a person can do a splendid bit of apostolic work by informing the priest of the sick person's condition. The priest has ways of tactfully disposing the sick person for the frequent reception of Holy Communion at home. Every parish priest has known of cases where the zeal and vigilance of neighbors has been instrumental in rendering a sick person's time of confinement spiritually profitable.

§ 10. *Holy Communion does for the supernatural life of the soul what food does for the natural life of the body.*

The phases of a person's supernatural growth and development parallel the phases of his natural growth and development. We need hardly call attention to the part that food plays in one's physical health and well-being. Holy Communion is the supernatural food of the soul. Food does four things for the body. Holy Communion does four things for the supernatural life of the soul. (1) It preserves strength. We shall see this more pointedly when we study the sacramental grace that the Holy Eucharist gives. (2) It promotes growth. There is only one type of growth in the supernatural life. It is the increase of sanctifying grace. While the other sacraments give us the grace won by Christ, the Holy Eucharist gives us Christ Himself as well. St. John records how Christ underscored It as a particularly fruitful means of grace. (3) It repairs spiritual harm done to the supernatural life of the soul. While it was not primarily instituted to remove mortal sin, it can repair spiritual harm in many different ways. It provides the actual grace inspiring one to remove venial sin and the temporal punishment due to sin. (4) It engenders delight. This may be described as an eagerness to advance in the love of God. A person who receives Holy Communion often does not have to be urged to use the other means of grace such as prayer and good works. He has a realization of their importance keener than one who rarely receives Holy Communion. He derives a positive delight and joy from a clear conscience. For him the observance of the Commandments is not a negative matter. He sees them to be what God intended them to be, namely, sign posts pointing the way to the goal that God has assigned to us.

Spiritual writers have written books on each of the four points that we have noted here as being effects of the reception of Holy Communion.

§ 11. *Holy Communion entitles one to the sacramental grace he needs to grow rapidly in the love of God.*

Where the love of God is, there also is sanctifying grace. Charity or love of God is not exactly the same as sanctifying grace but the two are concomitant. Any increase in sanctifying grace causes an increase in love of God.[8] All the sacraments give sanctifying grace to those who receive them worthily. Each sacrament also confers a special actual grace which no other sacrament can confer. Holy Communion gives the actual grace to grow *rapidly* in the love of God. None of the other sacraments can match the Holy Eucharist's power in enabling us to grow in the love of God. How is this effect produced? It would be wrong to think that Holy Communion's power to give actual grace ends as soon as the Sacred Species are dissolved. The very fact that one is in sanctifying grace entitles him to a continuous stream of actual graces. That stream keeps on coming even though the person rejects the help that the actual grace represents.

There is probably a proportion between one's store of sanctifying grace and the amount of actual grace he receives. The more sanctifying grace one has, the more actual grace to which he is usually entitled. Since Christ in the Holy Eucharist is the very Author of all grace, it follows that It is in Itself the most fruitful means of sanctifying grace. The more sanctifying grace one has, the more does God love him and is probably more inclined to give him greater and greater actual grace. The Holy Eucharist in Itself is, therefore, also the most fruitful means of actual grace that God has given to us. It differs from all other sacraments in that no other sacrament gives us the grace enabling us to grow in the love of God as rapidly as this one. We speak of the potential power of this Sacrament in comparison with the potential power of any of the other sacraments.

§ 12. *The first requisite for the fruitful reception of Holy Communion is that the person be baptized and have the use of reason.*[9]

In the treatment of all sacraments besides the Holy Eucharist, we note that the recipient must fulfill certain conditions necessary for valid reception. Those sacraments cannot exist apart from the person who receives them. The Holy Eucharist, however, can and does. Anyone who receives the Holy Eucharist receives the Body and Blood of Christ regardless of his age, his rationality, his freedom from sin, and so forth. But there are certain conditions that must be complied with to receive Holy Communion fruitfully or worthily.

It is generally estimated that a person reaches the use of reason when he is about seven years old. This estimate does admit of many variations. There is a great deal of confusion as to the precise meaning of the use of reason. It is more than the point when a child can be frightened away from committing certain acts. The use of reason is that stage of maturity when one can be taught to avoid a bad act because God forbids it or to perform a good act because God commands it. To be said to have the use of reason, it is not necessary that one *de facto* know what acts are good and what are bad. All that is necessary is that one have the capacity to be taught these things.

§ 13. *The second requisite for the fruitful reception of Holy Communion is that the recipient have an adequate knowledge of Christian doctrine.*[10]

We have seen in the last number that only persons with the use of reason may today be admitted to the reception of Holy

Communion. The First Commandment prescribes that all persons with the use of reason and not in danger of death are obliged to know the doctrines required by a necessity of precept. The binding force of this precept is a serious one.[11] The truths in question are those that one must know to pray well, to live well, to believe well, and to worship well. They consist of the Lord's Prayer, the Commandments, the Creed, and the sacraments one receives. These truths need not be remembered in set terms. It is sufficient to know them substantially. A person who once knew these truths but has now forgotten them is obliged under pain of sin to re-learn them. The parish priest has the right and duty to examine persons on this point before admitting them to the reception of Holy Communion. He can do this systematically in the case of converts and of children making their First Communion. Experienced confessors can often tell by the manner in which a penitent makes his confession as to whether or not he knows the truths of precept. If the penitent does not know them, the priest must caution him not to receive the Sacraments until the truths are re-learned.

It sometimes happens that the rapid approach of death or the low capacity for learning precludes the assimilation of the truths to be known by a necessity of precept. The minimum amount of knowledge that is required of such a person is knowledge of the truths to be known by a necessity of means and that he is receiving the Body and Blood of Christ under the appearances of bread. In these circumstances, it is not neglect that causes him to be ignorant of the truths to be known by a necessity of precept.

14. *The third requisite for the fruitful reception of Holy Communion is freedom from mortal sin.*

One who deliberately and freely receives Holy Communion while in mortal sin does more than receive this Sacrament unfruitfully. He receives It sacrilegiously. The sacrilege in this

case is a serious one. A person who is not conscious of th
mortal sin on his soul when he receives Holy Communio
does indeed receive Our Lord, but not at all sacrilegiously
since he is not conscious of being in sin. No one can commit
formally sacrilegious sin without knowing it, and wanting t
commit it. Such a man is actually the recipient of sanctifyin
grace indirectly or "accidentally," as the theologians call i
from this very reception of Holy Communion provided, o
course, that he has made at least a general act of imperfec
contrition before receiving It. The mortal sin that otherwis
would have blocked the entry of grace in the soul is now re
moved "accidentally" by the sacrament of the Eucharist, bu
it must still be confessed later.

A person who is in mortal sin and who wishes to receiv
Holy Communion must ordinarily first recover sanctifyin
grace by the reception of the sacrament of Penance.[12] It is tru
that an act of perfect contrition does remove even mortal sin
but Canon Law prescribes that in the case of one wishing t
receive Holy Communion, it must be removed by Penance
To disobey this law is itself matter for mortal sin. In extraor
dinary circumstances where there is a pressing need to receiv
Holy Communion but one cannot remove mortal sin by th
reception of Penance, one may make an act of perfect contri
tion and then receive. Example of this would be soldiers go
ing into battle, rapid approach of death, and so forth. A person
who finds himself at the altar rail about to receive Holy Com
munion and then remembers an unforgiven mortal sin on hi
soul may receive Holy Communion if he cannot return to hi
pew without causing serious scandal.

A person who validly received the sacrament of Penance
and then remembers having forgotten to confess a mortal sin
may receive Holy Communion even though he remembered
the sin soon after emerging from the confessional and could
easily have re-entered it to receive a fresh absolution. He must
however, confess this sin at the next confession if he still re
members it.

§ 15. *The fourth requisite for a fruitful reception of Holy Communion is that one observe the prescribed Eucharistic fast.*

The Church has the authority to lay down regulations that are to be observed in receiving or in administering the sacraments. She can make the observance of these regulations bind even under penalty of mortal sin. Her purpose in laying them down is to prevent abuse that might creep into the distribution of the sacraments. For centuries, the Church required the observance of a very strict fast on the part of persons about to receive Holy Communion. In 1953, its strictness was relaxed. The regulations in force today are listed here. A person may drink water or take medicine at any time before receiving Holy Communion. He may not drink liquids other than water for one hour before receiving Holy Communion unless sick, in which case he can take it without special permission any time before receiving. Liquids such as milk, coffee, tea, fruit juices, and other non-alcoholic drinks fall into this category. A person may not eat solid food such as bread, meat, eggs, cereal and the like, nor may he drink alcoholic beverages during the three hours preceding the reception of Holy Communion. It is to be noted with reference to paragraphs two and three that the one hour and the three hours mentioned must precede the time when Holy Communion is received. It is not the time of the beginning of the Mass at which Holy Communion is received.

It is a mortal sin deliberately and freely to receive Holy Communion after having disregarded the Church's regulations on the Eucharistic fast. The regulations need not be observed when Holy Communion is to be received as Viaticum. A person who finds himself at the altar rail and then remembers that he is not fasting may receive Holy Communion if he cannot return to his pew without serious scandal.

The Eucharistic fast is not broken by intravenous feedings, by smoking, or by swallowing food particles remaining in the mouth from a previous meal. It is broken by the chewing of gum, for this contains sugar. While taking any amount of food or drink is sufficient to break one's fast, the law forbids only those who have certainly broken their Eucharistic fast.[13] It does not bind those who have reason to doubt that they are not fasting.

§ 16. *The better one prepares to receive Holy Communion, the more grace does he receive from it.*

We must make a careful distinction between the amount of grace that the reception of Holy Communion can give and the amount It actually does give in particular cases. The amount of grace that Holy Communion gives is measured by the person's capacity to receive. A person has a limited capacity for grace by the very fact that he is a creature. He can obviously do nothing to remove this limitation. But he himself is the cause of any further limitation of his capacity for grace. The presence of venial sin or affection for sin lessens the grace that Holy Communion gives, for they lessen the active charity with which one can receive the Sacrament.[14] Venial sin is destroyed by a proper act of sorrow. Affection for sin is destroyed by implementing an effective plan designed to prevent the commission of even venial sin in the future.

One's capacity for grace is usually measured by the amount of grace already in the soul. This capacity is measured by one's active love of God. The more sanctifying grace one has in his soul, the more does he usually love God and God loves him. The implication here is very important. The more one increases in grace now, the more efficacious for him can be the means of grace he uses in the future. We cannot isolate the effects of spiritual exercises performed today from those performed in the future. Every means of grace, that is, prayer, sacraments and good works, can be used to prepare one for the better reception of Holy Communion. A thorough preparation is not necessarily replete with emotion and sentimentality as some falsely think it must be.

NOTES

1. *Summa Theologica,* Par. III, Ques. 80, Art. 11.
2. Canon 859.
3. Canon 861.
4. Canon 864.
5. *Summa Theologica,* Par. III, Ques. 82, Art. 4.
6. Canon 852.
7. Canon 863.
8. On the effects of Holy Communion, confer Tanquerey, *The Spiritual Life* (Tournai, Desclee and Co., 1930), p. 143 ff.
9. Canon 854, 1.
10. Canon 854, 1.
11. Noldin, *Summa Theologiae Moralis* (Ratisbon, Pustet, 1941), Vol. II, p. 13.
12. Canon 856.
13. Noldin, *Summa Theologiae Moralis* (Ratisbon, Pustet, 1940), Vol. III, p. 150.
14. *Summa Theologica,* Par. III, Ques. 79, Art. 8.

VIII

Penance

§ 1. *Penance is a sacrament of the New Law especially instituted to forgive sins committed after Baptism.*

The sacrament of Penance was always in use in the Church. For centuries, no notable heresies attacked either its existence or its nature. But in the Sixteenth Century, the leaders of the Protestant revolt did propound errors against it. The Church at the Council of Trent was obliged to set forth her teaching on the subject. She defined, "If anyone says that in the Catholic Church Penance is not truly and properly a sacrament instituted by Christ our Lord to reconcile the faithful, as often as they fall into sin after baptism, let him be anathema." (D-911)

Penance has all the notes of a sacrament. (1) The Church has defined and the Gospels tell us that it was instituted by Jesus Christ as a permanent rite. (2) It is an effective means of grace, for it was instituted to remove all sin committed after Baptism. After a person has been baptized, he is either in sanctifying grace or mortal sin. (3) It has a matter and a form. The matter of Penance is the contrition, confession, and satisfaction made by the penitent. Its form is the words of absolution pronounced by the priest over the penitent. (4) Penance entitles one to a special actual grace; namely, the supernatural help needed to keep the resolution to avoid sin that he has just made in confession. (5) The sacrament was confided by Christ to the Church, and so may be administered only with her authorization. The Church is competent to legislate as to the frequency with which her members are to receive this sacrament. (6) In physical life, people can fall gravely ill. Sin is the counterpart of grave illness. Medicine cures sickness. Penance is the supernatural medicine which cures the grave illness represented by sin.

§ 2. *Christ promised to give to the Church the power to forgive sin when He promised to grant Her the power to bind and to loose.*

We saw that Christ promised to institute the Holy Eucharist before He actually did so. He prepared the people ahead of time for the great Gift they were to receive. He did the same thing for the same reason with the Sacrament of Penance. In St. Matthew's Gospel, we read that Christ said to Peter, "I will give to thee the keys to the kingdom of heaven; and whatever thou shalt bind upon earth shall be bound also in heaven; and whatever thou shalt loose upon earth, it shall be loosed also in heaven."[1] (Matt. 16:19) He later repeated these words to the Apostles. (Matt. 18:18) Several things must be noticed about them. (1) The second passage cited excludes what is special to the first; namely, a promise of a primacy of power to Peter. Both passages clearly have reference to jurisdiction, for they speak of the power to bind and to loose. Jurisdiction means the right to direct others in the use of the just means needed to further one's progress toward his goal. The ultimate goal of man's existence on earth is to see God face to face. Sin most effectively prevents one from attaining this goal. The jurisdiction that Christ promised to give to His Church must include the power to forgive sin. (2) Only God can forgive sin, meaning that only He can institute the means by which sin is forgiven. The power that Christ promised in the two passages we quoted above was not the power to institute these means. It was the power and authority to use them after Christ had confided them to His Church. (3) In the passages where Christ promises to give power, we must notice that He in no way restricts its exercise. This implies that the Church would have the power as long as sin was an obstacle to salvation; that is, until the end of time. Then too, Christ did not give the Church power only over some sins. He gave it power over all sins,[2] for any serious sin is an effective barrier to salvation. He wanted the Church to have power to remove this barrier completely.

§ 3. *Christ fulfilled His promise to institute the sacrament of Penance when He actually gave the Church the power to forgive or to retain sins.*

The Council of Trent defines, "If anyone says that those words of the Lord Savior: 'Receive the Holy Spirit; whose sins you shall forgive, they are forgiven them; and whose sins you shall retain, they are retained' (Jn. 20:22) are not to be understood of the power of remitting and retaining sins in the sacrament of Penance as the Catholic Church has always understood from the beginning, but, contrary to the institution of this sacrament, distorts them to an authority for preaching the Gospel, let him be anathema." (D-913) There are several things to be noted about the Gospel verses quoted by the holy council. (1) Christ is empowering human persons to take His place in the act of forgiving sins. The use of the second person plural pronoun "you" explicitly indicates this. It would be correct to say that Christ makes Himself juridically or morally one with His human agent in the administration of Penance. (2) The power to forgive sin is issued to Christ's Church without any kind of limitation. The Church would have the power to forgive all kinds of sin regardless of their heinousness until the end of time. (3) In the passage quoted by the Council, Christ issues two distinct powers; namely the power to forgive and the power not to forgive. The second is just as real as the first. We shall see that it is far from being merely a negative power. (4) This passage from St. John's Gospel almost perfectly parallels those referring to jurisdiction in St. Matthew's Gospel quoted in the last number. This close parallel coupled with the fact that one points to the future and the other to the present, shows that they treat of the same thing; namely, the forgiveness of sin. (5) The fact that Christ was giving a means to destroy any and all sin until the end of time shows that He was confiding the power to the Apostles insofar as they were officials of His Church. In other words, He was confiding it to His Church. The Apostles received the power because they were officials of His Church. They would not have received it if they were not.

§ 4. *The positive power recorded in John 20:23 shows that Penance is the only means specially instituted to forgive sins committed after Baptism.*

The positive power is embodied in the words, "Whose sins you shall forgive, they are forgiven them." (John 20:23) The modern critical editions of the New Testament show that there was never any doubt as to the authenticity of this verse. It indicates that Christ instituted a clear-cut means to forgive sin. But from this fact, we can conclude that He precluded the existence of other means specially instituted to forgive sins committed after Baptism. In other words, a person who rejects Penance, rejects forgiveness. What advantage would there be in instituting several means to forgive sin? The conditions necessary for "new" means could not conflict with the conditions necessary for Penance, for truth cannot contradict truth. Now there would indeed be a conflict if the conditions for the "new" means would be more or less than those required for the valid reception of Penance. Any "new" means could not make the forgiveness of sin either easier or more difficult than Penance now makes it. If the conditions for the "new" means exactly paralleled the conditions for Penance, there would be no new advantage to souls accruing from it. The institution of such a means would be useless duplication. This in turn would make for confusion. It is difficult now to get people to learn and to remember the conditions necessary for the reception of one means. It would be doubly difficult for them to learn and to remember a second set of conditions. The result would be that instead of it being easier to obtain forgiveness, it would eventually become more difficult. To obviate these pitfalls, Our Divine Lord instituted only one special means to forgive sin after Baptism; namely, the Sacrament of Penance.

§ 5. *The negative power recorded in John 20:23 shows that Penance is the only means specially instituted to forgive sins committed after Baptism.*

The negative power that Christ gave to the Church with regard to the administration of Penance is a real power. The words of Christ are, "Whose sins you shall retain, they are retained." (John 20:23) This power underscores the fact that Christ instituted only one special means for the forgiveness of sins committed after Baptism. We prove it anew here. Whenever Christ gave any power, it was effective power; that is, it was completely adequate to perform the duty assigned. When Christ's ambassadors on earth retained sin, those sins were retained in heaven as well. The power to retain sin would not be an effective power if it could be circumvented by the use of means other than Penance. One means would cancel the effectiveness of the other means. The two powers that Christ gave His Church, namely, the power to forgive and the power to retain, must not be seen isolated from each other. One sheds light on the other. Christ brought out this

fact by placing them side by side. The two powers are mean-
ingful only if they are given to intermediaries or plenipoten-
tiaries of God who use them for the spiritual benefit of the
members of the Church. Apart from the use of the pronoun
"you," the existence of two powers shows that Christ placed a
third person between the penitent and God. That third person
must make a judgment as to which of his powers he must use
when a penitent approaches him for forgiveness. When a
sinner rejects the person empowered to administer Penance,
he rejects the sacrament of Penance itself. When he rejects
the sacrament of Penance, he makes it impossible to have his
sins forgiven. All this flows from the fact that Christ in John
20:23 gave the Church a two-fold power over sin.

§ 6. *There is literary evidence dating from earliest Christian
times proving the existence of the sacrament of Penance in
the Church.*

Christ instituted only one means for the forgiveness of sins
committed after Baptism, namely, the sacrament of Penance.
When early Christians refer to the means they used to have
their sins forgiven, they can only be referring to Penance. (1)
The *Didache* (60-100 A.D.) reads, "On the Lord's Day come
together, break bread and hold Eucharist, after *confessing
your transgressions* that your offering may be pure." (Ch. 14)
This passage strongly indicates the existence and use of a
means for the remission of sin. (2) A great deal has been written about the reference to the forgiveness of sin in *Hermas
Pastor* composed in about the middle of the Second Century.
The theme underlying the whole writing is that the Church
possesses the means to forgive sin. (3) Tertullian (c160-200)
speaks of the secret confession of sin, made to a priest or bishop
for the purpose of recovering the innocence one had received
by Baptism.[3] In the later years of his life, Tertullian's rigorism
drove him first to hold that certain sins *should* not be forgiven.

But his denials are noted in the history of dogma simply because they are denials of the commonly accepted teaching of the Church on Penance. (4) Origen (c180-225 A.D.) has especially clear evidence of a clear-cut means confided to the Church for the forgiveness of sins committed after Baptism.[4] He underscores the idea that all sins of every sinner can be absolved by the power given to certain members of the clergy after a secret confession of sins has been made. (5) We could cite evidence of the existence of the special means for forgiving sin in the writings of Clement of Alexandria (+211), St. Cyprian (+256), St. Basil (+379), St. John Chrysostom (+407), St. Ambrose (+397), St. Augustine (+430), and others. The statement that Penance as a sacrament first made its appearance in the Middle Ages indicates either ignorance or calumny on the part of the person making it.

§ 7. *Only God is competent to lay down the conditions required for the forgiveness of sin.*

In St. Luke's Gospel, we read that Christ said to the paralytic, " 'Man, thy sins are forgiven thee.' And the Scribes and Pharisees began to argue, saying, 'Who is this man who speaks blasphemies? Who can forgive sins, but God only?' " (Luke 5:20) Christ proved His divinity and His possession of the power to forgive sin by healing the paralytic. There are several premises for the conclusion stated in the proposition. (1) The sanctifying grace that one receives in Baptism creates a bond of supernatural love between God and the soul. That bond can be broken only by the commission of mortal sin, for every mortal sin is an implicit rejection and hatred of God. Only man can break this bond. (2) When a person commits a mortal sin, he not only rejects God's love, but he also rejects all future right to this love. He has no basis to claim the right that the bond of love be repaired. It follows from this that he may not lay down the requirements for the bond to be repaired. They must come from God, for only the one who can forgive can lay down conditions for forgiveness. (3) The requirements laid down by God are just and adequate. They are just, for any sincere person helped by actual grace is capable of meeting them. They are adequate, for they are fully capable of healing the bond of love broken by mortal sin. None of the requirements laid down for the valid administration of Penance is optional. It is strictly necessary. Any person who fails to meet all of them receives this sacrament unfruitfully. If he freely and deliberately neglects to meet all of them, he receives Penance sacrilegiously.

§ 8. *Penance was instituted by Christ to forgive any and all sins committed after Baptism.*

The Council of Trent defined, "If anyone says that in the Catholic Church Penance is not truly and properly a sacrament instituted by Christ our Lord to reconcile the faithful as often as they fall into sin after Baptism: let him be anathema." (D-911) We requote this definition here to show that the Church makes no distinction as to the sins that Penance is capable of forgiving. If Christ wished to limit the effectiveness of Penance, He could have done it on two counts. He could have made Penance powerless to forgive certain types of sins, and He could have limited the number of times that individuals could approach this sacrament. The Church teaches that He made no such limitations and the Gospel of St. John implicitly repeats this teaching.

There is solid testimony in ancient writings to the effect that all sins could be forgiven by Penance regardless of their heinousness. In some parts of the Church, it was the local practice not to absolve the sins of murder, adultery, and apostasy. But this was done for disciplinary reasons, and not because of a lack of power over these sins. When there was danger that the discipline would cause more harm than good, it was discontinued. Some persons objected to this change of discipline. It was then that Pope St. Callixtus (c.217-c.222 A.D.) reminded all that the Church by virtue of the power of the keys, has power to absolve even from these three sins.[5] In saying this, he was stating that there was no sin that could not be forgiven by Penance. The same distinction between power and practice is to be made on the frequency with which Penance could be received in the early centuries. The Church in ancient times always claimed the power to administer Penance, but in practice it was administered at longer intervals to impress upon the people an appreciation for the sacrament.

§ 9. *Christ instituted Penance to make the forgiveness of sin easier and surer.*

Criticism of the sacrament of Penance as the means of forgiving sin springs either from pride or ignorance. We list only a few reasons showing the wisdom of its institution. There are certain indispensable conditions necessary for the forgiveness of sin. Unless a person meets these requirements objectively, his sins are not forgiven no matter how subjectively convinced he is that he has recovered God's love and friendship. Christ saw that if people in general were left to their own devices, a great many of them would omit some of these requisites, thus making forgiveness impossible. When He entrusted the administration of Penance to priests, He provided added assurance that the sacrament would be received worthily. Confessors can attest to the fact that many confessions would be unworthily received if the priest did not remind penitents to make a proper act of sorrow and a firm purpose of amendment. They often must tell the penitent how to make these acts. Far from making the forgiveness of sin more difficult, Christ made it surer.

When Christ prescribed that a penitent must seek forgiveness through the hands of a priest, He provided him with a spiritual physician and father. As a physician of souls the confessor directs a penitent in the use of the correct method to deal effectively with such things as the occasion and habits of sin which may be a problem to the particular penitent before him. As a spiritual father, the confessor encourages the penitent to shun venial sin, mediocrity, and the neglect of the means of grace. A person's spiritual diseases are as particular as his bodily diseases. For effective cure of bodily disease, one seeks the individual attention of a physician. Christ saw that the effective cure of spiritual disease must be obtained by the individual attention of a spiritual physician administering the sacrament of Penance.

§ 10. *The reception of Penance in fact or in desire is necessary for salvation for all who have fallen into mortal sin after Baptism.*[6]

"Whose sins you shall forgive, they are forgiven them; and whose sins you shall retain, they are retained" (John 20:23) explicitly refers to the forgiveness of sin. "But he who loves me will be loved by my Father, and I will love him and manifest myself to him" (John 14:21) implicitly refers to the forgiveness of sin. These two passages are in complete harmony with each other, but the second must be interpreted in the light of the first. Christ said that charity, love of God, or perfect contrition can remove sin, but He never intended it to be used as a means to circumvent the reception of Penance. Perfect contrition does not circumvent Penance if it is accompanied by a sincere desire to receive Penance. In fact, one who does not have at least the implicit desire to receive Penance cannot be said to have perfect contrition.

The desire to receive Penance in the context discussed in this number can be either explicit or implicit. It is explicit when one longs to confess and to receive valid absolution. It is implicit when he longs to do all that God wants him to do to save his soul. The desire to receive Penance in fact must be a sincere one. It is certainly sincere if one seeks to receive absolution at the first opportunity he gets. But for how long can he postpone the actual reception of Penance and still be said to have the sincere desire to receive the sacrament? The answer is that he may not postpone it beyond the time when the Church law obliges those in mortal sin to receive valid absolution. This law says that all Catholics in mortal sin are seriously obliged to receive valid absolution within a year after committing mortal sin. Invincible ignorance excuses from blame in this matter.

§ 11. *The proximate matter of the sacrament of Penance is a sorrowful confession of sins.*

The Council of Trent defines, "If anyone denies that for the full and perfect remission of sins there are three acts required of the penitent, as it were, the matter of the sacrament of Penance; namely, contrition, confession, and satisfaction, which are called the three parts of penance—let him be anathema." (D-914) Every sacrament must have a matter and form. Penance is no exception. The three acts mentioned by the holy council are bound together in a single unit and are sometimes labeled "a sorrowful confession."[7] These three acts are so interdependent that modification in one of them has great influence on the others. If one is completely missing, the other two are stripped of their effectiveness; that is, they cannot be valid matter for Penance. The contrition necessary for the reception of Penance is the sorrow one has for having offended God. A person is not sincerely sorry for his sins if he refuses to take effective means that will prevent their recurrence, nor is he really sorry for his sins if he refuses to use the divinely appointed means for repairing the harm caused by sins. God alone is competent to lay down terms under which sin can be forgiven. We shall see that He requires that a penitent confess his sins to a duly authorized priest. The administration of Penance is a judicial process. The purpose of the sentence given in this judicial process is to repair at least in part the harm caused by sin. A penitent who refuses to accept the duty to make satisfaction destroys the judicial character of Penance, thereby preventing it from being an effective means for the forgiveness of sins.

§ 12. *A penitent must try to remember the kind and number of his mortal sins not yet directly forgiven by Penance.*

Unless extraordinary factors intervene, a person wishing to receive Penance must make a sincere examination of conscience. He is required to search for two things. He must try to recall the kind and number of his unforgiven mortal sins. By kind, we mean that he must try to remember the lowest species of each mortal sin together with any circumstance which adds a new malice to the basic act. The lowest species embodies that quality of a sin which makes it different from other sins against the same commandment or virtue. For example, heresy and external denial of one's faith are both sins against the same virtue, yet they are specifically different. A penitent must try to recall the kind and number of his mortal sins which, although they were indirectly forgiven, have not been directly submitted for absolution.[8] A sin is indirectly forgiven by an act of perfect contrition, or imperfect contrition with another sacrament, as when one makes an act of contrition after receiving Extreme Unction. A mortal sin is also indirectly forgiven if inadvertently forgotten in one's last reception of Penance or when it was not confessed because an impending disaster such as shipwreck precluded confession. There is a serious obligation to submit all mortal sins indirectly forgiven to the direct power of the keys.

A person examining his conscience must try to remember the number of times he committed the mortal sins that fall into the above categories. If he cannot remember the exact number of his mortal sins, he should try to determine their weekly or monthly average. The student should be thoroughly familiar with the principles laid down by moral theologians to determine the numerical distinction of internal and external sins.

§ 13. *In preparing for confession, a penitent need not recall all of his venial sins, nor the number of times that he committed them.*

The justification for the proposition lies in the nature of a venial sin. Strictly speaking, venial sin is a sin only by analogy, for it does not strip the soul of sanctifying grace. This grace can coexist in the soul with venial sin. When a person commits a venial sin, he shows that he does not love God as much as he should. It is an act of lukewarmness toward God. If grace can coexist in the soul with venial sin, it follows that one can receive new amounts of grace in spite of the presence of venial sin. A person examines his conscience in order to make the confession required for valid absolution. Since he need not confess all his venial sins to receive this absolution, neither is it necessary to recall all of them, nor the frequency with which each was committed.

Persons examining their consciences must make a clear distinction between venial sins and imperfections. Venial sins are matter for confession, but imperfections are not. Many penitents have sadly confused these two. A venial sin is a true human act. There is in it a slightly sinful object chosen with a measure of deliberateness and freedom. An imperfection completely lacks one of the elements necessary for a sinful act. In most cases, it is not a human act but the act of a human. For example, many think that anger as such is always sinful. This is not true. It is in itself an indifferent emotion which receives its moral coloring from concrete circumstances. We need scarcely emphasize the importance of knowing what constitutes a human act.[9] Any of the five impediments to a human act can lessen one's blameworthiness.

§ 14. *In examining his conscience, a penitent must determine whether or not a doubtful sin is truly doubtful.*

A person examining his conscience tries to discover his blame-worthiness before God for an act he has performed. This may at times be a difficult task. Perhaps the principles we discuss here will clarify matters. The first step is to learn if he doubted before he acted or after he acted. We learn from the study of moral theology that one may act only when one has a sub-jectively certain conscience. If he has doubt as to the permissi-bility of the act he is about to perform, he may not act. If he "takes a chance" on the objective goodness of an act, he is guilty of sin even though he later learns that it was objectively good. When he examines his conscience, he must list these acts as certain sins. For example, teen-agers engage in passionate kisses and embraces. If they are doubtful of the precise moral value of this act, they are most likely guilty of serious sin, for they act on a doubtful conscience.

It sometimes happens that a doubt as to blameworthiness arises after an act has been committed. The penitent must try to recall whether or not the three conditions for mortal or venial sins were verified when the act was performed. He must judge the act in the light of the knowledge he had when he committed it; and not in the light of the knowledge he has since acquired. If after diligent investigation, he still has at least one, good, solid reason for holding that the act was not a human act, he must list it as a doubtful sin. It is doubtful matter for confession and must be placed in a special category.

§ 15. *A scrupulous person must obey his confessor's directives as to how he is to examine his conscience.*

A scrupulous person finds it very difficult to make correct moral judgments. He tends to exaggerate blameworthiness. He is inclined to inflate venial sins into mortal sins and sinless acts into sinful acts. Scrupulosity is not sanctity! For a person who is scrupulous, the examination of conscience is a real chore. He is torn between the drive to be certain and a host of problems which defy certain solution. Such a person needs help. He must be given kind consideration; he should expect firm treatment. A scrupulous person cannot make up his own mind on the morality of an act he has committed. It must be made up for him. He should seek the advice of a confessor or a spiritual director whose judgment he trusts. He must then follow that advisor's directives to the letter. Disobedience will defeat the best advice of the most prudent confessor.

Scrupulosity may result from a "negative" approach to sanctity; that is, the person thinks that sanctity consists only in the avoidance of sin. In reality, any person who is in sanctifying grace is holy. He grows in holiness by more frequently and fervently using the various means of grace. A confessor will steer a penitent away from scruples by making him concentrate on the positive side of sanctity. A second antidote for the disease of scrupulosity is meditating on God's goodness and superabundant love for us. A scrupulous person tends to concentrate on God's justice, but then rides roughshod over His mercy. A third point is that the confessor may instruct a scrupulous person as to how he is to examine his conscience. Needless to say, the confessor has a right to demand that his directives be obeyed.

§ 16. *The first quality of the contrition necessary for Penance is that it be supernatural.*

At the very outset, we must call attention to the fact that sorrow for sin is not an emotional, sentimental experience. Many tears shed over sins are no proof that the penitent has great sorrow for his sins. These tears often indicate nothing more than a high-strung disposition. The type of sorrow is determined by the reason why a person is sorry. Natural reasons indicate natural sorrow; supernatural reasons indicate supernatural sorrow. For the valid reception of Penance, super-natural sorrow is absolutely necessary.

A person has natural sorrow for sin when he regrets having committed it because he sees that it will cause him to lose some temporal benefit. For example, a person has natural sorrow for his sin of theft because it has caused him to lose his friends, or his reputation, or his job. Natural sorrow is an ego-centric type of sorrow based on an erroneous appraisal of the meaning of sin, and is, therefore, insufficient for Penance.

A person has supernatural sorrow when he sees his acts for what they are, namely, offenses against Almighty God. He realizes that in committing a mortal sin he has rejected God in favor of a seriously forbidden object. He sees that in committing a venial sin he does not love God as much as he should. A person who has supernatural sorrow acknowledges the damage done to the bond of love by mortal or venial sin. He regrets his act and desires to take effective steps to repair that harm. Supernatural sorrow is theocentric and is based on a correct appraisal of the meaning of sin. It is certainly sufficient for Penance.

§ 17. *The supernatural sorrow for sin necessary for Penance may be either perfect or imperfect.*

The proposition states that either of the two types of super-natural sorrow is sufficient for the valid and fruitful reception of Penance. It is not necessary to have both of them. A person who has perfect sorrow for his sin does two things. He first sees his sin as being an offense against an infinitely good God—a God who is the source of all perfection. He then regrets having rejected God by mortal sin or having slightly offended Him by venial sin. The sinner now affirms that he loves God above all things and prefers Him to any finite good regardless of its magnitude.

Imperfect sorrow is also supernatural, for otherwise it

would not be sufficient for Penance. A person who has imperfect sorrow also does two things. He first sees that sin can separate him from God forever in hell or for a time in purgatory depending on its gravity. God has assigned us the goal of seeing Him face to face in heaven. At death, the soul flings itself at God and wants Him with every fibre of its being. To be separated from God causes excruciating suffering. After seeing that this possibility can befall him if he continues in his state of sin, the person who has imperfect sorrow fears this separation from God and the suffering that accompanies it. He detests and regrets his folly in having sinned because it was the first step toward a temporary or eternal separation from God. He then tells God that he never wants to be separated from Him. We fear to lose something that we love. In the case of imperfect contrition, it is God. When we tell God that we fear to lose Him in hell or in purgatory, we are telling Him that we love Him. Imperfect contrition is clearly based on love of God.

§ 18. *The contrition necessary for Penance must be universal for mortal sin, and at least partial for venial sin.*

The justification for the proposition lies in the nature of mortal and venial sin. When a person commits a mortal sin, he chooses to reject God in favor of a seriously forbidden object. The soul is completely stripped of sanctifying grace. The bond of love between God and the soul established by grace is broken by the commission of even one mortal sin. The contrition necessary for Penance must aim to repair this harm. It must extend to each and every mortal sin not yet forgiven. If the penitent excludes even one mortal sin from his act of sorrow, then none of them are forgiven. Mortal sins are destroyed by the infusion of sanctifying grace. If one unrepented mortal sin remains, it is capable of blocking the entry of the grace that would destroy the other sins.

Venial sin is an act of lukewarmness toward God. It does not strip the soul of sanctifying grace. In fact, it can coexist in the soul with this grace, and one can receive increases of this grace while in venial sin. Contrition is necessary for every valid reception of Penance. But when a penitent has only venial sins on his conscience the contrition need not extend to every one of them. No sin—mortal or venial—is forgiven without the proper sorrow for it. If a penitent has many venial sins, but is sorry for only some of them, then all are not forgiven even with the valid reception of Penance. In practice, a penitent should be sorry for all of his sins as they exist in the sight of God. There is a measure of risk to be sorry for only those sins that one remembers. If he is not at least implicitly sorry for all of his serious sins, his confession is at least unfruitful and can even be sacrilegious.

§ 19. *True contrition implies the intention to avoid all mortal sin in the future.*

It is impossible to separate true contrition from a firm purpose of amendment. Where there is no intention to take fully effective steps immediately to prevent the recurrence of mortal sin, there is no true sorrow in spite of the penitent's protestations to the contrary. The intention to avoid serious sin must extend to each and every mortal sin *without distinction*. The penitent is presumed to have this universal intention unless he explicitly excludes some mortal sin from it. Notice that the term "universal" here includes all mortal sins, and not only those being confessed. The intention not to avoid all mortal sin in the future can render the reception of Penance sacrilegious, for it lacks the proper sorrow. The person can even be guilty of new sins of desire.

A firm purpose of amendment means the effective desire to avoid all mortal sin for *all future time*. To intend to avoid mortal sin for a limited period of time is clearly insufficient.

It renders the reception of Penance invalid or sacrilegious. Many persons who are addicted to habits of serious sin strongly suspect that they will sin again in the future. May they approach the sacrament of Penance? If this person is here and now resolved to take fully effective means to prevent future sin, he may be absolved, for his suspicions do not stem from an ineffective intention.

A firm resolve to avoid mortal sin implies the intention to implement it immediately. The penitent must begin without delay to take all *necessary and effective* steps that will prevent the recurrence of the sin. Notice that these are not just "some" means or "any" means or means that the penitent "feels like taking." They are means that will work. There is no such thing as an "unbreakable" habit of mortal sin. In every case the persistence of such a habit is proof that the penitent has not taken the effective steps that a firm purpose of amendment demands.

§ 20. *Habitual sinners and recidivists may be required to follow a well-laid plan that will prevent the recurrence of mortal sin.*

A habitual sinner may usually commit the same mortal sin at least once a month. The number of times that he commits it forms a series. A recidivist keeps on falling back into a variety of mortal sins. When these penitents come to confession, the priest has good reason to suspect the firm quality of their past intentions to amend. He must prevent their repetition. Vague, hit-and-miss plans, indefinite "I'll trys" are no match for the stubborn situation of a habit of sin. Our Divine Lord never intended Penance to be a crushing burden for the penitent. But He never intended that confessor or penitent should ride roughshod over the requisite of a firm purpose of amendment. The confessor is perfectly justified in demanding that a habitual sinner or a recidivist formulate an effective plan to crush sin. If one plan is tried and proves ineffective, it must be scrapped and another one devised and put into practice. This process must be repeated as often as the situation remains out of control. The difficulty in most situations is that the penitent is long on devising plans but short on putting them into practice. If the penitent feels incompetent to formulate such plans, he should ask his confessor or his spiritual director for help. The plans of which we speak are indications of one's firm purpose of amendment; this in turn is an index of one's sorrow for sin. It should be devised before one enters the confessional, for then he can ask the confessor to check it. It is surprising how fast penitents can forget the duty to devise an effective plan after they have received absolution.

§ 21. *A penitent must fit his plan to avoid sin to the particular sin he resolves to avoid.*

A penitent knows his situation better than anyone else. He knows the vehemence of the temptations that assail him and the occasions of sin that he must face. He is the one primarily responsible for formulating a plan to cope with sin. The confessor can make suggestions or corrections but there just is not enough time for the confessor to formulate it in the confessional. In this number we suggest a few general plans. (1) Confessors agree that there is a proportion between frequency of sin and neglect of the Sacraments. A person who has long neglected the sacraments—has not received them for over six months—can plan to go to confession every Saturday for the next four weeks and then begin to make the Nine First Fridays. (2) A person who misses Mass should also start making the Nine First Fridays or at least going to the Sacraments at least once a month. Persons who receive the Sacraments at least once a month very rarely miss Mass. (3) Several plans are suggested for persons addicted to habits of impurity. It is suggested that they go to confession every week until the habit is broken; approach the same confessor; firmly control the eyes in looking and reading; avoid the occasion of sin, that is, persons, places, or things that experience has taught will lead to sin. (4) Another general plan to avoid sin is to start the practice of meditation. St. Robert Bellarmine wrote, "It is extremely difficult for anyone who neglects meditation to live long without sin." St. Teresa of Avila wrote, "No one who perseveres in meditation can continue to lead a bad or even an indifferent life." Ten minutes of meditation a day will do wonders, not only in helping one to avoid sin, but in helping him to grow in the love of God.

§ 22. *Although the purpose of amendment for venial sin need not be universal, it must be effective.*

A firm purpose of amendment is intimately bound up with proper sorrow for sin. Without the intention to avoid sin, no one can be said to have true contrition for his sins. Proper sorrow or contrition is an indispensable requisite for the reception of Penance. A penitent must make a firm purpose of amendment whenever he seeks absolution. This is true regardless of the gravity of the sins he has on his conscience. No purpose of amendment is worthy of the name unless it is effective. With habits of venial sin, one should devise at least a simple plan. The resolve to recite a prayer after sins of uncharitableness, profanity, and untruthfulness focuses attention on these sins, and eventually builds up resistance against them. It has been said that a person can reach a notable degree of sanctity if he will root out of his life one habit of venial sin a year.

The firm purpose of amendment necessary for Penance need not extend to each and every venial sin he confesses. But it must extend to at least one of them. The penitent must resolve to make some improvement in his observance of the Commandments. He clearly does this by determining to cut down on the frequency with which he has been committing venial sins. If he does not intend to take effective steps to do this, he can hardly be said to have a firm purpose of amendment. There are times when a penitent has no new venial sins to confess. He then fulfills the requisites for Penance by eliciting sorrow for past sins and resolving to continue his observance of the Commandments. If one will try to grasp the malice of venial sin, he will have little difficulty having the motivation for avoiding them.

§ 23. *The sacrament of Penance is administered only by a priest.*[10]

There is evidence dating from ancient times that only priests were the ministers of the sacrament of Penance. It appears in documents issued by the Holy See as early as the middle of the Fifth Century. Pope St. Leo the Great affirmed it in a letter issued in 452 A.D. The Council of Constance in 1418 A.D. repeated it when condemning the errors of Wycliffe and Hus. Pope Leo X restated it in 1520 against the errors of Luther, who held that in time of necessity, anyone, even children, could absolve from sin. The Council of Trent in 1551 defined, "If anyone says that priests who are in mortal sin do not have the power of binding and loosing, or that not only priests are the ministers of absolution . . . . : let him be anathema." (D-921)

There is ample evidence in works of ancient ecclesiastical writers testifying that priests administered Penance. Origen of Alexandria (+256 A.D.) wrote that sins are remitted by Penance "when the sinner drenches his pillow with his tears—and is not ashamed to confess his sin to one of the Lord's priests and ask him for a remedy."[11] In the Fourth Century, St. John Chrysostom (+407 A.D.) affirmed that "priests have the power of forgiving sins, that is to say, not merely the power of declaring them remitted, but that of truly remitting them; that anyone who wishes to be cured must show his wounds to the physician and that confession blots out sins completely."[12] A great many ancient writers state that Penance is administered by the bishop, but their statements must not be interpreted to mean that priests could not receive the bishop's permission to absolve. This point shall be explained in the next number.

§ 24. *There are a number of censures that a priest may not absolve in ordinary circumstances without special faculties from competent authorities.*

The Code of Canon Law[13] lists over forty ecclesiastical crimes that a priest cannot absolve without special faculties. We list only the more common ones. Even some of these occur only rarely. (1) Abuse of the Sacred Species. This must not be interpreted as the sacrilegious reception of Holy Communion. (2) Apostasy, heresy, or schism. The persons openly profess their errors. (3) Suspicion of heresy. In this case the person has committed an act that smacks of heresy. The Church wants that person to show good faith by rectifying the situation or fall under the penalty for heresy. (4) Publishing, defending, reading, or keeping books expressly condemned by the Holy See. (5) Publishing notes and commentaries on Sacred Scripture without due permission. (6) Adhering to Masonic or similar condemned societies. (7) Attempting marriage before a non-Catholic clergyman. (8) Agreeing to educate one's children as non-Catholics. (9) Deliberately handing one's children over to a non-Catholic minister for Baptism. (10) Violently attacking clerics or religious. (11) Procuring an abortion. (12) Interfering with the freedom of clerical and religious vocations. Church Law also permits the ordinary of a diocese to name a few reserved sins which may not be absolved in ordinary circumstances without special faculties. The purpose of the reservation is to impress upon the mind of the sinner the seriousness of his sin. It is impossible to list them, for they vary from

one diocese to another. In many dioceses, it is a reserved sin for
a Catholic to attempt marriage before a civil magistrate or to
obtain a civil divorce without ecclesiastical permission.

§ 25. *A priest must have faculties in order to absolve from sin.*

The priest about to administer the sacrament of Penance possesses a two-fold power, namely, the power to forgive and the
power to retain. To use either of them would be an exercise
of jurisdiction. This jurisdiction was given by Christ in its
fullness to Peter and his successors. The Roman Pontiff may
permit or forbid any priest in the Church from administering
Penance. He may also reserve the absolution of any sin to himself. Without due permission, no one may absolve from a sin
that the Pope has reserved in this manner.

We read in the Gospel that Christ also conferred jurisdiction on the other Apostles and their successors, namely, the
bishops. Their exercises of jurisdiction must be in accordance
with that of the Sovereign Pontiff. Bishops who are in positions of ordinary authority may also permit or forbid any
priest under their jurisdiction from administering Penance.
These bishops may also reserve to themselves the absolution
of certain sins.

No priest can validly absolve from sin without the jurisdiction to do so. This jurisdiction to absolve is often referred to
as faculties. They must be obtained from the superior who has
ordinary jurisdiction over the priest who seeks them. This superior is the ordinary of the diocese for diocesan priests; it is
the provincial for regular priests.

The reason why certain sins are reserved by the Holy See or
by Ordinaries is to impress upon penitents the gravity of their
crime and the far-reaching harm it can cause. In cases where
scandal has resulted, the ordinary may feel that he must give
the situation special attention and designate special means to
repair the harm. Any priest has permission to absolve one in

danger of death even from those sins which are reserved to higher authorities at other times.

§ 26. *Christ prescribed that a penitent must confess his sins to a priest in order to receive absolution.*

We could cite several instances dating even from ancient times where the Holy See reminded the faithful that confession of one's sins to a priest as a condition for absolution was prescribed by Christ Himself. With characteristic clarity, the Council of Trent defined, "If anyone says that sacramental confession was not instituted by divine law nor is necessary for salvation; or says that the manner of secretly confessing to a priest alone, which the Catholic Church has always observed from the beginning and still observes, is alien to the institution and the mandate of Christ, and is a human invention: let him be anathema." (D-916)

With regard to sin, Christ gave the Church two distinct powers, namely, the power to forgive and the power not to forgive. Matthew 18:18 refers to the power to bind and to loose; John 20:23 refers to the power to forgive and retain. When the priest sits in the confessional he possesses both of these powers. When a penitent approaches him, the confessor must ask himself which of the two powers he must use. It is contrary to all reason for him to act blindly or arbitrarily. He can make an intelligent judgment only if he knows the nature of the case before him. He cannot read the penitent's mind. The only way for him to learn the nature of the case is if it is revealed to him. The easiest and simplest way to do this is by making a secret confession to the priest. The penitent must reveal all that the confessor must know to make a sound judgment as to whether he should absolve or not absolve. The kind and number of at least mortal sins, proper sorrow, firm purpose of amendment, and acceptance of penance all pertain to the nature of the case. These are the valid reasons for holding that Christ Himself requires that penitents seeking forgiveness through the sacrament of Penance make a confession to a duly, authorized priest.

§ 27. *The confession of sins necessary for penance must be truthful.*

In ordinary circumstances, a penitent is obliged under penalty of serious sacrilege to confess the kind and number of all his certain mortal sins not yet directly submitted for absolution. If he deliberately hides even one of them, then none is forgiven and a new mortal sin is added. A penitent who cannot remember the exact number of these sins should confess their weekly or monthly average. This procedure will very likely help habitual sinners to determine the approximate number of their sins. If a penitent later learns that the exact number is greater than the approximate number, he must confess the others in his next confession. If the exact number is less than the approximate number, he need not confess the sins anew. In denoting the frequency with which sins were committed, penitents are to avoid vague expressions as "all the time," "now and then," "several," "a few," and so forth.

A confession is not deliberately incomplete when conditions —usually of a physical nature—make it extremely difficult to reveal all mortal sins. We can easily imagine that it is very difficult to make an integral confession when one has sustained a severe wound, or is extremely weak, or is dying.

One may then confess in a general way but must make an integral confession when he next receives Penance and can make the integral confession. The great embarrassment of having to confess certain sins is no legitimate reason for making a non-integral confession.

A penitent does not commit a sacrilege even if he deliberately fails to confess all his venial sins or the number of times that each was committed.

§ 28. *A penitent's confession to a priest should be made in secret.*

There is evidence in the works of ancient Christian writers that the confession of sins made in connection with Penance was made in secret. St. Basil the Great (+379), St. Ambrose (+397), and St. Augustine (+430) give testimony of this practice in their day. In 459 A.D. Pope St. Leo the Great in a letter to an inquiring bishop stated, "With regard to Penance, what is demanded of the faithful is clearly not that an acknowledgment of the nature of individual sins written in a little book be read publicly, since it suffices that the state of conscience be made known to the priest in secret confession" (D-145). Secret confession, of course, is the practice in the Church today.

A confession is public if it can be overheard by outsiders; it is secret if it cannot be overheard by them. Penitents are not obliged to make public confessions. In fact, in cases where it is necessary to receive Penance but the confession cannot be made secretly, it need not be made integrally. For example, a person injured in an auto accident is brought into the emergency room of a hospital. The doctors and nurses who must work on him would overhear his confession. He, therefore, need not make an integral one to the priest. Writers classify a confession made through an interpreter as a public confession.

In ordinary circumstances, a confession should be made orally. For a good reason, it can be made in writing or by gestures.

§ 29. *A person who receives Penance invalidly or sacrilegiously must confess all the mortal sins he should have confessed.*

In Penance, sin is removed by the infusion of sanctifying grace. We have already seen that the conditions for valid and fruitful reception of this sacrament are exactly the same. We have also studied what these indispensible requisites are. A person who presents invalid matter to the priest cannot receive Penance. If absolution is pronounced over him, no grace is infused and no sin is forgiven. He must approach this sacrament anew in order to receive its benefits.

A distinction must be made between a simply invalid reception of Penance and a sacrilegious reception. In the case of the simply invalid reception, the penitent must repeat the confession and also supply the requisite that he had unconsciously omitted. He did not commit a sacrilege, for his involuntary ignorance prevented him from performing a human act. In the case of the sacrilegious reception, the penitent must not only repeat his confession and supply the requisite that he had deliberately omitted, but must also confess and elicit proper sorrow for a new sin, namely, the sacrilege of deceiving the priest into pronouncing absolution invalidly.

§ 30. *A penitent who approaches penance with no new mortal sins on his conscience may confess venial sins or sins already absolved.*[14]

The distinction between mortal and venial sins was noted even in ancient times. In 1520, Pope Leo X condemned Luther's error that venial sins should not be confessed. The Council of Trent defined, "If anyone says . . . . that it is not lawful to confess venial sins; let him be anathema."(D-917) In 1304, Pope Benedict XI issued the instruction, "Although it is not necessary to confess the same sins a second time, nevertheless, because of the shame which is a large part of repentance, we consider it of benefit to repeat the confession of the same sins."(D-470)

When a penitent confesses only venial sin or sins absolved in past confessions, he is not dispensed from having the requisites for every reception of Penance. He must have proper contrition and a firm purpose either to improve or to continue his sinlessness.

Spiritual writers advise that we occasionally make a general confession. They recommend it when an individual enters a new state in life or on the occasion of a retreat or day of recollection. Penitents sometimes think that they are bound under penalty of making a bad confession to repeat in this general confession every mortal sin they have committed. This is not true. In a general confession, one may confess as many or as few of the already absolved mortal sins as his devotion dictates. The urge to make general confessions at very frequent intervals is usually the sign of a tendency to be scrupulous. The direction of a prudent confessor in these situations is of paramount importance.

§ 31. *A confessor has a right and a duty to question a penitent who he suspects of having made a faulty preparation for confession.*

A penitent is required to present valid matter to the priest for absolution. He, namely, the penitent, is the one primarily charged with the responsibility of seeing to it that an adequate preparation is made. He is the one who freely approaches the confessor to have his sins forgiven. The confessor has the right to expect that the penitent has spent enough time and diligence in making the preparation required. It would be a wonderful thing if confessors could take all penitents as they should be. Unfortunately, they cannot. A great many penitents approach the sacrament of Penance very poorly prepared. Many of them have scarcely examined their conscience. Some have forgotten and neglected to re-learn the Act of Contrition. Some have no real sorrow for their sins, nor have they made a firm purpose of amendment. Some penitents have devised a clever vocabulary designed to hide the gravity or number of their mortal sins. A confessor can easily tell when the penitent has made a faulty preparation for confession. Now a confessor is responsible to God for every absolution he pronounces. In many cases, the only way that he can assure himself that the penitent has the requisites for a good confession is by questioning that penitent. It is a very distasteful chore thrust upon the confessor. Some penitents resent being questioned especially about matters pertaining to the Sixth Commandment. They feel that it embarrasses them. But in practically every case, it is the flimsy, slip-shod preparation on the part of the "penitent" that occasioned and caused the questioning—a task that the confessor would gladly like to be spared. The preparation necessary for confession is ordinarily neither intricate nor difficult. It does, however, require a measure of sincerity and conscientiousness on the part of the penitent. In some cases, it gets neither.

§ 32. *A confessor is bound under penalty of grave sacrilege to refuse absolution to persons unfit to receive it.*

A person is unfit for absolution when he cannot receive it validly. He lacks one of the indispensable requirements for the reception of Penance. There are two sets of requirements for Penance. The remote requirements are that the penitent has received Baptism of water and explicitly knows and believes the articles of faith that a person in his condition must know and believe. A confessor may not absolve a person who is ignorant of those truths that must be believed by a necessity of means. A person in ordinary circumstances is to have explicit knowledge of those truths that must be believed by a necessity of precept.

The proximate requirements are that the penitent present valid matter for absolution. Penitents are unfit for absolution when they do not confess sins but only imperfections, when they fail to make a proper act of sorrow or purpose of amendment or refuse to accept the penance that the priest imposes.

In these cases, the confessor is not merely justified in refusing absolution. He is required under penalty of grave sacrilege to refuse it. When a penitent has fulfilled all the requirements for valid reception of Penance, a confessor is duty-bound to administer the sacrament unless external factors intervene. We occasionally hear the expression, "I went to confession but the priest refused to give me absolution." This expression is perhaps most unfair and most misleading. That "penitent" might rephrase his statement to read, "I went to confession, but I refused to accept the absolution that the priest wanted to give me."

§ 33. *A confessor has the duty to impose a salutary penance for sins confessed.*

The administration of Penance is a judicial act requiring a judgment and the pronouncing of a sentence. The purpose of the sentence imposed is to help repair the harm caused by sin, and to prevent its recurrence in the future. When a person commits a mortal or venial sin, he contracts a debt of guilt and a debt of punishment. Absolution removes the guilt, but it does not necessarily remove all of the punishment.[15] The Council of Trent defined, "If anyone says that the whole punishment together with the guilt, is always pardoned by God, and that the satisfaction of penitence is nothing other than faith, by which they perceive that Christ has made satisfaction for them; let him be anathema." (D-922) The satisfaction which the priest imposes removes at least part of the temporal punishment due to sin. If the debt of punishment is not removed before death, it is removed by suffering in purgatory.

Reason dictates that unless extenuating circumstances intervene, there must be a balance between the gravity of the sin and the magnitude of the satisfaction imposed. Mortal sin calls for notable satisfaction; venial sins call for slight satisfaction. A notable satisfaction is a work which the Church prescribes under penalty of serious sin. For example, the Church obliges us under penalty of mortal sin to assist at Mass on Sunday. A confessor can impose the assistance at a Mass as satisfaction for a serious sin. We are obliged to abstain from meat on Friday; a confessor can impose a day's abstinence as satisfaction for mortal sin. Other examples could be cited. The Church permits confessors to impose a relatively grave penance, that is, one which though not grave in itself is grave to this particular penitent because he is, for example, sick.

§ 34. *A penitent who refuses to accept the satisfaction imposed by the priest receives penance invalidly; he sins if he accepts it but then refuses to perform it.*

A clear distinction must be made between refusing to accept the satisfaction imposed by the priest and accepting but then refusing to perform it. The administration of Penance is a judicial act. The satisfaction imposed by the confessor flows from the judgment he has just made. If the penitent refuses to accept the satisfaction imposed by the priest, he would be refusing to do his essential part toward completing the juridical act. Without this sentence, there would be no juridical act; without a juridical act there would be no reception of the sacrament of Penance. If the penitent gave the priest the false impression that he was accepting the penance imposed, and the priest pronounced absolution, the "penitent" would be guilty of a sacrilegious reception of this sacrament.

Sins are forgiven when the sentence to make satisfaction is accepted and absolution is pronounced. If the penitent later fails or refuses to carry out the sentence to make satisfaction, the forgiven sins do not revive. But he is bound under obedience to perform that penance. If the penance was imposed for mortal sin, the penitent is bound under penalty of mortal sin to perform it. If it was imposed for venial sin, he is bound under penalty of venial sin to perform it. Unless the confessor prescribes otherwise the penance imposed by the priest as satisfaction for sin may be performed at any time, even after the penitent has received Holy Communion or fallen into a new mortal sin. It should be performed as soon as it is conveniently possible so that it will not be forgotten.

§ 35. *A confessor is obliged to maintain strict silence about everything a penitent reveals to him.*[16]

The information revealed by a penitent in confession is in itself matter for a natural secret. Since Christ prescribed that sins be revealed to a confessor, it follows that the positive divine law also obliges that secrecy be kept. (1) The obligation to maintain silence on confession matters binds the confessor, interpreters, and everyone who even accidently overheard the confession being made. It does not bind the penitent himself. (2) Persons who must maintain silence may not divulge the gravity, species, or number of sins confessed, the gravity of the penance imposed, the names of accomplices even unwittingly given, and other details used to explain sins. The confessor may not reveal that he refused to give absolution to a particular penitent. Information may not be divulged that would discourage the penitent from making future confessions even though it did not pertain to the present confession, as for example, revealing that a particular penitent was scrupulous. (3) Persons who must remain silent about confessional matters may not reveal this information either directly or indirectly. It is revealed directly when the revealer links the penitent with a specific sin. It is revealed indirectly when, for example, the speaker reveals a sin with such details that the listeners can guess the identity of the sinner. The same would be true if the confessor revealed the identity of one of his penitents to a person who would then know what sins were confessed. The same would be true if a confessor acted in the light of information he received from a confession, thereby revealing sins or a penitent to those observing the actions of the priest.

§ 36. *A confessor who directly violates the seal of the confession commits a mortal sin and is excommunicated most specially reserved to the Holy See.*[17]

No reason whatsoever can ever justify a confessor in breaking the seal of confession. It must be kept inviolate even in the face of fine, imprisonment, torture, and death. We read that St. John Nepomucene was martyred for refusing to break the seal to the king of Bohemia. In recent times, a French priest spent more than twenty years in the infernal penal colony of Devil's Island and died there rather than break the seal to prove that he was innocent of the crime of which he was accused.

A priest who directly violates the seal of the confession commits a grave sacrilege and is excommunicated most specially reserved to the Holy See. There is no excommunication more severe than this one. Without permission, a confessor may not even speak to a penitent about the penitent's own confession outside of confession. The seal is not broken, however, when the priest speaks to a penitent in confession about matters that he has learned from this penitent's past confessions.

Persons other than the confessor who overhear a confession being made and then divulge the information are guilty of mortal sin. The law says that they are to be given a salutary punishment and even excommunicated. The seal of the confession is intended to make confession easier. It is also intended for the penitent's protection. The penitent may give the confessor and others permission to speak about the contents of a confession he made. This permission must be given explicitly and freely. It may never be presumed. Catholics have always approached the confessional with the complete assurance that no detail of their confession would ever be divulged.

§ 37. *Penance confers sanctifying grace and its own special actual grace.*

Penance was especially instituted to take away sin committed after Baptism. It does this by infusing sanctifying grace into the soul. If the soul is already in grace, it receives an increase of grace from the reception of Penance. The Council of Trent teaches that this sacrament can be received even by one not in serious sin. Like all other sacraments, Penance confers on its recipient a title to a special actual grace called sacramental grace. Each sacrament was instituted to meet a special crisis in our life when we stand in need of supernatural help. Penance is no exception. It confers the sacramental grace one needs to keep the resolution to avoid sin which he has just made in confession. We saw the sweeping nature of the resolve to avoid all mortal sin and to improve in avoiding venial sin. Actual grace works on one's intellect and will. The actual grace of Penance works on the intellect of the penitent by giving him a better insight into the heinousness of sin. It enlightens his mind to see what steps he must take to prevent the recurrence of sin. It shows him how to devise a plan aimed at rooting out a habit of sin. This grace also works on the penitent's will. It shows him that the salutary thoughts of the mind are to be put into practice. It strengthens his will so that he can choose and follow a plan that is useful or necessary to avoid sin and the occasion of sin. Like the actual grace one receives from other sacraments, the actual grace which Penance confers can be wasted and even rejected, for it does not compel one to act against his free will.

§ 38. *A Catholic may receive Penance as often as he wishes; he must receive it within a year after falling into mortal sin.*

Neither God's law nor the Church's law limits the frequency with which a Catholic may receive Penance. He may receive it several times a day. The custom in parishes of scheduling the hours and days for confession is merely an arrangement made for the convenience of the people. Priests are willing to hear one's confession at any reasonable hour. A practical Catholic goes to confession at least once a month even if he has no new mortal sin to reveal.

There is evidence dating back to the Fourth Century regarding the custom of going to confession at least once a year. The Lateran Council of 1215 A.D. put this custom in the form of a law. Today, the Church obliges a Catholic to go to confession within a year after falling into mortal sin. The person who disobeys this law is guilty of a new mortal sin. The year must be computed from the day a mortal sin is committed. Catholics who have committed no new mortal sin are not obliged to go to confession even once a year.[18]

The Church's law binds all in mortal sin regardless of their age. Children are to receive a certain amount of catechetical instruction before being admitted to the reception of the sacraments. Parents sin if they have neglected to see to it that their children are properly instructed in time to comply with the law to go to confession when obliged.

The law obliging Catholics to go to confession is distinct from the one obliging Catholics to receive Holy Communion during the Easter season. One who neglects to make his Easter duty commits a mortal sin. He can commit a second one if he neglects to go to confession for more than a year after committing a serious sin.

§ 39. *It is most advisable for a penitent to use a precise formula in making his confession.*

We have tried to impress upon the mind of the student that confession is not the mechanical recitation of sins as they are listed in a theology text. A confessor must have a grasp of the penitent's subjective estimate of those sins and must have assurance that the penitent is truly sorry for them. A precise formula for confession can go a long way in eliminating many questions that a confessor would otherwise be obliged to ask. The formula for confession that is set down here forces the penitent to make adequate preparation for the reception of the sacrament. If the penitent does not use this formula, after he has been taught how to use it, then he can be suspected of not having made a thorough preparation. It reads:

1. **Bless me, Father, for I have sinned. It has been_____ since my last confession.**

Children say: **I am_____years old.**

Adults say: **I am married or single.**

2. **These are my mortal sins . . .** *confess them.*
These are my venial sins . . . *confess them.*
These are my doubtful sins . . . *confess them.*

3. **I am sorry for all my sins because they have offended God who I love more than anything else and because I fear to lose Him forever in hell or for a time in purgatory. I now resolve and plan to avoid all sin in the future.**

Explanation of Part One: (1) Telling how long it has been since one's last good confession enables the confessor to "size up" the penitent in a general way. For example, if it has been a long time but very few sins of any kind are confessed, the priest can suspect a poor examination of conscience. (2) When the priest knows a child's age, he has a better insight into the child's subjective estimate of his act. For example, an eight year old child will probably judge stealing a quarter to be a mortal sin, whereas an eighteen year old child probably will not. It is often impossible for the priest to guess even approximate age from the tone of a child-penitent's voice. (3) The married or single status of adult penitents is an invaluable bit of information to the confessor in many instances. A penitent's status can add new malice to basic acts. Then too, knowing a penitent's status can suggest questions necessary to complete the integrity of a confession. For example, a married man confesses frequently missing Mass. This leads the priest to inquire about the possibility of added sins of scandal to his children.

Explanation of Part Two: (1) Mortal, venial, and doubtful sins must be kept distinct in confession. The difference between mortal and venial sins is one of essence, not of degree. The Council of Trent implies that the confessor must know whether the penitent considers his act to be a mortal sin or a venial sin. It would be a most serious mistake to think that all penitents correctly judge the malice of sinful acts. A survey of college freshmen conducted over a period of fifteen years revealed that from twenty to thirty per cent of them were under the impression that taking God's name in vain is always a mortal sin. Confessing one's sins according to the formula set down above, not only gives the confessor the information he must have, but it also gives him an opportunity to correct a false conscience. (2) In confessing, mortal or venial sins that were certainly committed must never be thrown in with doubtful sins. They must be kept distinct, for certain sins are valid matter for absolution, whereas doubtful ones are not.

Explanation of Part Three: (1) The concluding prayer is really an act of perfect and imperfect contrition. It is carefully worded to insure that the act of sorrow will be universal, supreme, and supernatural. Penitents—especially children—are apt not to race through this act of contrition in meaningless fashion when they know that the priest is listening to them. (2) Recidivists and habitual sinners are the cause of most grave concern to confessors. Their purpose of amendment is often vague, indefinite, and therefore, often ineffective. They must have a clear-cut plan to prevent the recurrence of sin. The last sentence of the prayer reminds them to formulate it.

§ 40. *The Church has defined that she has the power to grant indulgences.*

About a hundred years before Luther's break with the Church, the Holy See condemned John Wycliffe's errors on indulgences.[19] But Luther made certain abuses in the grant-on indulgences. The Council of Trent took steps to correct the abuses practiced by some of the members of the Church's hierarchy, but at the same time restated her teaching on this topic. It said, "Since the power of granting indulgences was conferred by Christ on the Church, and she has made use of such power divinely given to her, even in the earliest times, the holy Synod teaches and commands that the use of indulgences, most salutary to a Christian people and approved by the authority of the sacred Councils, is to be retained in the Church, and it condemns those with anathema who assert that they are useless or deny that there is in the Church the power of granting them." (D-989)

An indulgence is the remission of at least part of the temporal punishment due to sin granted by the Church for the performance of a specified good work. Two things are to be noted in connection with this subject. The first is that an indulgence is not the remission of the guilt of sin, for this is the purpose of Penance. An indulgence can be granted without any reference to Penance and is certainly no substitute for Penance. The second is that an indulgence remits temporal punishment due to sin before God. It has effects beyond the earthly sojourn of a person. Some have falsely said that an indulgence is merely the permission to omit the good works imposed on sinners in ancient times to impress on them the heinousness of their sins and to insure that they would repair the scandals they caused. This interpretation would have us believe that indulgences have no effect on the spiritual state of a person after death.

§ 41. *Several conditions must be fulfilled before one can gain an indulgence.*

The Church has enacted legislation to prevent abuse from creeping into the granting of indulgences. (1) The person must be baptized and free from excommunication. (2) He must

be in the state of sanctifying grace at least before he finishes
the good work prescribed for the gaining of the particular indulgence. (3) He must be subject to the ecclesiastical authority who has granted the indulgence. Any Catholic can gain
a papal indulgence. Indulgences granted by a bishop may be
gained by his subjects even though they sojourn outside his
diocese or by strangers who sojourn within his diocese unless
the concession states otherwise. (4) The person must have at
least a general intention to gain the indulgence. The intention
to do this which one includes in his morning offering is certainly sufficient to fulfill this condition. (5) He must perform
the good works at the appointed time and in the manner prescribed by the wording of the concession. (6) No one who
gains indulgences can apply them to living persons besides
himself. Unless stated otherwise, all indulgences granted by
the Holy See may be applied to the Souls in Purgatory. (7) A
plenary indulgence is the remission of all the temporal punishment due to one's sins. A partial indulgence is remission of
part of this punishment. The former may be gained only once
a day; the later can be gained often on the same day. (8) If confession is required for the gaining of an indulgence, it can be
made within eight days preceding or following the day of the
indulgence. If Holy Communion is required, It may be received either on the day preceding or within eight days following the day of the indulgence.

§ 42. *Scriptural proof that the Church has power to grant indulgences is contained in St. Matthew's Gospel.*

Christ gave His Church the power to grant indulgences when
He endowed her with the fullness of power in spiritual matters. In Matthew 16:19 Christ said to His Church through St.
Peter, "And I will give thee the keys of the kingdom of heav-
en; and whatever thou shalt bind on earth shall be bound in
heaven, and what ever thou shalt loose on earth shall be loosed

in heaven." In this passage Christ promises to give to His Church the full authority and the complete means necessary for her to carry out her task of sanctifying and saving souls. The means referred to are of two kinds. They are the means that will positively promote sanctification and the means that will remove obstacles to sanctification. The first set of means could be rendered ineffective and even useless unless accompanied by the second set. Sin is the thing that hinders and even precludes sanctification. Christ gave His Church power to remove this obstacle to sanctification. But sin has two phases, namely, the guilt of sin and the punishment due to sin. After Baptism, the guilt of sin is removed by the sacrament of Penance. If Christ had not also given the Church power to remove the temporal punishment due to sin, He would have endowed her with only incomplete power over sin. The Gospel text quoted above shows that Christ imposed no such limitation on His Church's power. It follows that the Church's fullness of power in spiritual matters includes the power to grant indulgences. The Church has been in conscious possession of this power from ancient times and we have literary evidence dating from Ante-Nicene times that she made abundant use of it.

NOTES

1. *Summa Theologica*, Par. III, Ques. 84, Art. 3.
2. Sins against the Holy Spirit (cf. Matt. 12:32) are said to be unforgivable because these sins imply a final rejection of God's grace. Confer the exegesis of this verse in *A Catholic Commentary on Holy Scripture*, p. 874 cf.; also *Summa Theologica* III, Ques. 86, Art. 1 and 3.
3. Cayré, *Manual of Patrology* (Tournai, Desclée & Co., 1936), Vol. I, p. 242.
4. Daniélou, *Origen* (New York: Sheed & Ward, 1955), p. 68 ff.
5. D-43 Tertullian writes, "I also hear that an edict is published and is indeed final. Evidently the Supreme Pontiff (Callixtus) because he is the bishop of bishops, declares, I forgive the sins of adultery and fornication to those who have performed the penance." (*De Pudicitia*.cl).
6. *Summa Theologica*, Par. III, Ques. 84, Art. 5.
7. On this point cf. also St. Thomas, *Summa Theologica*, Par. III, Ques. 90, Arts. 1-3.

8. Canon 901.

9. Alexander, *College Moral Theology* (Chicago: Henry Regnery Co., 1958), pp. 7-55.

10. Canon 871.

11. *Com. in Lev.* 2-4.

12. cf. Tixeront, *History of Dogma* (St. Louis: Herder, 1926), Vol. II, p. 185.

13. Canon 2314-2405.

14. Canon 902.

15. *Summa Theologica*, Par. III, Ques. 86, Arts. 4 & 5.

16. Canon 889-890.

17. Canon 2369.

18. Davis, *Moral and Pastoral Theology* (London: Sheed & Ward, 1945), Vol. III, p. 346.

19. cf. D-622.

IX

Extreme Unction

§ 1. *Extreme Unction is a sacrament of the New Law whereby sin and its remains are removed from the soul of one in danger of death through the anointing and prayer of a priest.*

The oldest known reference to Extreme Unction in documents issued by the Holy See dates from the beginning of the Fifth Century. It is also found in documents of the Ninth, Twelfth, Thirteenth, and Fifteenth Centuries. The Council of Trent was merely repeating traditional Church doctrine when it defined, "If anyone says that Extreme Unction is not truly and properly a sacrament instituted by Our Lord Jesus Christ, and promulgated by blessed James the Apostle, but is only a rite accepted by the Fathers or a human fiction; let him be anathema."(D-926)

Extreme Unction has all the notes of a true sacrament. (1) The holy council defined that this sacrament was instituted by Christ. He alone can institute a means of grace, for He alone merited the grace. (2) It has a definite external rite consisting of matter and form. The matter is the anointing of the five senses with oil of the sick. The form is the prescribed prayer that accompanies the anointings. (3) Extreme Unction has a place in man's spiritual life. It fortifies him to face the awful transit from this life to the next one. It confers the sacramental grace necessary to enable one to enter heaven immediately after death. (4) There are conditions that must be com-

194

plied with to insure valid and fruitful reception. By a valid reception, a person receives title to sacramental and sanctifying grace. Because of this special title, the sacrament cannot be repeated within a fixed period of time. (5) Extreme Unction is validly administered by the priest. Authorization by the church is necessary for the priest to administer it lawfully.

§ 2. *The existence of Extreme Unction can be proved from the Epistle of St. James in the New Testament.*

We saw that the existence of Extreme Unction appears in documents issued by the Holy See dating back to ancient times. It is not mere coincidence that every one of those documents either cites or quotes the pertinent passage in St. James' Epistle. That passage reads, "Is any one among you sick? Let him bring in the presbyters of the Church, and let them pray over him, anointing him with oil in the name of the Lord. And the prayer of faith will save the sick man, and the Lord will raise him up, and if he be in sins, they shall be forgiven him" (James 5:14). The Church teaches that this passage is not to be interpreted to mean that St. James instituted the sacrament, but that he promulgated it.

Several things are to be noticed about this passage. (1) The sickness referred to is a serious one for the ailing person is presumed unable to go to the priest. The priest must come to him. (2) The rite must be performed by a priest. It allows no exception to this even though the sickness is an emergency. (3) The matter of the sacrament is anointing with oil; the form is the prayer of the priest. (4) The passage is most explicit in stating that the rite is an effective means of grace. The anointing and prayer are the cause of the sick person's sins being taken away if there are any such on the soul. Another effect of the sacrament is that it causes the sick person to be "saved." Writers say that "saved" here means that it can liberate a sick person from the evils that press upon him. What are these particular evils? They may be listed as temptations to despair, fear of death, affliction of mind, remorse, inability to cooperate with God's grace, fear of the approaching judgment, and so forth.

§ 3. *There is evidence in the works of early Christian writers of the existence and use of Extreme Unction in the first centuries of the Christian Era.*

There is not as much evidence for Extreme Unction in ancient Christian literature as there is for some of the other sacraments, but there is enough evidence to prove that it was used in the early Church. There are good reasons to explain this existence of Extreme Unction was known throughout the Church because St. James' Epistle was known and used throughout the Church. There was never any doubt raised as to the textual integrity of the pertinent verses 14 and 15. They are found in all critical editions of the New Testament and without significant variants. (2) In 1894, there was found at the Mt. Athos Monastery in the Aegean Sea, the *Sacramentary of Serapion* dating back to the fourth century. This was a kind of a ritual of prayers used in the administration of the sacraments. It also contains the prayer used to bless the oil of the sick. This is obviously the oil used in Extreme Unction. (3) The import of St. James' words are so clear that early writers who treated of Extreme Unction were content merely to quote them. They were quoted by Tertullian (+220), St. Cyril of Alexandria (+444), St. John Chrysostom (+407), St. Caesarius of Arles (+543), and St. Bede the Venerable (+735). The testimonies of these writers take on added significance when we consider that they span almost six centuries and both the Latin and Greek world. (4) There is much Christian literature in defense of doctrines that were attacked by heretics. The history of dogma reveals that the first heresy to attack the existence of Extreme Unction was the one advanced by the leaders of the Protestant revolt in the Sixteenth Century.

Hence there was no need for apologetical literature on this subject in early times.

§ 4. *Extreme Unction was instituted to help a gravely sick person to die well.*

Extreme Unction can prepare the soul of a dying person to go to heaven immediately after death. Besides giving him sanctifying grace, this sacrament can provide the help to meet two sets of obstacles to dying well. Notice that this does not mean that everyone who is anointed uses to the maximum all the helps provided him. He must cooperate with them. Lack of cooperation lessens the benefits he receives.

A dying person may have mortal or venial sin on his soul or he may still have temporal punishment due to sins already forgiven. These are clearly obstacles to his immediate entry into heaven. Extreme Unction can give the actual grace that enlightens the mind and moves the will to make the act of sorrow needed to take away any sin. In cases where persons are too weak in body to make this act of sorrow, Extreme Unction may even give the necessary physical strength to make it.

The approach of death often brings with it new and peculiar obstacles to dying well. Gravely sick persons are often seized by great remorse for their sins and great fear of God's judgment. While these experiences are often very salutary, they can shade off into temptations against the virtues of faith and hope. Extreme Unction can give actual grace to meet these and other temptations to sin. This sacrament can give the help to clear away existing obstacles to immediate entry into heaven and to prevent new ones from developing.

§ 5. *The removal of sin is an accidental but true effect of Extreme Unction.*

The removal of sin is an accidental effect of Extreme Unction because, although it can remove it, this sacrament was not primarily instituted for this purpose. When we say that the removal of sin is a true effect of this sacrament, we mean that it has the inherent power to do so. It does not merely prepare one to use the means that forgive sin. Justification for holding that Extreme Unction can forgive sin is found in St. James' Epistle we quoted above. The passage reads, ". . . . and the Lord will raise him up, and if he be in sins, they shall be forgiven him." (James 5:15)

Extreme Unction's power to forgive sin is effective against both mortal and venial sin. But this is an accidental effect of Extreme Unction. The sacrament primarily instituted to take away sin is Penance. When we studied Penance we saw that no one may circumvent that sacrament and yet have sins forgiven. The term "circumvent" here means that no one may deliberately reject or neglect Penance. One does not circumvent Penance when one recovers sanctifying grace by making an act of perfect contrition with the desire to receive Penance when the law obliges him. The roles of Penance and Extreme Unction in the forgiveness of sins can be harmonized. Extreme Unction can indeed take away sin but not when it is used as a means to circumvent Penance. Extreme Unction may be used to take away mortal sin only when Penance can not be used. We must not forget the Extreme Unction is primarily a sacrament of the living and only accidentally a sacrament of the dead. If it were primarily a sacrament of the dead, then it would duplicate and even conflict with Penance.

§ 6. *A conditional effect of Extreme Unction is restoration of bodily health.*

A conditional effect does not take place every time the cause is placed. Besides the operation of the cause, other factors must be present for the effect to take place. In this number, we study what "other factors" must be present before Extreme Unction brings about the effect of restoring one to bodily health. There can be no doubt that this is an effect of this sacrament for the Council of Trent says that those who receive Extreme Unction "sometimes attain bodily health, when it is expedient for the salvation of the soul." (D-909) In its statement, the Council tells us that the condition necessary for Extreme Unction to bring about bodily health is that "it be expedient for the salvation of the soul." The Church has not further explained this expression, nor has she definited how completely Extreme Unction can restore bodily health. Theologians have advanced several opinions on the subject. In restoring bodily health, the sacrament utiltizes the natural sources of restoration of the body. Extreme Unction will not bring about bodily health if these sources are exhausted. The next question is to try to determine how completely bodily health can be restored. There is clearly a tie-up between the spiritual and physical effect of Extreme Unction. The latter is subordinated to the former. It would seem that Extreme Unction can give a person the bodily strength he needs to make full use of the spiritual opportunities that the sacrament provides the sick person.[1] The degree of strengthening of the body will vary from person to person. It is conditioned on the reserved strength remaining in the body and how much strengthening is needed to make full use of the spiritual benefits to which one is entitled by receiving this sacrament.

§ 7. *For a valid reception of Extreme Unction, one must be baptized, have reached the use of reason, desire to receive the sacrament, and be in danger of death from a wound or disease.*

(1) To receive Extreme Unction validly, one must be baptized, for Baptism confers the right to participate at least passively in the priesthood of Christ, that is, it entitles one to the capacity to receive the fruits of the Cross. (2) The recipient of Extreme Unction must have reached the use of reason, that is, he has been able to distinguish right from

wrong. Normal children can make use of this power at about the age of seven. Extreme Unction was instituted to restore perfect spiritual health. A person who has never had the use of reason is incapable of committing the sins that destroy the perfect spiritual health he received in Baptism. Notice that this condition does not mean that one must have the use of reason while he is receiving Extreme Unction. (3) A person must desire to receive Extreme Unction, but it need be only a habitual intention. This is the desire where the person once makes the intention to receive this sacrament and never retracts it. It may persist even for many years. Persons who rejected this sacrament while they were conscious may be anointed conditionally after they have lapsed into unconsciousness. (4) The word "sickness" used in connection with Extreme Unction has a wider meaning than we commonly attach to it. It embraces disease to be sure, but also wounds, and even old age.[2] One can be anointed when they have already attacked the body and will probably cause death. Notice that certainty of death is not required. All that is needed is that there be a well-founded belief that the cause at its present strength can produce death. If there is reason to doubt the seriousness of the sickness, Extreme Unction may be administered conditionally.[3]

§ 8. *For a fruitful reception of Extreme Unction, one must receive it validly and have sorrow for his sins.*

Every sin carries with it a debt of guilt and a debt of punishment. No debt of guilt that a person contracts is remitted unless he is sorry for it. This is true of all personal sin taken away by Baptism, and remitted either by the actual reception of Penance, or by perfect contrition with the desire to receive Penance. But the debt of punishment usually remains after the debt of guilt has been taken away.

Extreme Unction was primarily instituted to remove the

remains of sin from the soul of a person in danger of death. The proposition says that Extreme Unction cannot be received fruitfully unless one has sorrow for his sins. When must this act of sorrow have been made? If the person has only a debt of punishment to be taken away, he made the necessary act of sorrow at the time when the debt of guilt was taken away. The force of the act of sorrow for that sin continues indefinitely, for the debt of guilt can never revive.

It may well happen that a person about to be anointed has both debt of guilt and debt of punishment to be taken away. A distinction must then be made as a debt of guilt for venial sin or that for mortal sin. If he has only venial sins, and makes an act of sorrow, he can indeed receive Extreme Unction fruitfully but the debts are remitted only for those sins for which he has sorrow. It is possible therefore to receive Extreme Unction fruitfully and still retain even the debt of guilt for some venial sins. The sorrow needed for venial sin is imperfect contrition. If a person has mortal sin on his soul, he must make an act of sorrow covering all unforgiven mortal sins, but imperfect contrition for them is sufficient in the reception of Extreme Unction.

§ 9. *One can receive the fruits of Extreme Unction even after he has received the Sacrament unfruitfully or sacrilegiously.*

A person who receives Extreme Unction validly receives a true sacrament. The sacrament cannot be repeated within a fixed period of time, but it can be received unfruitfully. The reception of this sacrament confers a title to the spiritual benefits that Christ intended this sacrament to give.

If a person received Extreme Unction validly but completely lacked the sorrow needed for fruitful reception, he could receive the fruits at a later date, that is, in the same sickness, provided the title to these fruits had not expired. If the cause for the unfruitful reception was not a sacrilege committed in the reception, one receives the fruits of Extreme Unction by later making at least an act of imperfect contrition. If a forgotten mortal sin caused the unfruitful reception of Extreme Unction, this act of sorrow must be accompanied by at least an implicit desire to receive Penance. This situation is very often verified in cases of persons who are anointed while unconscious but who later regain consciousness.

A person who freely and deliberately receives Extreme Unction with unforgiven mortal sin on his soul commits a grave sacrilege. But he does receive a title to the fruits of this sacrament which lasts as long as the sacrament cannot be repeated. In this case, one must make either an act of perfect contrition with the desire to receive absolution or at least imperfect contrition with the actual reception of absolution.

A person who refuses to receive Extreme Unction while he is conscious may be anointed conditionally after he lapses into unconsciousness. The condition that the priest has then is that he intends to administer the sacrament provided the sick person who had refused now changed his mind but cannot express his intention because of great weakness.

§ 10. *Extreme Unction entitles one to the special actual grace he needs to withstand the peculiar temptations and fears that may accompany the danger of death.*

Some effects of Extreme Unction look to the past, for the sacrament was primarily instituted to remove from the soul of a person in danger of death the remains of sin already committed and forgiven. But some effects of Extreme Unction look to the immediate future. This sacrament entitles the recipient to special sacramental grace needed to cope with a very serious situation or crisis, namely, the danger of death. The Council of Trent said, "For, although 'our adversary seeks' and seizes throughout our entire life, occasion 'to devour' our souls in every manner, yet there is no time when he directs

more earnestly all the strength of his cunning to ruin us completely, and if possible, to drive us also from faith in the divine
mercy, than he sees that the end of life is upon us." (D-907)

The sacramental grace of Extreme Unction enlightens the
intellect to appraise correctly the meaning of the bodily sufferings the person endures and the death he faces. It teaches him
that these things can be the occasion of great spiritual merit.
It gives him a sense of security by enabling him to grasp the
value of this sacrament itself to a person in danger of death.
It suggests to him what he must do to receive the full benefit
of the sacrament.

Extreme Unction does not take away the temptations that
accompany the danger of death, but it gives one all the actual
grace he needs to overcome them. These are often temptation
to commit sins against faith, that is, sins such as disbelieving
or doubting a truth taught by the Church. Persons in danger
of death are often tempted to despair of God's mercy or to
blaspheme Him, or to rebel against His providence. The
sacramental grace of Extreme Unction can also strengthen
one's will to act upon the salutary thoughts suggested to the
intellect. We see, therefore, how this great sacrament projects
its power into the future.

§ 11. *The matter of Extreme Unction is anointing with the
oil of the sick. The form is the prayer of the priest that accompanies the anointings.*

St. James' Epistle clearly states both the matter and form of
Extreme Unction. The pertinent verse reads, "Let him bring
in the presbyters of the Church, and let him pray over him,
anointing him with oil in the name of the Lord. And the prayer of faith will save the sick man." (James 5:14)

The remote matter of Extreme Unction is olive oil expressly blessed for the administration of the sacrament. The bishop
blesses it on Holy Thursday.[4] The Holy See may empower a

priest to bless it. It is called the "Oil of the Sick." The proximate matter of Extreme Unction is the anointing of the five senses in the form of a cross. The order of anointing is the eyes, ears, nostrils, lips, hands, and feet. If any of the bodily members are missing, the priest anoints the part of the body adjacent to the missing member. If lack of time does not allow him to anoint each of the senses, he may anoint only the forehead.[5] This last method of anointing is used very often in the emergency rooms of hospitals.

The form pronounced by the priest while he makes the prescribed anointings must embody a prayer. It reads, "Through this anointing and His most tender mercy, may the Lord pardon thee whatever faults thou hast committed by sight, by hearing . . . ." The form is repeated with each anointing. When there is only one anointing, the form pronounced is, "Through this holy anointing may the Lord pardon thee whatever faults thou has committed." The prayer used in the form is one of petition. The Council of Trent anathematizes those who hold that the rite, that is, the combination of matter and form used by the Church today is an essential variation from the one set down in St. James' Epistle.

§ 12. *Although Extreme Unction is not in itself absolutely necessary for salvation, there may be a grave obligation to receive it.*[6]

As a sacrament of the living, Extreme Unction increases sanctifying grace in the soul of its recipient. If a person in danger of death is already in grace, there is no serious obligation for him to be anointed. But Christ did not institute any of the sacraments to have them disregarded by those who could and should receive them. A person already in the state of grace commits a venial sin if he neglects to receive Extreme Unction.

We have seen that Extreme Unction looks to the immediate

future of a person in danger of death. The Council of Trent reminds us of the especially trying crisis such a person faces. He will likely be subjected to peculiar and severe temptations. Extreme Unction entitles one to the special actual grace that no other sacrament can give. It is the special grace given to meet those special temptations. If a person in danger of death but in sanctifying grace feels that he will not be able to conquer these temptations without the grace of Extreme Unction, he is bound under pain of mortal sin to receive this sacrament.

A person in danger of death and in mortal sin is in serious obligation to receive Extreme Unction if he cannot recover sanctifying grace in any other way. He would be bound to make at least an act of imperfect contrition before lapsing into unconsciousness or being anointed. It is surprising how many adult Catholics have only vague notions of the nature of obligation to receive Extreme Unction. They cause harm to themselves and great sorrow to the Church.

§ 13. *Those who attend the sick are obliged to see to it that a sick person has the opportunity to receive Extreme Unction.*

It often happens that a gravely sick person is physically unable to call a priest. The duty then devolves on those who attend him. These are such persons as the members of the family, doctors, nurses, and the like. The duty may even bind a friend or a neighbor. If possible, a sick person is to be anointed while he is still conscious. We have seen that definite conditions must be met for a fruitful reception of Extreme Unction. If neglect in calling the priest is the cause of the sick person receiving the sacrament unfruitfully, those responsible for the neglect may be guilty of mortal sin. The virtue of Charity can bind one under penalty of serious sin. It very often happens that sick persons must be helped to fulfill the conditions for fruitful reception. Those attending him should give him the assistance he needs to recall those truths to be known by a necessity of means, to make an act of contrition, and to elicit the desire to receive the sacraments. Some theologians hold that the sick person should also make an act of faith. Unless the sick person has already made these acts he should immediately be helped and urged to make them, for he may lapse into unconsciousness before the priest arrives.

A person who is apparently dead may be anointed at least conditionally as long as two hours after apparent death has taken place. Apparent death is accompanied by such phenomena as heart stoppage, or cessation of breathing, and so forth. Real death takes place when the soul leaves the body. Since real and apparent death may not coincide, we give the person the benefit of the doubt and anoint him at least conditionally. The condition is that he is still alive.

§ 14. *Extreme Unction can be validly received only once during the same danger of death.*

Extreme Unction was instituted to provide a very sick person with all the special actual grace he needs to withstand the temptations that may try him during this crisis. The title to sacramental grace that he receives in Extreme Unction is valid as long as the crisis lasts. For this reason, one can receive this sacrament only once during the same danger of death from the same sickness. It is difficult at times to determine whether a person who was once anointed is now in the same danger of death or in a new one. This is often the case when considering the situation of persons who have a grave but lingering illness, such as cancer. Our best guide in resolving this question is the practice permitted by the Church. She says that a person who was anointed and lives for more than a month in the same physical danger may receive a fresh anointing. Those who attend the sick person should keep a record of the date when the sacrament was last administered.

Extreme Unction is the sacrament for the gravely sick, and

not only for those who are on their death bed. One reason many persons do not ask for Extreme Unction is because they think it is only for those who are certain to die. They feel that they are not that sick. They think that they will soon get well. Parish priests have a great deal of experience in dealing with such cases. Those who attend the sick should call a priest to a gravely sick person even though the sick person will resent it. Priests very often have no difficulty in getting such sick persons to receive all the sacraments. They have a great deal of experience in handling very delicate situations such as these.

§ 15. *Any priest can validly administer Extreme Unction; the parish priest lawfully administers it in ordinary cases.*

In Greek the term "presbyter" is a noun meaning "an older person." In Christian contexts, it means a "priest." This is its meaning in all ancient Christian literature. And this meaning was universally accepted until the Sixteenth Century. It was then that the leaders of the Protestant revolt raised the baseless problem as to the identity of the presbyters mentioned by St. James in the passage on Extreme Unction. The Council of Trent then defined, "If anyone says that the priests of the Church, whom the blessed James exhorts to be brought in to anoint the sick are not the priests ordained by a bishop, but elders by age in each community, and for this reason a priest alone is not the proper minister of Extreme Unction: let him be anathema." (D-929) The definition states that Extreme Unction has no extraordinary minister as Baptism and Confirmation have.

In the Latin rite, only one priest may administer Extreme Unction to the person about to receive it. In some Oriental rites, one priest can administer it to a given person, but several priests may together administer the single sacrament.

In ordinary cases, Extreme Unction is lawfully administered by the parish priest of the place where the person resides. But even when there is no sudden need, Extreme Unction can be lawfully administered by any priest with at least the presumed permission of the pastor or ordinary. In cases of emergency, valuable time should not be wasted with the formality of procuring the pastor's explicit permission. Those attending the sick person should call the nearest priest available. Priests are bound in justice or in charity to administer this sacrament.[7]

§ 16. *Extreme Unction does not remove the debt of guilt or the debt of punishment of one who sins after having been anointed but in the same danger of death.*

Extreme Unction can remove even mortal sin after it has been received unfruitfully, that is, by the reviving sacrament. It might erase the debt and punishment of the sins committed before the sacrament was received. But it does not remove new sins committed after the sacrament was received even though they were committed during the period when the sacrament could not be repeated. Nor can Extreme Unction remove the debt of punishment of these new sins. The debt of guilt of the new mortal sins must be removed by absolution or perfect contrition with the desire to receive absolution. Venial sin can be removed by at least an act of sorrow. The debt of punishment for these new sins can be taken away at least in part by the penance imposed by the priest in confession, or by prayer, indulgences, and voluntary sufferings.

The sick should be exhorted not to waste the splendid opportunity to gain merit by enduring their sufferings patiently. Love marks God's dealings with us. The pains and sufferings He sends us are no exception to this rule. Less than what He sends will not sanctify or save us. More than is necessary will never come. It is a paganistic view to look upon pain as being intrinsically evil. Jesus Christ could have redeemed the world in glory. He chose to redeem it in shame and suffering. Pagan

barbarism could devise no more cruel or shameful way to put
a person to death than crucifixion. And in a very difficult passage, St. Paul urges us to endure suffering "to fill up what is
wanting in the sufferings of Christ."

NOTES

1. Zoltan Alszegethy, S. J., *L'Effetto Corporale dell'Estrema Unzione* (Rome:
Gregorianum, 1957), Vol. 38, pp. 385-405.
2. Canon 940.
3. Canon 942.
4. Canon 945.
5. Canon 947.
6. Canon 944.
7. Canon 939.

X

Holy Orders

§ 1. *Holy Orders is a sacrament of the New Law whereby bishops, priests, and deacons are formed into a hierarchy distinct from the laity in the Church.*

In the pagan religions of pre-Christian times there were persons specially set apart from the others who were charged with the duties of conducting worship of the false gods. In Judaism, the tribe of Levi was consecrated to the worship of the true God. But in the early days of the Christian era, a tenet of the Montanist heresy held that there was no distinction between clergy and laity. This was an unusual heresy, for the notable heresies of ancient times such as Donatism, Arianism, Nestorianism, and practically all the others admitted a clear-cut distinction between the clergy and laity. In the Sixteenth Century, Luther, wishing to found a church completely stripped of "Catholic" doctrines, denied the existence of Holy Orders. He then had to find a Scripture passage to justify his denial. He took a passage from St. Peter's *First Epistle* completely out of context and tried to make it serve his purpose. It reads, "You, however, are a chosen race, a royal priesthood, a holy nation, a purchased people." (I Peter 2:9)

To prevent anyone from being confused by the errors of Luther, the Council of Trent repeated the Church's uniform

doctrine. "If anyone says that Orders or Sacred Ordination is
not truly and properly a sacrament instituted by Christ the
Lord, or that it is some human contrivance, devised by men
unskilled in ecclesiastical matters, or that it is only a certain
rite for selecting ministers of the word of God and of the sacraments: let him be anathema." (D-963) Substantially the same
teaching appears many times in official documents of the
Church issued in different centuries before the Sixteenth.

§ 2. *Holy Orders has all the notes of a true sacrament distinct
from all the other sacraments.*

The Council of Trent in the definition quoted in the last
number explicitly states that Holy Orders has the first requisite of a sacrament, namely, institution by Jesus Christ. (1) It
has a matter and form necessary for making the conferring of
it an external, sensible rite. The matter is a special imposition
of hands on the person receiving it. The form is the prayer
accompanying the imposition of hands. (2) There are definite
conditions that must be complied with to insure valid, fruitful
and lawful administration. (3) Holy Orders was instituted to
meet a distinct need in the life of the Church. It empowers
certain individuals to carry on the work assigned to the
Church, namely to teach all men what they must believe and
do to be saved, and to distribute to all men the means of
grace. (4) This sacrament entitles its recipient to all the special
actual grace he needs to perform the duties imposed upon him
by the reception of this sacrament. Since these are special
duties, they require that the one performing them have special
grace. Holy Orders confers an actual grace that no other sacrament can confer. (5) Holy Orders is a permanent rite or sacrament. Our Divine Lord authorized individuals to carry on His
work by conferring upon them this sacrament. This is the
only way that the power to teach and to sanctify will ever be
transmitted. Since the Church will always need such individ-

uals, it follows that Holy Orders is a permanent sacrament and will be conferred in the Church until the end of time. Every one of these points has been solemnly defined by the Church at one time or another.

§ 3. *Holy Orders imprints on the soul an indelible mark by virtue of which the sacrament cannot be repeated.*

The truth embodied in the proposition was solemnly defined by the Church with the words, "If anyone shall say that in Holy Orders there is not imprinted on the soul a sign, that is, a certain spiritual and indelible mark on account of which it can not be repeated: let him be anathema." (D-852) The nature of the mark imprinted in Holy Orders can best be studied in the light of the marks conferred in Baptism and Confirmation. All three marks confer upon a degree of participation in the priesthood of Jesus Christ. The participation conferred in Baptism is principally passive. It enables one to receive the fruits of Christ's priesthood. The participation conferred in Confirmation is an active one but an active one of lower grade. It empowers one to profess publicly the faith in Christ. Holy Orders confers on its recipient active participation of higher grade. The participation conferred by Holy Orders starts where the participation conferred by Confirmation stops. This is why a new sacrament is needed to confer them.

Holy Orders itself confers varying degrees of power, which in turn indicate varying degrees of higher participation in Christ's priesthood. These steps taken together form what is called a hierarchy of Orders consisting of the episcopacy, the priesthood, and deaconship. There is also a hierarchy of jurisdiction in the Church consisting of two grades, namely the primacy of power invested in the Roman Pontiff and the power of ordinary jurisdiction invested in the bishops. In this chapter, we speak of the hierarchy of Orders, for the hierarchy of jurisdiction is studied in courses in apologetics.

§ 4. *Holy Orders entitles its recipient to the sacramental grace he needs to participate fully in the priesthood of Christ.*

Holy Orders was primarily instituted, not for the private benefit of its recipient, but for the benefit of the Church in general. It is to make him a better instrument for the sanctification of souls. This is true of all three orders of the hierarchy. The sacramental graces suggest salutary thoughts to the intellect, and they strengthen the will to reduce these suggestions to action. Those in Orders are charged with the task of teaching revealed truth. The actual graces they receive enlighten their minds to grasp ways of explaining those truths, to devise plans to spread the faith, and to counteract error. "Do not be anxious how or wherewith you shall defend yourselves, or what you shall say, for the Holy Spirit will teach you in that very hour what you ought to say." (Luke 12:11) The clergy is to exhort the laity to make better use of the means of grace. Sacramental grace strengthens the will of those in Holy Orders to persevere in the face of many obstacles in pastoral work.

All the Encyclicals of the recent Holy Fathers insist that Holy Orders is also intended to help a priest live a holy, personal, priestly life. They point out the almost unparalleled opportunities that he has to grow in the love of God.

§ 5. *There is clear evidence dating from earliest Christian times proving the existence in the Church of a hierarchy consisting of bishops, priests, and deacons.*

Those who might find it too intricate a task to sift through the works of early Christian writers for evidence of the hierarchy have been assured of its existence by the teaching authority of the Church. At the Council of Trent, the Church defined, "If anyone says that in the Catholic Church a hierarchy has not been instituted, which consists of the bishops, priests, and ministers (deacons): let him be anathema." (D-966)

The clearest and most abundant evidence of a hierarchy of orders in the Church in Apostolic times appears in the seven letters of St. Ignatius of Antioch written before 107 A.D. The letters were dispatched to seven Christian communities while their author was on route from Syria to martyrdom in the Colosseum at Rome. In those seven brief letters he tells us no less than fourteen times that the hierarchy consists of bishops, priests, and deacons. In the letter to the Magnesians, we read "Be zealous to do all things in harmony with God, with the *bishop* presiding in the place of God and the *presbyters* in the place of the Council of the Apostles and the *deacons,* who are most dear to me." In the famous eighth chapter of his Epistle to the Smyrneans he writes, "See that you all follow the *bishop,* as Jesus Christ follows the Father and the *presbytery* as if it were the Apostles. And reverence the *deacons* as the command of God." When we put all of St. Ignatius' testimonies side by side, there can be no doubt that these three are the only orders of hierarchy. He writes to the communities of Ephesus, Magnesia, Tralles, Rome, Philadelphia, Smyrna, and to Polycarp with such a casualness about the hierarchy that it is abundantly clear that he was not telling them anything new. In fact in every instance he presupposes that they know the position of the hierarchy in their own community.

§ 6. *The episcopate is a distinct order in the hierarchy superior to the priesthood.*

The term "episcopate" is derived from a Greek noun meaning "an overseer" or "a superintendent." In examining this term in ancient documents, we must not think that a member of this episcopacy, that is, a bishop, was merely a layman invested with a certain amount of power as members elect someone to be president of an organization. A bishop is one who indeed oversees, but he has received a distinct power of Orders. It is easy to prove the existence of this rank in the Church. (1) The

Council of Trent defined, "If anyone says that the bishops are not superior to priests . . . or that the power which they have is common to them and to priests . . . : let him be anathema." (D-967) Needless to say, this teaching appears very often in official documents of the Church issued before this definition. (2) St. Paul implied the existence of this order for he lists the qualities of a good bishop. He writes, "For a bishop must be blameless as being the steward of God, not proud, or ill-tempered." (Titus 1:6) There is evidence in the *Acts* and *Epistles* proving the existence of the Order of Bishop. (3) The testimony of ancient Christian literature on this point is simply overwhelming. St. Ignatius of Antioch states no less than fifty-eight times in his seven extant letters that the episcopacy exists and that it is superior to the priesthood. (4) There is clear archeological proof of the existence of the Order of bishop from earliest times. In 1854, DeRossi discovered the famous Crypt of the Popes who reigned in the Third Century. Inscriptions on the six marble slabs sealing the tombs show that the persons interred there were bishops.

§ 7. *A bishop possesses the fullness of the power that can be received by the reception of Holy Orders.*

The principal powers of a bishop are listed here. (1) In the last number, it was pointed out that the episcopate is superior to the priesthood. It follows that a bishop has all the powers of a priest plus powers that a priest does not have. (2) In 451 A.D., the Council of Chalcedon defined (D-150) that a bishop alone can consecrate another bishop. Today a bishop is forbidden under penalty of excommunication to consecrate another bishop unless directed to do so by the Holy See. If he did this without the directive of the Holy See, the consecration would be valid but not lawful.[1] (3) In 1439, the Council of Florence taught that only a bishop can ordain a priest or a deacon. (D-701) (4) In 1551 the Council of Trent defined that the bishop alone is the ordinary minister of Confirmation. (D-873) (5) The bishop is the ordinary consecrator of the oils of the sick, of the oil of catechumens, and holy Chrism. (6) Besides having the fullness of the power of orders, the bishops are the successors of the Apostles. They are, therefore, invested with ordinary authority to teach. When Christ commissioned the Apostles to teach, He commissioned them as a group. When all the bishops taken as a group teach a doctrine, it is covered by the endowment of infallibility. God then protects them from error when teaching faith and morals or a doctrine needed to protect or explain revealed truth. As individuals, bishops are not infallible, as the Church's condemnation of the errors of such bishops as Nestorius and Jansenius clearly proves. Bishops are the official teachers and official spiritual rulers in their own diocese. All other teachers there teach by the authority of the local bishop. The proof of the Roman Pontiff's primacy of jurisdiction over even all bishops is given in Apologetics.

§ 8. *The Order of Bishop is conferred by a distinct rite of consecration.*

Special matter and form are used in conferring the Order of Episcopate. The matter is a special imposition of hands of another bishop. We find no other matter universally considered essential. In times past, some thought that the imposition of the book of the Gospels on the shoulders of the man being consecrated was necessary. The form reads, "Accomplish in thy priest the fullness of thy ministry and endow him with the adornments of complete glorification, and sanctify him with the dew of heavenly anointing."

The bishop receives in his consecration a new and distinct indelible mark on his soul. This mark entitles him to all the sacramental grace he needs to carry out his duties as a bishop. If he is in sanctifying grace, he receives a constant flow of these actual or sacramental graces. If he is in mortal sin, he does not receive these graces by virtue of this mark until he again recovers sanctifying grace. Some theologians hold that he does receive some, but only congruously.

One bishop by himself can validly consecrate another bishop. In the rite of consecration today, there are three bishops.[2] One is called the consecrator. The other two are called co-consecrators. Today, the Holy See selects the priests who are to be made bishops. In ancient times, the clergy and even the laity often elected him. We read how St. Ambrose was elected bishop of Milan while still a catechumen and how the people of Alexandria by acclamation designated St. Athanasius to be their bishop.

§ 9. *The priesthood is an order in the hierarchy distinct from and superior to deaconship.*

In early Christian writings, the priests of the church—as opposed to priests of the Old Law—were often called "presbyters." This term is derived from the Greek noun meaning "elders." While any serious student would have no difficulty noticing that it is a technical noun in early Christian literature, it was seized upon by some leaders of the Protestant revolt to try to give justification to their elimination of the distinction between clergy and laity. The Council of Trent defined, "If anyone says that there is not in the New Testament a visible and external priesthood . . . . but only the office and bare ministry of preaching the Gospel . . . : let him be anathema." (D-961) This definition was not the first time that the Church officially stated that the priesthood was a distinct order in the hierarchy. We find it in statements of the Roman Pontiff as early as 416 A.D.

The existence of the order of presbyterate or priesthood is clearly contained in Sacred Scripture. We read, "On arriving at Jerusalem, they were welcomed by the church and the apostles and the *presbyters* and they proclaimed all that God had done with them." (Acts 15:5) Again, "Now I exhort the *presbyters* among you—I, your fellow-presbyter and witness to the sufferings of Christ." (I Peter 5:1) Finally, "Is any one among you sick? Let him bring in the presbyters of the Church." (James 5:14) The presbyters are mentioned six times in the New Testament. There are two very revealing notes about these six times. In every instance the noun is in the plural and in every instance the plural noun is preceded or modified by the article. We know that the Greek language does not use the article indiscriminately. It says, "the presbyters" and in so doing, it denotes a definite order in the hierarchy. They were not merely "elders," for the Scripture tells that they performed sacred functions that lay men could not perform.

§ 10. *The Apostolic Fathers clearly show that the presbyterate or priesthood was a rank in Holy Orders distinct from that of episcopacy or deaconship.*

The importance of the Apostolic Fathers lies in the fact that they are so very old and that they give witness to the belief of the Church in earliest times. They are singularly free from speculation and attempts to explain Christian doctrine. They hand down truths just as they received them. The outstanding witness of this group for the topic we now discuss was St. Ignatius of Antioch (107 A.D.) It was in Antioch in Syria that Christ's followers were first called Christians. It was the center of Christianity before St. Peter went to Rome. St. Ignatius was the second or third bishop of Antioch after St. Peter, who once had his See there. He was also a disciple of St. John the Evangelist. In his letters, St. Ignatius touches upon many doctrines, but he makes his greatest contribution when he tells us of the composition of the hierarchy in existence in the First

Century. He mentions the "presbyters" twenty-three times in his epistles. Twenty-two of these times the term appears in the same sentence with the term "bishop." We quote several passages to illustrate our point. "For it is right that each of you and especially the *presbyters* should refresh the bishop to the honor of the Father, of Jesus Christ, and of the Apostle."[3] Again, "so do you do nothing without the bishop and the *presbyters*."[4] Finally,—"that you may be joined together in one subjection, subject to the bishop and the *presbytery*."[5] In practically every instance, St. Ignatius uses the article with the plural of the noun as was done in the *Acts* and *Epistles*. The two dove-tail perfectly. There is the same testimony on the presbyters in the *First Epistle of Clement of Rome* and in the *Epistle of St. Polycarp*. Both of these documents are also among the Apostolic Fathers, but the testimony is not as abundant in these sources as it is in the epistles of St. Ignatius.

§ 11. *A priest alone has the power to celebrate Mass, and to administer Penance and Extreme Unction.*

The proposition lists the powers proper to a priest. It does not include the extraordinary powers that he can receive by special delegation. (1) A priest in any religion is one who offers a sacrifice to God. This was true of the pagan priesthood and the Judaic priesthood of the Old Law. The priesthood of the New Testament is linked to the Holy Sacrifice of the Mass. At the Last Supper, Christ offered the first Mass and then empowered priests to repeat this sacrifice. The Council of Trent defined, "If anyone denies that by these words: 'Do this in commemoration of me' Christ did not make the Apostles priests, or did not ordain that they and other priests might offer His own body and blood: let him be anathema." (D-949) A priest can always say Mass validly, but he would commit a sacrilege if he did so when his Ordinary forbade him. (2) The same holy council solemnly defined that only a priest can administer Penance and Extreme Unction. "If anyone says that . . . not only priests are the ministers of absolution . . . let him be anathema." (D-920) "If anyone says that the priests of the Church, whom blessed James exhorts to be brought to anoint the sick, are not the priests ordained by a bishop . . . . let him be anathema." (D-929) (3) A priest is the ordinary minister of solemn Baptism and the extraordinary minister of Confirmation. (4) Although the priest does not administer the sacrament of Matrimony when received by two Catholics, he must ordinarily witness it for it to be valid. A priest also blesses and preaches, but these are not functions that require priestly ordination. Persons other than priests can be empowered to perform them.

§ 12. *The priesthood is conferred by a distinct rite of ordination.*

The priesthood is a true sacrament conferring special powers. Those powers are less than those of a bishop, but more than those of a deacon. The ordination of a priest has a special sacramental matter and form. It confers an indelible mark on the soul of the man who is ordained. Because of this mark, the sacrament cannot be repeated.

In 1947, a Constitution of Pope Pius XII declared that the only matter necessary for the ordination of a priest was the imposition of hands of the bishop. There was a great deal of discussion as to whether or not the handing over of the paten and Chalice was essential to the rite. The questions raised by those discussions are now settled. At the ordination of a priest, there are two impositions of hands, but only the first is necessary for the validity of the sacrament. Sacred Scripture clearly states that the matter of this ordination is the imposition of hands. St. Paul writes to Timothy saying, "I admonish thee to stir up the grace of God which is in thee by the laying on of my hands." (II Tim. 1:7) The same truth is contained in numerous works of the Fathers.

The form pronounced during the ordination of a priest reads, "We beseech Thee, Almighty Father, invest these Thy servants with the dignity of the priesthood. Do Thou renew in their hearts the spirit of holiness, that they may hold the office, next to ours in importance, which they have received from Thee O Lord, and by the example of their lives point out a norm of conduct." The meaning of the words of this form fixes the intention of the bishop.

§ 13. *Deaconship is an order in the hierarchy of the Church inferior to that of the priesthood.*

There is ample evidence in the official documents of the Church, in Sacred Scripture, and in Christian literature to prove that deaconship was always considered a true sacrament. In 1091 A.D. Pope Urban II said officially, "Let no one be chosen in order of succession into the episcopacy, except one who has been found living religiously in sacred orders. Moreover, we call sacred orders the diaconate and the priesthood." (D-356) The same truth was stated in documents issued or approved by the Holy See before and after this one.

There are several references to deacons in the New Testament. We read "Paul and Timothy, servants of Jesus Christ, to all the saints in Christ Jesus that are at Philippi, with the bishops and deacons." (Phil. 1:1) The Council of Trent says that Scripture refers to deacons in the *Acts of the Apostles*. The passage reads, "They chose Stephen, ..., and Philip and Prochorus and Nicanor and Timon and Parmenas and Nicholas. . . . These they set before the apostles, and after they had prayed they laid their hands upon them." (Acts 6:5) We have called attention to the singular importance of the evidence of the existence of the hierarchy found in the epistles of St. Ignatius of Antioch. (107 A.D.) His testimony on the existence of deaconship as an order of the hierarchy is also clear and abundant. He refers to deacons no less than seventeen times. We quote several of them: "And they also who are *deacons* of the mysteries of Jesus Christ must be in every way pleasing to all men."[6] "And if you have the will, it is not impossible for you to do this for the sake of the Name of God, even as the neighboring Churches have sent bishops and other presbyters and deacons."[7] Several other Apostolic Fathers contain evidence of the existence of deacons.

§ 14. *Deaconship is conferred by a distinct ordination; deacons are ordained to assist bishops and priests in the discharge of their sacred duties.*

The ordination of a deacon has a distinct sacramental matter and form. The matter of this ordination is the special imposition of hands of the bishop. That this is the matter for the ordination of a deacon is seen from the clear testimony of *Acts of the Apostles.* In 451 A.D. the Council of Chalcedon said, "When a deacon is ordained, let the bishop alone, who blesses him, place his hands above his head, because he is consecrated not for the priesthood, but for the Ministry." (D-150) The form pronounced by the bishop at the ordination of a deacon reads, "Send forth upon them, we beseech Thee, O Lord, the Holy Spirit that they may be strengthened by Him, through the gift of the sevenfold grace, unto the faithful discharge of Thy service." In ordination, a deacon receives an indelible mark upon his soul.

The proposition states that a deacon is ordained to assist bishops and priests. He hands the Chalice to the celebrant at Mass and sings the Gospel. He may be delegated to preach. A deacon is the extraordinary minister of Holy Communion and solemn Baptism. In ancient times, deacons had the duty of administering the Church's charities. Ancient Rome was divided into seven districts for the distributing of charity. Each district was administered by a deacon. The first of these seven was called the Archdeacon and he was sometimes elected pope. Pope St. Callixtus I was a deacon in charge of one of these districts before being elected pontiff. While a deacon he undertook the construction of the largest Roman Catacombs, namely the one that still bears his name. It was this cemetery that became the burial place of the popes of the Third Century and whose tombs were discovered by DeRossi in 1854 A.D.

§ 15. *Subdeaconship and the other lesser orders are not sacraments.*

The earliest extant evidence in documents issued by the Holy See for the existence of the orders referred to in the proposition is a letter from Pope St. Cornelius I to Fabius, bishop of Antioch, in 251 A.D. It is certain that these orders were instituted by the Church some time before the middle of the Third Century. Each is conferred by a special rite. (1) In the Latin rite, subdeaconship is a major order; in the Oriental rites, it is a minor order. A *subdeacon* prepares the water for the ministry of the altar, assists the deacon and washes altar linens used at Mass, that is, purificators and corporals. (2) The *acolyte* assists at Mass by carrying the candle and handing the wine and water to the subdeacon. (3) The *exorcist* is empowered to lay his hands on persons possessed by the devil and then read the exorcisms approved by the Church. (4) The *lector* is commissioned to read the Scriptures publicly in Church, to sing the lessons at Mass, and to teach Christian doctrine. (5) The *porter* is charged with guarding the doors of the Church, with calling the faithful to services and with excluding the unworthy from sacred functions. In ancient times, the members of these orders filled very real needs. Their functions were more or less related to the Mass so that St. Thomas said that these orders could be called "sacraments" in the wide sense. The Church, of course, never considered them on a par with the orders instituted by Christ. Although subdeaconship and the other orders are not absolutely necessary for the valid reception of the sacrament of Holy Orders, the Church prescribes that men advancing toward the priesthood must receive them.

§ 16. *A man becomes a cleric by the reception of tonsure.*

The rite of tonsure is of purely ecclesiastical origin. It was in existence as early as in the Fifth Century. The ceremony consists in the cutting of a portion of the candidate's hair and pronouncing him now to be a cleric. In some European countries, the tonsure is worn throughout life. In the United States it is not worn.

While tonsure is not even one of the minor orders, it confers several important rights in Canon Law. These rights flow from the fact that the person is no longer a simple layman, but one set aside for the service of God and of the Church. (1) Any one who lays violent hands on a cleric is excommunicated reserved to the ordinary. The law, however, does not preclude legitimate self-defense.[8] (2) Anyone who sues a cleric in Civil Court without due permission is also excommunicated with an excommunication reserved to the ordinary. Canon Laws lay down the limits of the clerical immunity. A cleric may, however, be sued in ecclesiastical courts. The reason for this law is that the bad publicity that results from such a suit does great harm, not merely to the individual, but to the clerical state in general.[9] (3) A cleric is exempt from civil duties foreign to the clerical state. They are such duties as military service and serving on a jury. Many countries respect this regulation, but some do not.[10] (4) By tonsure, a person is incardinated into a diocese and is subject to its ordinary.[11] He is then qualified to receive benefices, jurisdiction and sacred orders. The rights and privileges listed here belong to the clerical state.[12] They may not be waived by individual clerics without proper permission from competent superiors.

§ 17. *At the reception of subdeaconship clerics of the Latin rite take a promise of perfect and perpetual chastity.*

A celibate clergy has always been the glory of the Church and the envy of her enemies. The example of Christ and His Virgin Mother are indications of the greatness of the virtue of chastity. The Council of Trent defined, "If anyone should say that the married state is higher than the state of celibacy or virginity or says that it is better and more blessed to marry than to remain in celibacy or virginity; let him be anathema." (D-980) St. Paul explicitly stated "He who is unmarried is concerned about the things of the Lord, how he may please God. Whereas he who is married is concerned about the things of the world, how he may please his wife; and he is divided." (I Cor. 7:32)

In earliest times, there were many celibates among the clergy. The oldest extant evidence of legislation requiring perfect chastity of those in sacramental orders dates from the Third Century. It is Canon 30 of the Council of Elvira in Spain enacted in 295 A.D. In 385 A.D. Pope St. Siricius prescribed it for all in sacramental orders in the Latin rite. By the Twelfth Century perfect and perpetual chastity was required of all subdeacons of the Latin rite. The legislation for Oriental rites is not the same as that for the Latin rite. Benedict XIV (1740-1758) forbade Uniate subdeacons, deacons, and priests to contract marriage after ordination. In 1929, the Holy See directed that no married man of a Uniate rite in the United States would be allowed to be ordained a deacon or priest. Notice that the legislation for Latin and for Orientals is not the same even in the United States. Perpetual chastity is the promise required of the Latin clergy. Perpetual celibacy is the promise required of the Oriental clergy.

§ 18. *To be validly ordained, the subject for ordination to the priesthood must be a baptized male who intends to receive this sacrament if he has reached the use of reason.*[13]

We must carefully distinguish between valid, fruitful, and lawful ordination. The proposition lists the conditions necessary for valid ordination. It is by divine law that only males can be validly ordained or consecrated. The "deaconesses" of ancient times did not receive any sacred orders of any kind. The "priestesses" of ancient times invariably belonged to pagan or heretical sects. A candidate for ordination must be baptized, for Baptism is the gateway to the reception of the other sacraments. A third condition for valid reception of Holy Orders is that one who has reached the use of reason must consent to it.

For fruitful reception of Holy Orders a man must be validly ordained and must be free from mortal sin. If he receives Holy Orders sacrilegiously, he does indeed receive the sacrament, but does not receive its grace until the sin is removed by absolution or perfect contrition.

In ancient times even more than in modern times, the Church has had to make a judgment on the validity of the Orders of schismatic clergymen. While it is perfectly possible for a schismatic bishop, priest or deacon to be validly ordained, it is the Church's policy to investigate each one of them before labeling it valid. The case is slightly different with the validity of Anglican orders. In 1896, Pope Leo XIII had competent historians and theologians investigate this question based on the defect of form and intention used in these ordinations. He said, "We pronounce and declare that ordinations enacted according to the Anglican rite have hitherto been and are invalid and entirely void." (D-1966)

§ 19. *For lawful ordination a candidate for Holy Orders must be free from the impediments laid down by the Church.*[14]

In laying down the impediments for ordination the Church is guided by her vast experience. She wishes to avoid those factors that will hamper a cleric in his work. As we shall soon see, these impediments do not necessarily imply moral fault or sin on the part of the person. We list some of them. (1) Bodily defect which will hinder a cleric in the performance of his work. For example, the loss of fingers preventing a priest from breaking the Sacred Host at Mass. (2) Engaging in secular business enterprises. (3) Illegitimacy, unless legitimated by subsequent marriage of parents. (4) Insanity and epilepsy, unless a dispensation is granted after the malady has been overcome. (5) Prospect of proximate draft into military service. (6) Recent conversion to the faith unless the ordinary judges otherwise. (7) A non-Catholic parent as long as he or she persists in error. (8) Loss of reputation, and the loss still persists. The Church at times permits a dispensation from some of these irregularities when there is clear indication that they will not hinder the performance of the cleric's duties. The ordinary is required to make careful inquiry into their possible existence before he may ordain a man. It is for this reason that the Church prescribes that banns be announced in the candidate's parish before he receives subdeaconship, deaconship, and priesthood. Any person knowing of the existence of these impediments in a candidate for major orders is bound in conscience to reveal them to the proper authorities.

§ 20. *A bishop is forbidden to ordain a man without positive evidence of his fitness to perform the duties of the clerical state.*[16]

It is not enough that a candidate for Holy Orders be free from irregularities or even serious sin. These are negative qualifications. The bishop must have clear evidence of a candidate's positive qualifications. A candidate must not only be free from mortal sin but free from any habit of mortal sin. He must have made good progress in the practice of virtue and mortification. The daily schedule of the seminary is designed to foster these qualities.

A candidate must have successfully completed the studies in sacred science prescribed for those who seek ordination. These courses are fixed by the congregation of seminaries and universities in Rome. They are principally studies in theology and philosophy, but also include courses in Sacred Scripture, history, canon-law, classical languages and others. They are almost perfectly uniform in all seminaries throughout the world. Many of the courses are conducted in Latin. The oldest extant evidence of a seminary dates from the middle of the Seventh Century in Spain, but the greatest progress for the uniform education of priests was made by the directives of the Council of Trent.

Church law prescribes that a candidate for Holy Orders shall have reached the proper age.[17] The prescribed age for sub-deaconship is twenty-one years; for deaconship it is at least twenty-two; and for priesthood it is at least twenty-four years. When the situation warrants it, it is possible to receive a dispensation from the regulations of the age required of a candidate for sacred orders.

§ 21. *The call to the priesthood is the greatest vocation that man can receive from God.*

A vocation receives its dignity from its purpose. There is no greater privilege given to man than the priest's power to offer Holy Mass. St. Thomas stated that no act is greater than the consecration of the Body of Christ. St. Albert the Great wrote, "Forasmuch as no act can be more excellent than the consecration of the Body of Christ, there can be no order higher than the priesthood."[15]

The priest is an indispensable instrument in the sanctification of men. A very good barometer of the spirituality of a parish is the frequency with which people receive Penance and Holy Communion. And these sacraments must be received from the hands of a priest. The enemies of Christ are keenly conscious of the role of the priest in the life of a Catholic. They wholeheartedly subscribe to the saying, "Smite the shepherd, and the sheep of the flock will be scattered" (Matt. 26:31). They know that they can destroy the souls of Catholics by destroying the lives of their priests.

A priest is a teacher of revealed truth. He is an important member of the Church which Christ commissioned with the words, "Go, therefore, and make disciples of all nations . . . . teaching them to observe all that I have commanded you" (Matt. 28:19). "He who hears you, hears me; and he who rejects you, rejects me" (Luke 10:16). Christ underscored their importance by coming in person to deliver them to us. They are truths whose primary aim is not to unlock the secrets of nature, or to solve sociological problems, or to secure political tranquility, but to save souls. And the priest is deputized to double for Christ to teach these very truths.

§ 22. *High school and college students who think they have a vocation to the priesthood or religious life are urged to foster it in every possible way.*

In His providence, God gives out enough vocations for the work of the Church to be carried out adequately. And yet it has always been true that "the harvest indeed is great, but the laborers are few." (Matt. 9:38) The reason may be that these vocations are being rejected by those whom God calls. Students who think they have a vocation should by all means foster it. A vocation is like a garden. The positive side requires tilling the soil, planting and watering the plants. The negative side requires the removal of weeds and the killing of insect pests that will destroy the crop. (1) On the positive side, a student should devise a daily rule of life designed to promote his love of God. He will include in it frequent and possible daily assistance at Mass and reception of Holy Communion, rosary, meditation, visits to the Blessed Sacrament, spiritual reading, and mortification. He should keep daily check on how often and how well he performs these spiritual exercises. It is advisable for him to have a regular confessor and spiritual director. (2) On the negative side, the student will foster a vocation by avoiding anything that will endanger it. He will, of course, stay away from mortal sin and make determined war on venial sin. Other dangers to vocation are frivolous entertainment in mixed company, love of ease, thirst for pleasure, reluctance to make sacrifices and to practice self-denial. Some young people with a vocation must foster it and preserve it in the face of bitter opposition from parents. (3) Three things are listed as being indications of a vocation. They are good health, a normal amount of intelligence, and a desire to serve God in this special way.

NOTES

1. *Summa Theologica Supp.*, Ques. 38, Art. 1.
2. Canon 954.
3. *Ad Trall.* 12.
4. *Ad Mag.* 7.
5. *Ad Eph.* 2.
6. *Ad Trall.* 2.
7. *Ad Phila.* 10.
8. Canon 119.
9. Canon 120.
10. Canon 121.
11. Canon 111.
12. Canon 118.
13. Canon 968.
14. Canon 974.
15. *Com. In IV Sent.* 24, 30.
16. Canon 973.
17. Canon 975.

XI

Matrimony

§ 1. *Matrimony is the sacrament by which a baptized man and a baptized woman are united in a valid marriage.*

In the Ante-Nicene period the moral practices of Christianity were strongly tinged with asceticism. It is not surprising to find a number of errors held by heretics that would forbid anyone from taking even the legitimate pleasures of marriage. In the Second Century, the Montanists at first forbade all marriages, but later forbade only second marriages.[1] After he became a heretic, Tertullian held second marriages to be a species of adultery.[2] Tatian as an Encratite condemned marriage as fornication.[3] In modern times, Luther held marriage to be a "worldly thing." For the most part these opinions erred on the side of severity. Many modern heretics err on the side of laxity. A number of neo-pagan sociologists have attempted to destroy the concept of marriage by replacing it with the notion of "free-love." They have poisoned the minds and destroyed the souls of many college students.[4]

The Church has had to repeat the teaching of revelation on marriage many times in the course of history. Those who attack marriage as a natural institution *a fortiori* attack it as a sacrament. In 1139 A.D., the Second Lateran Council condemned the Neo-Manicheans for their errors on marriage. In 1184, the Council of Verona anathematized those who held

231

that Matrimony was not a sacrament. In 1563 A.D., the Council of Trent repeated the Church's traditional teaching in the face of the new attacks on the sacramental system. It defined: "If anyone says that Matrimony is not truly and properly one of the seven sacraments of the evangelical Law, instituted by Christ the Lord, but that it has been invented by men in the Church, and does not confer grace: let him be anathema." (D-971) The holy council goes on to make a clear distinction between marriage as a natural contract and marriage as a sacrament.

§ 2. *It cannot be conclusively proved from Sacred Scripture that Matrimony is a sacrament.*

God delivered His revelation to the Church in both written and spoken form. All that we must accept is not in written form, that is, in Sacred Scripture. There is absolutely no reason to be alarmed because of the scarcity of evidence on Matrimony as a sacrament in the New Testament. A number of Scripture passages touch upon marriage, but it cannot be conclusively proved that they, taken singly or collectively, refer to marriage as a sacrament. Christ said, "For this cause a man shall leave his father and mother, and cleave to his wife, and the two shall become one flesh. Therefore, now they are no longer two, but one flesh. What therefore God has joined together, let no man put asunder." (Matt. 19:6) A second passage often quoted is from St. Paul's *Epistle to the Ephesians*. It reads, "Husbands, love your wives, just as Christ also loved the Church . . . . For this cause a man shall leave his father and mother, and cleave to his wife; and the two shall become one flesh. This is a great mystery. I mean in reference to Christ and to the Church. However, let each one of you also love his wife just as he loves himself; and let the wife respect her husband." (Eph. 5:25-33) Both Christ and St. Paul are speaking of marriage.

It is interesting to note that none of the Latin or Greek Fathers use these passages to prove that Matrimony is a sacrament. The Council of Trent quotes the passage from the *Epistle to the Ephesians,* but adds that in it St. Paul "intimates" or "hints" the sacramental character of Matrimony. The council does not say that the passage proves it.

§ 3. *The Latin and Greek Fathers of the ancient Church teach that Matrimony is a sacrament.*

Many of the Fathers wrote extensively on marriage. Tertullian composed several monographs on it. St. Basil, St. Gregory of Nazianzus, and St. John Chrysostom in the East; St. Ambrose, St. Jerome, and St. Augustine in the West made important contributions to the early literature on the subject. They treat of the nature, ends, and properties of marriage. But a great deal of what they write could be applied to marriage as a natural contract. It is difficult to find passages in their works where they say that Matrimony is an effective means of both sanctifying and actual grace. The question is, "How can we be sure that they are writing about the sacrament and not about the natural contract?" The answer is simple. We know that these Latin and Greek Fathers are referring to the sacrament because otherwise they would have little reason or incentive to treat of it. These men were theologians, not sociologists. It is difficult to see how St. Ignatius of Antioch (107 A.D.) could be referring only to a natural contract when he said that the bishop's permission was necessary for Christians to marry. He wrote, "But it is right for men and women who marry to be united with the consent of the bishop, that the marriage be according to the Lord, and not according to lust."[5] As theologians, they were concerned principally with questions of the supernatural order and man's relationship to this order. The indispensable element of the supernatural order is grace. When they treat of marriage, its nature, its properties and ends, they are treating of something intimately connected with grace. What connection is possible between marriage and grace? The obvious one is marriage as a means of grace. This is precisely what a sacrament is. When these Fathers treat of marriage, they are treating of it as a sacrament. Far from there being a scarcity of evidence on this subject in their writings, their works are full of such evidence. Its probative force is great even though it is only implicit.

§ 4. *Matrimony has all the elements necessary for a true sacrament.*

Judging merely from externals, it would be difficult to see the distinction between marriage as a natural contract and Matrimony as a sacrament. But in Matrimony there are verified all the necessary elements for a true sacrament. (1) The Church has solemnly defined that it was instituted by Jesus Christ. When Christ refers to marriage, He is referring to a sacrament. (2) The matter is the persons who marry insofar as they mutually give each other as spouses; the form is also the persons who marry insofar as they accept each other as spouses.[6] It was perhaps this peculiar matter and form, differing so much from that of, for example, Baptism, that made it difficult for the Fathers to notice Matrimony's similarity to the other sacraments. (3) This sacrament has its own deputized ministers. They are the very persons who marry. All the sacraments were confided to the Church. She can lay down regulations as to when this sacrament may be administered and received. Her authorization affects the lawfulness and sometimes even the validity of the contract. (4) Matrimony was instituted to have a very definite supernatural role in society. The primary goal of Matrimony is to enable married persons to beget and to educate their children to be citizens of the kingdom of God. And in the process, they themselves grow in sanctifying grace. (5) As a sacrament, Matrimony confers grace. It entitles one to the sacramental grace needed to fulfill the purpose of the sacrament. This grace enlightens the intellect and strengthens the will to fulfill the duties which this state of life imposes. It furthermore enables one to overcome the peculiar temptations to sin that this state of life may occasion.

§ 5. *The primary purpose of marriage is the orderly propagation of the race.*

The Sixth Commandment of God prescribes that an individual's primary purpose in taking sex pleasure must be for the benefit of the race. Since the primary purpose of marriage is the orderly propagation of the race, it follows that those who contract valid marriage acquire a right to perform the act of generation.[7] They may perform incomplete sexual acts provided these acts are proximately or remotely directed to the act of generation. The contracting parties, that is, the husband and wife, mutually acquire this right in justice.[8] Either may ask the other to perform the marital act. The spouse who is asked must cooperate if the one asking reasonably and seriously makes the request. It is a mortal sin to refuse cooperation under these conditions. There are several instances when even a serious request is unreasonable. It may then be refused without sin. A person who has committed adultery may ask to perform the marital act, but the innocent spouse who is thus asked is not obliged to cooperate. A request is also unreasonable when made by an insane or drunken spouse, when the request is made too frequently, or when there is great danger of serious contagion or bodily harm.[9] Notice that in these cases, the request is for the act of generation. The spouse *may* refuse to cooperate. But that spouse *is obliged* to refuse a request to practice birth control or to cooperate in any other unnatural sin. Persons living in an invalid marriage have not acquired any right to the act of generation. Between them, it is at least fornication. It may even be adultery as when one party had contracted a valid marriage, obtained a divorce, and then attempted this second marriage.

§ 6. *The orderly propagation of the race includes fulfillment of the duties to care for the bodies, minds, and souls of children.*

Children have bodies, minds, and souls that must be trained, developed, and preserved from harm. When they are minors, they lack the maturity and means to do these things for themselves. These tasks devolve on those persons responsible for the child's coming into this world. A child's care requires continuous cooperation on the part of parents. As a rule, the duties can be performed satisfactorily only in a stable union where responsibility is fixed and definite.

Since married persons have a right to the act of generation, they have a duty to care for the children born to them. (1) There is little difficulty in grasping the duty to care for the bodies of children. Parents are obliged to provide them with adequate food, clothing, shelter, and medical attention. They sin if their improvidence or laziness prevents them from fulfilling these duties. (2) The duty to educate children depends on the child's ability to learn and the parents' ability to provide. God does not give talent and opportunity without imposing the corresponding duty to make use of them. The education that parents must provide their children should teach them, not only how to make a living, but also how to live.[10] (3) Caring for the souls of children means that parents must see to it that the children receive the sacraments when they are obliged to do so, that they develop virtues that will stand them in good stead in later life, and that they are shielded from the moral dangers that threaten them. In providing a good Catholic outlook on life, there is no substitute for the Catholic school at every intellectual level.[11] The best efforts of Catholic educators will be defeated unless there is sincere cooperation from parents.

§ 7. *The secondary purpose of marriage is the mutual love of husband and wife.*[12]

Love is defined as seeking another's spiritual or temporal welfare. Married people have a positive precept to love each other. They must take definite means to secure their spouse's well-being of body and soul. If they do not know what these means are, they are obliged to learn them and use them. Husband and wife are to encourage each other in the practice of the Catholic religion. They can do this in a whole host of ways. They can urge each other by word or by example to receive the sacraments frequently, to recite the rosary daily, to practice mortification, to avoid sin and so forth. If one can truthfully say that his or her spouse is a better Catholic for having married, then he or she can say that they loved their spouses. We cannot emphasize too strongly that the precept of love is a positive one. Spouses must work actively to fulfill it. With too many persons, it is either neglected or fulfilled in a hit-and-miss fashion.

It is sinful for husband and wife to obstruct the temporal or spiritual welfare of their spouses. They commit a double sin if they do serious unjust bodily harm to their spouse, ruin their reputation, prevent them from observing the Commandments and so forth. When one spouse insists that his or her unwilling spouse practice birth control and is successful in this insistence, that spouse is clearly guilty of the extra sin of scandal. Scandal consists of doing anything which of its nature will lead another to commit sin. It is a sin against the virtue of charity, and it carries with it the obligation to repair the spiritual harm that was caused. Spouses guilty of this sin may partially repair the harm by urging the other to seek absolution.

§ 8. *The first property of marriage is that it is one.*

The properties of marriage were assigned to it by God. No human authority, such as the state, can add or subtract any of them. The property of oneness means that one man can be married to one woman at one time. The Second Council of Lyons in 1274 A.D. said, ". . . . concerning matrimony, it (the Church) holds that neither one man is permitted to have many wives, nor one woman many husbands at the same time." (D-465) The Council of Trent defined, "If anyone says that it is lawful for Christians to have several wives at the same time, and that it is not forbidden by any divine law: let him be anathema." (D-972) This Council quotes Christ's words on this point. They read, "Have you not read that the Creator, from the beginning, made them male and female, and said: 'For this cause a man shall leave his father and mother, and cleave to his wife.'" (Matt. 19:4)

Polyandry is one woman having several husbands at one time. This practice is opposed to the Natural Law, for it is contrary to both purposes of marriage. The woman eventually becomes incapable of bearing children. It is easy for any of the "husbands" to disclaim the responsibility of educating a child that may be born. It is obvious that such a practice is contrary to the secondary purpose of marriage.

Polygamy is one man having several wives. This practice is not contrary to the Natural Law, but it is certainly contrary to the Positive Divine Law as promulgated by Jesus Christ. The primary purpose of marriage would not be excluded by such unions, but the secondary purpose would be rendered impossible of fulfillment. The law forbidding polygamy was promulgated by Christ. It, therefore, binds, not only Catholics, but all non-Catholics as well. Included here are pagans and infidels as well as heretics.

§ 9. *The second property of marriage is that it is indissoluble.*

In itself, the indissolubility of marriage means that man and woman bind themselves to be husband and wife until death breaks the bond. There is evidence that this doctrine on marriage was included in official ecclesiastical documents as early as the Third Century. (D-52) It was repeated on several occasions during the Middle Ages. When Henry VIII denied it in practice and incorporated his denial as a tenet of the Anglican creed, the Council of Trent was forced to restate the ancient truth. It defined, "If anyone says that the bond of Matrimony can be dissolved because of heresy, or grievous cohabitation, or voluntary absence from the spouse: let him be anathema." (D-975) The same Council then proceeded to anathematize anyone who says that adultery dissolves the bond thereby freeing the innocent spouse to contract a new marriage. (D-977)

The words of Christ on marriage are clear to anyone who has the sincerity to see the plain meaning of the words. "And I say to you, that whoever puts away his wife, except for immorality, and marries another, commits adultery; and he who marries a woman who has been put away commits adultery." (Matt. 19:9) St. Paul writes, "But to those who are married, not I, but the Lord commands that a wife is not to depart from her husband, and if she departs, that she is to remain unmarried or be reconciled to her husband. And let not a husband put away his wife." (I Cor. 7:10) These two passages cannot contradict each other, for both are inspired writing. In fact, they are in perfect harmony with each other. Some have tried to justify their own erroneous opinions by fastening on the "exceptive" clause in the passage from St. Matthew's Gospel.[13] In that passage, Our Lord is saying that the prohibition against separating from one's spouse admits of some exception, but that the prohibition against this person remarrying admits of no exception. Heretics trying to find justification for divorce and remarriage in these passages can find little comfort in the clear fashion that the Latin and Greek Fathers interpret them. This whole case is a perfect example of how heretics first choose an opinion and then seek Scripture passages which they think will justify them in it.

§ 10. *Matrimony entitles its recipients to the sacramental grace they need to fulfill the purpose of this sacrament.*[14]

The sacrament of Matrimony is more noble than the natural contract of marriage. Matrimony as a sacrament lifts the institution of marriage into the supernatural realm. The children are to be begotten and raised to be eternal citizens of the kingdom of God; they are to be taught to practice the supernatural virtues. Husband and wife are duty-bound to pour out their love for each other by working for the other's sanctification and salvation. These are obviously duties imposed only on those who marry. The very act that imposes them must also give them the title to the supernatural helps needed to fulfill them. Couples assume the duties on the reception of the sacrament of Matrimony. The title to this special actual grace of Matrimony remains as long as the sacramental bond remains undissolved.

So long as married persons are in sanctifying grace, the actual grace continues to flow into their souls in a never-ending stream. The influence of the sacramental grace on the intellect is that it suggests thoughts to parents showing them how they can best use their authority to command their children and exact discipline. It teaches them to perceive the nature of the sins that weaken and destroy the true meaning of marriage. Grace will direct them to what they must do to secure the maximum temporal and spiritual welfare of their spouses. Sacramental grace will give them all the supernatural strength they need to fulfill the purpose of marriage and to withstand those temptations which assail married persons with particular vehemence.

§ 11. *The Church wisely prescribes that certain preparations be made before a marriage may be contracted.*

The regulations laid down by the Church pertaining to the preparation for marriage are the fruit of her vast experience. None is useless or arbitrary. (1) An investigation is to be made as to the person's fitness to marry. He or she is questioned to ascertain the absence of impediments that would render the proposed marriage invalid or unlawful.[15] Most dioceses in the United States have a printed questionnaire that must be filled out, sworn to, and signed by the prospective bride and groom. (2) Catholics who wish to marry must produce a fresh baptismal record, that is, one that is less than six months old, for any previously contracted valid marriage is noted on this record. They must also produce First Communion and Confirmation certificates to prove that they were raised as Catholics. Any difficulty in obtaining these documents should be explained to the priest, for then affidavits may have to be substituted for the actual certificate. (3) Persons who wish to marry must ordinarily produce two trustworthy witnesses who have known them well since they were fourteen years old and who will testify under oath that the prospective bride or groom is free to marry. (4) The Church prescribes that whenever needed, the persons about to marry are to receive six instructions explaining the nature, purpose, and obligations of marriage.[16] (5) The banns of Matrimony are to be announced in the parish of the bride and groom for three Sundays and Holy Days before the marriage.[17] The purpose of these banns is to discover impediments that would block the marriage. Anyone knowing of their existence is bound in conscience to notify the pastor.[18] No banns are announced for mixed marriages.[19] (6) Persons about to marry are to obtain a civil license and they are to deliver it to the priest authorized to witness the marriage.

§ 12. *For the valid reception of Matrimony, both parties must be baptized, be free from invalidating impediments, and observe the proper form.*

The proposition lists the conditions necessary for the reception of the sacrament of Matrimony. (1) In order to receive this sacrament, both parties must be validly baptized, for this is the indispensable requisite for the reception of any sacrament. Furthermore, Matrimony is a sacrament that can be administered only by a baptized person. It follows that when one of the parties is not bapitzed, he or she cannot receive nor administer Matrimony. (2) Marriage is a sacrament which can be easily abused and distorted. Some of the attacks could be aimed at its purpose and at its properties. In some instances, an attempted marriage could even be used to attack a higher virtue. To prevent this sacrament from being used contrary to the way it should be used, certain impediments have been laid down by God and by the Church. Some of these impediments are of such a nature that they completely block the contracting of the marriage. It is obvious that both parties who enter marriage must be free from all invalidating impediments. (3) All of the sacraments were confided to the Church. The Church's authorization is necessary for anyone to confer or to receive a sacrament. The purpose of this authorization is to prevent the misuse of any sacrament. The Church has laid down certain definite regulations that must be met before her authorization is given. One of these reads that Catholics can receive the sacrament of Matrimony only when it is contracted before an authorized priest and two witnesses. Failure to comply with this regulation prevents the conferring or receiving of Matrimony and constitutes a serious sin of disobedience.

§ 13. *There are thirteen impediments which can block the marriage of a Catholic.*[20]

We list the thirteen impediments which block the marriage of a Catholic. Some of them can even block the marriage of a non-Catholic, for they were laid down by God. The Church can and sometimes does grant a dispensation from impediments of ecclesiastical origin. (1) Males under sixteen and females under fourteen can not validly marry. (2) Apart from a Pauline or Petrine privilege, a person still bound by a previous valid marriage is not free to contract a new one. (3) Without proper dispensation, a Catholic cannot validly marry a non-baptized person. (4) A person incurs an invalidating impediment if he or she commits adultery with the promise of a future marriage to that accomplice in sin. This is called the impediment of "crime." Divorced persons who attempt marriage while their spouses are still living obviously incur it. (5) Blood relatives within certain degrees are forbidden to marry. These degrees are all those in the direct line and all within the third degree in the collateral line, that is, all up to and including second cousins. (6) Persons bound by affinity cannot validly marry without a dispensation. Affinity is relationship by marriage. The degrees of affinity involved are all the blood relatives of one's spouse in the direct line and up to and including first cousins in the collateral line. (7) The impediment of spiritual relationship renders a marriage invalid unless a dispensation was granted from it. This impediment is contracted between a baptized person and his godfather or godmother in solemn Baptism. (8) Public propriety is an impediment which renders a marriage invalid. This arises when two persons live in an invalid marriage or in public and notorious concubinage. These must obtain a dispensation to marry. (9) The five other invalidating impediments to marriage recur less frequently. We include them here for the sake of completeness. They are sacred orders, solemn vows, impotency, abduction, and legal adoption if the civil law of a country also makes it an invalidating impediment.

§ 14. *The consent necessary for a valid marriage must be deliberate, free, and true.*

The matter and the form of the marriage contract are contained in the mutual consent of the contracting parties. The consent necessary for a marriage consists of an agreement between man and woman whereby each gives to the other and receives from the other the perpetual and exclusive right to the marital act. (1) This consent must be deliberate. This means that the contracting parties should know that marriage is a permanent contract entered into for the procreation, and education of children. Writers discuss how detailed this knowledge need be. The validity of very few marriages is questioned on the grounds that one of the parties was ignorant of its primary purpose. (2) The consent given in marriage must be freely given. Fear or force invalidates the consent when it is the cause of the consent given.[21] In other words, the person would not have given the consent if these factors were absent. This fear is not a concomitant fear which merely accompanies but does not cause the consent to be given. (3) The consent must be true. A contracting party expresses externally what he intends internally. There is no pretence, deception, or lying as to the sincerity of the consent. Affianced persons sometimes lie to each other as to their age, wealth, and so forth. Consent given under these false impressions still makes for a valid marriage unless it was made a condition to the consent. Deceptive answers as to one's virginity do not in themselves invalidate the consent necessary for marriage. Some reliable moralists hold that a girl, for example, can sinlessly give negative answers to all questions on this subject on the grounds that the inquirer knows what answers he will get even before he asks the questions.

§ 15. *Catholics can validly marry only before an authorized priest and two witnesses.*[22]

It is an extremely wise regulation of the Church that prescribes that Catholics can contract a marriage only before a priest and two witnesses. It is one way of seeing to it that those marrying will be free from invalidating impediments and that they will have clear notions of the state of life they enter. The priest who is to witness the marriage is obliged to see to it that all of the Church's regulations have been complied with. The form of marriage must be observed, not only when two Catholics receive the sacrament of Matrimony, but also when a Catholic marries a baptized non-Catholic or a non-baptized person. Failure to observe it renders the marriage invalid in the eyes of God and in the eyes of the Church. It remains invalid even though the state recognizes it as being valid.

Baptized non-Catholics and unbaptized persons are not bound to observe the form of marriage when they do not marry Catholics. Provided they are free from the invalidating impediments laid down by God, they can contract a valid and lawful marriage before a civil magistrate or a non-Catholic clergyman. These marriages, of course, are also valid in the eyes of the Church. Many falsely think that the Church does not recognize the validity of non-Catholic marriages and that they can always be "dissolved" to clear the way for the persons to marry Catholics.

The two persons who witness the marriage of a Catholic besides the priest must be at least fourteen years of age and must themselves be Catholics unless the ordinary of the diocese permits otherwise. The other members of a wedding party, that is, ushers and bridesmaids, need not be Catholics.

§ 16. *The priest before whom Catholics contract marriage must be duly authorized to witness the marriage.*

A great deal of confusion would arise if any priest indiscriminately were permitted to witness a marriage. It would then be difficult to fix responsibility for seeing to it that the Church's regulations on marriage had been observed. To prevent this sad state of affairs from developing, the Church clearly points out what priests are authorized to witness a marriage.

When both parties of the marriage are of the same rite, the pastor of the bride is authorized to witness the marriage. This is true of the Latin rite and of each of the five Oriental rites. Keep in mind that an Oriental Byzantine Catholic is of a different rite than, for example, an Oriental Melchite. In some dioceses, all priests appointed to the parish of the bride receive this authorization from the ordinary.

It sometimes happens that two persons of the same rite do not wish to marry in the parish of the bride or they wish to marry before a priest other than those stationed at the parish of the bride. The pastor of the bride must grant another priest permission to witness this marriage.[23] Let us consider the consequences of a marriage without this permisison. If the priest who witnessed the marriage has jurisdiction in the place where the marriage is contracted, but does not have the permission of the bride's pastor, the marriage is valid but unlawful. If he lacks jurisdiction to witness marriages in the place where he witnessed the marriage, that marriage is invalid.

If two person of different rites marry, they are to contract marriage in the parish of the groom. The pastor of the groom may permit the marriage to be contracted outside his parish or he may delegate an outside priest to witness the marriage. If a priest witnesses without permission the marriage of two persons who are of another rite than he is that marriage is invalid.

§ 17. *While Matrimony was instituted to increase grace, it can under certain conditions give first grace.*

Matrimony is a sacrament of the living, that is, it was instituted to increase grace in the souls of those receiving it. But if one receives it in mortal sin, he does not irretrievably lose the grace that he should have received. A person consciously in mortal sin must recover the state of grace by Penance or an act of perfect contrition before he may receive the sacrament of Matrimony. He is guilty of serious sacrilege if he deliberately receives the sacrament in mortal sin. But he may subsequently receive the grace of Matrimony by Penance or perfect contrition.

A person who receives Matrimony while unconscious of the mortal sin on his soul does indeed receive the sacrament but does not receive its grace unless he had made at least an act of imperfect contrition. His forgetfulness of the presence of this sin does not in itself remove it. The person who receives Matrimony while unconscious of his mortal sin does not commit a sacrilege. His forgetfulness of the presence of this sin or the lack of knowledge about the existence of such a sin, does not of itself, of course, remit that sin. But since the person who thus received Matrimony is actually not aware of that mortal sin, he cannot possibly be guilty of a sacrilege in thus receiving the sacrament of marriage. He even receives the grace of this sacrament indirectly or "accidentally," provided he has made at least an act of imperfect contrition.

A Catholic who enters into a natural contract of marriage while consciously in mortal sin does not commit a sacrilege, for he does not receive a sacrament. It is, however, quite possible for such a person to be guilty of a mortal sin for acting on a false conscience.

§ 18. *A Catholic who attempts marriage before a civil magistrate or a non-Catholic clergyman seriously breaks the law of the church.*

The Church is competent, that is, she has divine authorization to lay down regulations governing the marriages of validly baptized persons. We have seen that she seriously commands that all Catholics must marry before a priest and two witnesses. This binds those entering a natural contract or a sacramental union. We discuss here the consequences that befall those Catholics who choose to disregard this regulation. (1) A Catholic who attempts marriage before a civil magistrate, that is, a justice of the peace, is not married in God's eyes, nor in the eyes of the Church. Moreover, such a person is guilty of mortal sin. A priest may not ordinarily absolve it without special permission of the ordinary. Children who are born to parents in this "marriage" are illegitimate until they have been legitimatized. (2) A Catholic who attempts marriage before a non-Catholic clergyman is not married in God's eyes, is guilty of mortal sin, and is excommunicated.[24] This sin and censure can be removed only with the permission of the ordinary. Children born of this "marriage" are illegitimate until properly legitimatized. An excommunicated person loses his rights as a Catholic. Two of these are the right to receive the Sacraments and the right to a Christian burial. But he is not free of his duties as a Catholic. For example, he must still assist at Sunday Mass, make his Easter duty, abstain on the appointed days, and so forth.

§ 19. *A Catholic who has failed to observe the prescribed form in marrying may have his "marriage" revalidated.*[25]

In discussing this proposition, we presume that the only factor that rendered the marriage invalid was the failure to observe the prescribed form, that is, marrying before a priest and two witnesses. They can even receive the sacrament of Matrimony. Practically the same preparation must be made for a marriage to be revalidated as would have been made if it had been properly contracted. But there is a new factor in connection with the revalidation. Catholics who attempt marriage before a civil magistrate or a non-Catholic clergyman are most likely guilty of an added sin of scandal. Parish priests can attest that persons who attempt marriage can rarely keep it a secret. Their parents, relatives, friends, and acquaintances soon learn of it. If this is done frequently in a locality, people lose their horror for such a grievous sin. This in turn opens the flood gates for the sin to be repeated by other couples. The harm done by the scandal may be multiplied and perpetuated. Scandal carries with it the obligation to repair so far as possible the harm that has been done. The priest who revalidates the marriage should outline a plan designed to repair the scandal caused by the attempted marriage. He may suggest or even insist that the Catholic persons receive the sacraments weekly for a month or two after the revalidation. When an attempted marriage has been properly revalidated, the children already born are rendered legitimate.

§ 20. *The Church strongly opposes the contracting of mixed marriages; she reluctantly permits them in order to prevent greater evils from taking place.*[26]

A "disparity of cult" marriage is one contracted by a Catholic with a non-baptized person. A "mixed religion" marriage is one contracted by a Catholic with a baptized non-Catholic. The Church's opposition to them grows out of her long distasteful experience with them. St. Augustine deplored in his day the spiritual harm resulting from these unions. Some early provincial councils expressly forbade them. Mixed marriages have been the occasion of incalculable harm to souls. At least half of them have proved spiritually harmful to Catholic spouses. The promises made to the bishop so that a dispensation would be granted for the marriage to take place are often forgotten or repudiated. In a great many cases, the Catholic spouse has lived to see his or her faith made the target of scoffing ridicule. They have often heard the insistence on the practice of birth control enforced by the threat of divorce or infidelity. Non-Catholic spouses very often refuse to let the children be baptized as Catholics, receive catechism instruction, or attend a Catholic school. They often demand that the children be allowed to grow up as pagans and then "pick" their own religion. In most cases, the children continue to live as pagans throughout life. Mixed marriages have been the cause of many Catholics first losing their faith and then their souls. It is a small wonder that the Church strongly opposes them. She reluctantly permits them in order to salvage as much as possible of a bad situation. The distasteful experiences of parish priests with mixed marriages would fill many volumes of well authenticated material. The best way to counter-act them is for parents to discourage their children from dating non-Catholics. The children should then realize that their parents are not trying to deprive them of happiness, but are trying to insure it. Children themselves should make a rule in their lives to avoid these dates.

§ 21. *Under well-defined circumstances validly married Catholics may temporarily and sometimes permanently separate from their spouses.*

There is a great deal of confusion even in the minds of Catholics as to the meaning of "separation of spouses." A permission to separate does not in itself imply a permission to obtain a civil divorce. The permission to obtain a civil divorce in turn does not imply permission to remarry. Separation means that spouses cease to cohabit; they cease to share bed and board.

An innocent spouse may separate immediately from a spouse who is certainly guilty of adultery.[27] The innocent party need not seek the permission of the ordinary to separate in this case. But it is wise even then to seek this permission. An innocent spouse may not seek separation on the score of the spouse's adultery, if he or she is guilty of the same sin, or if he or she has forgiven the guilty party. Forgiveness in this case is shown by continuing to live with the guilty party after learning of the sin. In cases of doubtful adultery, the matter must be submitted to the judgment of the ordinary before separation is permitted.

An innocent spouse may temporarily separate from a spouse when cohabitation with that spouse is a proximate cause of grave physical or moral danger to the innocent members of the family.[28] Examples of physical harm are extreme cruelty or the great likelihood of contracting a serious disease. Examples of spiritual danger are the insistence that spouse or children be raised as heretics or live as pagans or that the guilty spouse is a proximate occasion of mortal sin. Alcoholics often qualify as causes of both physical and moral dangers to the rest of the members of the family. The ordinary must judge each case and then decide if there are grounds for a temporary separation. An innocent spouse may separate even without waiting for the ordinary's decision if the conditions listed above are grave, urgent, and there is great danger in delay. When the causes that led to the temporary separation no longer exist, separated spouses are obliged to resume cohabitation. Hasty separations often create more problems than they solve.

§ 22. *It is possible for a natural marriage contract to be raised to the status of a sacramental union.*

We have seen that a natural marriage contract and a sacramental union are both valid in the eyes of God and of the

Church. But although they have many points in common, there are many differences between the two. Almighty God has assigned to us the goal of seeing Him face to face. He has provided means that will help us at every turn to attain this goal. Very prominent among these are the sacraments. It is possible for a Catholic to marry an unbaptized person. Even though the marriage is valid, it is not a sacrament. The Catholic party is not entitled to the sanctifying and sacramental graces of the sacrament of Matrimony. This is no small loss when we realize the potential supernatural benefit that can accrue to one who receives the sacrament. But a natural marriage contract can be elevated to the status of a sacramental union. This is accomplished automatically when the unbaptized spouse receives valid Baptism. The parties are not even obliged to renew their marriage vows. The same situation would prevail if two pagans living in a natural marriage were validly baptized. The case is slightly different when a Catholic marries a baptized non-Catholic in the proper way. Both of the parties do indeed receive the sacrament of Matrimony, as do two validly baptized non-Catholics who properly marry. These facts play a prominent part when we come to consider the conditions necessary for a Pauline or Petrine privilege.

§ 23. *The Church exacts certain definite promises before permitting a mixed marriage to be contracted.*[29]

We list the promises that both parties to a mixed marriage must make under oath. A party that takes the oath while not intending to keep the promises is clearly guilty of perjury. (1) Both parties agree to adhere to God's law which forbids divorce and attempted remarriage. (2) Both parties agree to live a life in accordance with God's law which forbids the practice of artificial birth control. (3) The non-Catholic promises not to interfere with the spouse's practice of the Catholic religion. (4) Both promise that all the children born to them will be baptized and educated as Catholics, and, if possible, in a Catholic school. The non-Catholic parent promises to do this even in the event of the death of the Catholic parent. This means a great deal more than a non-Catholic's non-interference in the Catholic education of the children. It means that he or she must actively promote and facilitate it. (5) In the event that the spouses separate and cannot secure the spiritual welfare of the children, they agree to permit third persons, such as godparents, to fulfill this duty. (6) Both parties agree that there will be no marriage ceremony other than the one that takes place before the priest. (7) The Catholic party promises to lead the non-Catholic spouse to the True Church by his or her good example, prayers and frequent reception of the sacraments. Too often, the Catholic spouse miserably fails or neglects to keep this last promise. Both parties sign the above promises. The document is then sent to the ordinary. If he has no reason to suspect perjury or insincerity on the part of the persons, he grants a dispensation for the mixed marriage to be contracted. The same promises must also be made by a Catholic who wishes to marry a person who was baptized as a Catholic but was never raised as one.

§ 24. *A validly married Catholic must obtain the ordinary's permission to file for a civil divorce.*

In the last number, it was pointed out that in certain cases, a spouse may immediately separate from his or her spouse even without the ordinary's permission. But this must not be interpreted as meaning that an innocent spouse may straightway file for a civil divorce.

Regardless of how valid his or her reason for separation may be, a Catholic spouse living in a valid marriage must obtain the ordinary's permission even to file for a civil divorce. There is a very wise reason for this regulation. Married people are often too impetuous at the first sign of domestic difficulty. Many times, they take hasty courses of action and then spend a lifetime regretting them.

Persons who petition the ordinary for permission to file for a civil divorce must have a clear-cut cause for their request. It must be so grave that it cannot be removed by temporary separation. Accompanying the request for permission must be the statement of the petitioner made under oath that he or she will still consider himself or herself married in God's eyes and will never never attempt to remarry after a civil divorce has been obtained.

A validly married Catholic who even files for a civil divorce without the ordinary's permission commits a reserved mortal sin. If they obtain a civil divorce with or without the ordinary's permission and then attempt to remarry, they are guilty of mortal sin. They clearly enter an adulterous association. Sometimes the ordinary justifiably refuses to give permission for a civil divorce. He thinks that he has reason to fear the possibility that the person will proceed to attempt remarriage. Every parish priest knows how very well-founded these fears often are. The only reason why the ordinary will allow a civil divorce is to permit such things as the settlement of property and other civil effects to be taken care of. It is clearly forbidden for such "divorced" persons to "date" other persons. A confessor would be perfectly justified to refuse absolution to those who persist on doing so.

§ 25. *A Catholic living in an invalid marriage may obtain a civil divorce without the ordinary's permission and then contract a valid marriage.*

The truth embodied in this proposition has very often been misinterpreted by laymen. A Catholic who lives in an invalid marriage is obviously not married in God's eyes. A civil divorce that he or she obtains does not loose a marital bond, for no bond exists. They need not obtain the ordinary's permission to file for a civil divorce, for that permission is necessary only for Catholics living in a valid marriage. It must not be forgotten that this person committed at least a reserved sin in attempting marriage. The scandal that has been caused cannot be overlooked.

A Catholic who was invalidly married is to obtain a decree of nullity before he or she may contract a valid marriage with another person. This decree is given by the authority of the ordinary after due investigation has proved that the attempted marriage was really invalid. Failure to obtain this decree after attempting marriage before a civil magistrate renders a new marriage valid but unlawful. Failure to obtain it after attempting marriage before a non-Catholic clergyman also renders a new marriage valid but unlawful. The small charge made for conducting the investigation usually does not cover the expenses incurred by the diocesan matrimonial court. It is a small fraction of the expense incurred in obtaining a civil divorce.

Non-Catholics who attempt marriage while bound by invalidating impediments are not married in God's eyes. They too may obtain a civil divorce and then validly marry another person—even Catholics—before a priest and two witnesses.

§ 26. *A natural marriage contract can be dissolved when the conditions for the Pauline privilege are verified.*[30]

This privilege derives its name from the fact that it appears in an epistle of St. Paul. The exact passage is *First Corinthians* 7:12ff. Notice that it is a privilege, not a right. It can be refused even though the conditions for it are present. Five conditions must be verified for the Pauline Privilege. (1) Both spouses were not baptized when they married. They were pagans. (2) After their marriage, one spouse was converted and baptized, but the other spouse remains unbaptized. (3) When the one became a Christian, the one who remains a pagan refused to be converted and then departed from the converted spouse. This "departure" may consist of one of several things. It may mean that the pagan refuses to live with the baptized person. It may also mean that the pagan continues to live with the baptized person but refuses to do so without serious sin or offense to God. This may include such practices as refusal to educate the children as Catholics, trying to make the Catholic party apostatize, or being a constant and proximate occasion of mortal sin to the convert. (4) The pagan spouse must be asked if he or she wishes to be converted and is willing to live peacefully with the converted party without offense to God. The pagan must refuse to do both of these things. (5) Permission to remarry may then be granted by a competent ecclesiastical authority, but the converted person may marry only a Catholic. The previous natural contract is dissolved when the converted party actually contracts a new and sacramental marriage.

§ 27. *Natural contracts between non-Catholics can be dissolved by the supreme authority of the Holy Father so that the parties can contract a sacramental marriage.*

Dissolving a natural bond to make way for the contracting of a sacramental bond is in no way a violation of God's law. The marriage bond is intrinsically indissoluble, but in certain cases it can be extrinsically dissolved by competent authority. We saw that God permitted it in certain cases in the Old Testament. The Pauline Privilege is another example of a natural bond dissolved extrinsically. The case we consider here is called the Petrine Privilege or dissolution of the bond in favor of the faith. Several conditions are necessary for it. (1) A valid natural contract exists between a pagan and a baptized non-Catholic. If both of the parties are bap-

tized non-Catholics, there is no room for this privilege, for
they live in a sacramental marriage. (2) The two parties separate and then one of them is converted to Catholicism, but if
it is the pagan who is converted, he or she must not yet have
been baptized. The converted person then desires to contract
a sacramental marriage with a Catholic. The Holy Father is
petitioned to dissolve the natural contract. If he grants the request, the natural contract is thereby dissolved. The converted
party may then be baptized if a pagan. The two baptized
Catholics may then contract a sacramental marriage. (3) The
Holy See is most careful not to grant this permission when it
will cause scandal, for it can be easily misinterpreted by
those who misunderstand it. It takes a long time—several
years—for these cases to be processed and a judgment returned.

§ 28. *As a rule, Catholics may not assist at marriages contracted or attempted before a non-Catholic clergyman.*

Catholics assist at a marriage when they take active part in it,
that is, they are the official witnesses, and not merely attend-
ants or spectators. A Catholic may not be the official witness in
even a valid marriage being contracted before a non-Catholic
clergyman. The reason for this is that a Catholic may not actively participate in a distinctly non-Catholic ceremony. They
may be merely present at it when the conditions for the
double effect permit it. Those conditions are as follows: the
Catholic may only be passively present; there must be no
danger that the ceremony or its concomitant activities will
be detrimental to his faith; his presence will not confirm
others in their error; there must be a grave reason for being
there.

Under no circumstances may a Catholic participate in an
attempted marriage of a Catholic or a non-Catholic. If they
are the official witnesses, that is, best man or maid of honor,
they are clearly cooperating in sin. If they are not in official
capacities, their very presence may easily be the source of

scandal, for it can be interpreted by others as putting their stamp of approval on this act. This element of scandal must be considered in determining the permissibility of attending the reception of those who have attempted marriage.

Catholics do not need permission to be official witnesses at the marriage of two non-Catholics properly contracting marriage before a civil magistrate. In charity, they should avoid scandalizing those who would misinterpret their action.

§ 29. *Sacramental marriages can be contracted at any time during the year, but without a dispensation, they may not be solemnized during closed times.*[31]

The proposition implies that a marriage is not invalid simply because it was contracted during those periods when marriages may not be solemnized. (1) A couple contracts a valid marriage by observing the form prescribed by the Church. It is solemnized when the contracting of the marriage is accompanied by a nuptial Mass and nuptial Blessing. (2) The closed times are from the First Sunday of Advent to Christmas Day and from Ash Wednesday to Easter Sunday. The Ember Days are not closed times but they do present somewhat of a concomitant difficulty because they are days of fast and at least partial abstinence. (3) The Church wishes that sacramental marriages be accompanied by a certain degree of solemnity such as Mass and so forth. In fact, the ordinary must usually give permission for a sacramental marriage to be contracted without them. On the other hand, he must give his permission for a marriage to be solemnized during closed times. The nuptial Blessing is not given to the bride if she is contracting a second marriage.

§ 30. *The Church is competent to lay down regulations that Catholics must observe when they marry.*

When we say that the Church is competent to lay down marriage regulations, we mean that she is empowered by God to do so. Rules would mean very little if the legislator did not also have the power to punish those who violated them. The purpose of a law is not to restrict liberty but to direct those subject to it to their ultimate goal. Christ endowed the Church with authority to make any law that would promote the spiritual welfare of her members. He confided to the Church the means of grace, that is, the seven sacraments. When the Church legislates regarding the sacraments, it is always with the aim that we will derive the greatest benefit from them. It is well to keep in mind that the Church's legislation is incorporated in her Code of Canon Law. This code is covered by her endowment of infallibility. We have God's assurance that the code contains no error against faith and morals. In drawing up these regulations on marriage, the Church has made use of her vast experience in dealing with human beings. Jurists who have studied the laws have been greatly impressed by their prudence and clarity. The Church has the authority to attach a sanction to the violation of her laws. She has done this with regard to her laws on marriage. Some of them are suggested directives or bind under penalty of only venial sin. Others bind under penalty of mortal sin and even reserved mortal sin. A last category must be observed under penalty of mortal sin plus excommunication. We can get an accurate estimate of the importance of a law by noticing how severely the Church punishes those who deliberately violate it.

§ 31. *As far as the marriage of Catholics is concerned, the state is competent to legislate only on its civil effects.*[32]

The proposition must not be interpreted to mean that the state has unlimited authority to make laws pertaining to the marriage of non-Catholics. There is a hierarchy of authority in existence. The higher supercedes the lower. If a law made by a lower authority contradicts one made by a higher authority, the former must be disregarded.

God's authority is supreme. He has laid down certain regulations on marriage which bind all human beings on the face of the earth. These laws are incorporated in the Natural or in the Divine Positive Law. God has endowed the Church with authority to legislate on matters pertaining even indirectly to the spiritual welfare of her members. The binding force of those laws is the same as though they were made by God. The Church has stated that her laws bind all Catholics even when they seek to contract marriage with non-Catholics.

Civil authority has no power to pass legislation which contradicts God's law or the Church's law on marriage. When the state does this, it attempts to usurp power. Those civil laws must be disregarded. But the state has the duty to keep temporal order, and there are many things about a marriage which fall into the temporal sphere. The state is perfectly competent to legislate in this matter. Examples of these are the manner that spouses can hold property, the official registration of the marriage for legal purposes, alimony, custody of children in case of dispute, pre-marital blood test, and others. It has no authority to dissolve valid marriages and permit the parties to attempt new marriages.

NOTES

1. *Cayré, Manual of Patrology* (Tournai, Desclee, 1936), Vol. I, p. 106.
2. *De Exhortatione Castitatis,* Bk. I, 2, 5; *De Monogamia,* Bk. I, 2, 14.
3. cf. Eusebius *H. E.,* Bk. IV, 28.
4. Gilbert, *Crucifying Christ in Our Colleges* (San Diego: Danielle, 1935), p. 110 ff.
5. *Ad Polycarpum* V.
6. St. Thomas Aq. *Supp.* Ques. 45, Art. 1-5.
7. Canon 1013, 1.
8. St. Thomas Aq. *Supp.* Ques. 64, Art. 1-2.
9. Noldin, *Summa Theologiae Moralis* (Ratisbon, Pustet, 1940), Vol. III, p. 93.
10. Pope Pius XI Encycls. *The Christian Education of Youth,* 1929, and *On Christian Marriage,* 1930.
11. Canon 1374.
12. Canon 1013, 1.

13. *A Catholic Commentary on Holy Scripture* (New York: Nelson & Son), 1953, p. 885.

14. St. Thomas Aq. *Supp.* III, Ques. 42, Art. 3.

15. Canon 1020 and 1021.

16. Canon 1033.

17. Canon 1022-1025.

18. Canon 1027.

19. Canon 1026.

20. Canon 1042.

21. Canon 1087.

22. Canon 1094.

23. Canon 1096.

24. Canon 2319.

25. Canon 1133.

26. Canon 1060. Accurate statistics compiled in connection with his work by Rev. Joseph Toth, O.F.M. chaplain of Cleveland City Hospital for over forty years, show that about 43 percent of children born to parents in mixed marriages are not properly raised as Catholics.

27. Canon 1129.

28. Davis, *Moral and Pastoral Theology* (London: Sheed and Ward, 1945), Vol. IV, p. 228 ff.

29. Canons 1061-1062.

30. Canons 1120-1127.

31. Canon 1108.

32. Canon 1016.

Epilogue

"Wisdom has built for herself a house."
PROV. 9:1

Man has searched the earth, the air, even the sun and stars in his never-ending quest for knowledge. He has sent expeditions to the ends of the earth to wring secrets from rocks. He has measured the distance to the planets and the depth of the ocean. But in spite of this feverish activity, he realizes that learning is not precisely the same as wisdom, and secretly suspects that he may be mistaking the counterfeit for the real.

The student who examines pagan thought in search of truth encounters bits of wisdom buried in a seething mass of contradictions and doubts. The pagan answers to the questions "What are we here for?" and "Where are we going?" drive him first to frustration and then to despair. Modern pagans who try to divorce their search for truth from a search for the Infinite Truth are most pitiful. They attempt to disguise their intellectual bankruptcy in a labyrinth of pointless speculations, meaningless theories, and scientific mirages.

Socrates asked "What is wisdom?" and Pilate asked "What is truth?" All wisdom is truth, but not all truth is wisdom. Wisdom is that truth that enables one to evalue correctly all other truth. It places all the branches of learning in the correct relationship to each other. Its vision is completely unobstructed. A person standing at the base of a pyramid can see only one of its sides. The higher he climbs the more he can see. If he stands on the apex he can see all four sides. Truth is like a pyramid. The material sciences form its base, and philosophy forms its upper parts; but only wisdom, that is, theology, stands at the apex correctly evaluating all truth.

Who can teach the world the wisdom that it seeks? In the famous painting "The School of Athens," Raphael represents the philosophers who contributed to Greek thought. In the middle of the picture, Plato and Aristotle stand side by side. Plato points to the heavens; Aristotle points to the earth. What are they trying to say? Perhaps they are telling us that from heaven must come the wisdom that will enable us to evaluate the truths of earth. Unless the Lord build the edifice of truth, in vain do they labor who build.

Wisdom not only enlightens one; it also enlivens him. The pagans who thirsted for truth were also thirsting for life. They were not only crying out, "O Lord, that we may see" but also, "O Lord, that we may live." They not only wanted to be rid of darkness. They also wanted to be rid of death. And Jesus Christ, in His infinite love for us, came to give us both.

Few persons have been more favored with a deeper insight into the meaning of the "new light" and "new life" in Christ than was St. Paul. And see what a reaction it caused. It was like touching a spark to a powder-keg. He simply burst into flame. In reading his epistles we see that he has caught sight of something so big, so wonderful that it completely absorbs his attention and his energies. He wants to tell everyone, everywhere, and in every way what he has found. He chafes and frets because the words he must use are too weak, clumsy, and inadequate to describe its stupendous greatness. And just as the runner bringing good news of victory at Marathon ran all the way to Athens, delivered his message, and then dropped dead, so too St. Paul breathlessly delivered his message until he too was stilled by death.

For nineteen centuries, Holy Mother Church has sent missionaries to the ends of the earth to proclaim the same message that Christ proclaimed. To a world seeking truth, the Church preaches wisdom; to a world sitting in the shadow of death, she offers supernatural life. The individual no less than the world will find both light and life if they but translate into action the motto of St. Paul's life, "For to me to live is Christ and to die is gain" (Phil. 1:21).

Bibliography

Alexander. *College Apologetics*. Chicago, Henry Regnery Co., 1954.

Alexander. *College Moral Theology*. Chicago, Henry Regnery Co., 1958.

Apostolic Fathers, trans. by Kirsopp Lake, 2 vols. London, Heinemann, 1930.

A Catholic Commentary on Holy Scripture. Philadelphia, Thos. Nelson & Sons, 1953.

Catechism of the Council of Trent, trans. by Callan-McHugh. New York, Wagner, 1937.

Cayre. *Manual of Patrology*, trans. by Howit, 2 vols. Tournai, Desclee & Co., 1936.

Danielou. *Origen*, trans. by Mitchell. New York, Sheed and Ward, 1955.

Davis. *Moral and Pastoral Theology*, 4th ed., 4 vols. London, Sheed and Ward, 1945.

Denzinger. *The Sources of Catholic Dogma*, trans. by Deferrari. St. Louis, Herder, 1957.

Grossi-Gondi. *I Monumenti Cristiani* (Italian). Rome, Gregorian University Press, 1923.

Lebreton. *The History of the Primitive Church*, trans. by Zeiller, 2 vols. New York, MacMillan, 1949.

Leeming. *Principles of Sacramental Theology*. Westminster, Newman, 1956.

Marucchi. *Manual of Christian Archeology*, trans. by Vecchierello. Paterson, St. Anthony Guild, 1935.

McAuliffe. *Sacramental Theology*. St. Louis, Herder, 1958.

Noldin. *Summa Theologiae Moralis*, 27th ed., 3 vols. Ratisbon, Pustet, 1941.

Pohle-Preuss. *The Sacraments*, 4 vols. St. Louis, Herder, 1938.

Pourrat. *Theology of the Sacraments*, trans. from French. St. Louis, Herder, 1930.

265

Prat. *The Theology of St. Paul,* trans. by Stoddard, 2 vols. London, Burns, Oates & Washbourne, 1942.

Quasten. *Patrology,* 3 vols. Westminster, Newman, 1960.

Ricciotti. *Life of Christ.* Milwaukee, Bruce, 1947.

Ricciotti. *Paul the Apostle.* Milwaukee, Bruce, 1953.

St. Thomas Aquinas. *Summa Theologica,* trans. by English Dominicans, 3 vols. New York, Benziger, 1947.

Smith. *The Teachings of the Catholic Church,* 2 vols. New York, MacMillan, 1949.

Tixeront. *History of Dogmas,* trans. from French, 3 vols. St. Louis, Herder, 1930.

Woywood. *A Practical Commentary on the Code of Canon Law,* 2 vols. New York, Wagner, 1941.

Index

absolution, faculties needed for, 174
Acts of Apostles, 77
adjuration, 9
Albert the Great, St., 228
Alexandrine rite, 64
Ambrose, St., 103, 158, 178, 217
amendment, purpose of, 169, 172
Anglican Orders, 226
Anglicanism, 16, 25
Antiochean rite, 64
Appallinaris, 2
apostles, 8, 19, 21, 27, 50, 95
apologetics, 1, 11, 22, 216
Apostolic Fathers, 218
Arianism, 210
Armenian rite, 64
Athanasius, St., 217
attritian, 42
Augustine, St.: apostolicity, 15; Baptism, 51; confession, 178; form of Baptism, 62; marriage, 249; penance, 158; universality, 17
authorship of Gospel, 8
Avila, St. Teresa, 172

Baptism: by aspersion, 62; by immersion, 61; by infusion, 61; by non-Catholics, 67, 69; ceremonies of, 63; definition of, 48; delay in, 66, 67; effects of, 53, 56; form of, 62; godparents for, 65, 71; in Scripture, 50; in Tradition, 51; mark of, 55; matter of, 60, 61; minister of, 70; name given in, 73; necessity of, 49; of converts, 69; of desire, 74; of infants, 51; private, 71; reception, 53, 68; record of, 74; solemn, 71
Basil the Great, St., 109, 142, 158, 178
Bauer, 9
Bede Venerable, 196
Bellarmine, St. Robert, 172
Benedict XIV, Pope, 225
beneficiaries of Mass, 127
Bible, 4, 20

birth control, 42
bishops, 19, 214 f.
blasphemy, 10
Bonaventure, St., 75
Byzantine rites, 64

Caiphas, 9
Caesarius, St., 196
Callixtus, St., 160
Calvinism, 26, 94
Canon of New Testament, 7
Catacombs, 102
catechisms, 17, 72
causality, proof from, 3
censures, 64, 174
Chalcedon, Council of, 215, 222
charity, 68
chrism, 83
Christ: accused of blasphemy, 10; claimed divinity, 9; commands to receive sacraments, 137, 153, 160, 176; founded a Church, 13, 18; instituted sacraments, 26; miracles of, 10; Mystical Body of, 14; priesthood of, 35, 79; profession of faith in, 80
Church: apostolicity of, 15; authority of, 2, 25; decrees of, 17; duty to legislate, 136, 258; hierarchy of, 213; indulgences, 190; infallibility of, 3, 19; marks of, 14; name of, 19; nature of, 13; organization of, 13; power to grant indulgences, 190; sanctity, 18; unity of, 17; universality, 16
Classics, Manuscripts of, 7
Clement of Alexandria, 8, 158
confession, 164
Confirmation: definition of, 76; effects of, 77, 79; form of, 84; grace of, 80; in Scripture, 77; matter of, 84; minister of, 88; notes of, 77; reception of, 85; sacrament of, 26, 33, 74 f.; sponsors in, 89

conscience, 43, 165
consent in marriage, 244
Constance, Council of, 140, 173
contingency, proof from, 3
contrition, 54, 87, 163, 166, 168
cosmology, 27
critics of Gospels, 8
creeds, 17, 68
Cyril of Alexandria, St., 196
Cyril of Jerusalem, St., 101
Cyprian, St., 70, 78, 102, 114, 158

Dacetists, 95
deaconship, 221
degrees of perfection, proof from, 3
De Rossi, 215
design, proof from, 3
desire, baptism of, 74
Didache, 25, 60, 61, 101, 113, 121, 157
divorce, 251
Donatists, 29, 210
doubtful sins, 165
duties of godparents, 72
duty to hear Mass, 129

Easter Duty, 138
Elvira, Council of, 225
episcopacy, 214
essence of Mass, 123
Eutyches, 2
Evangelists, 7, 8, 79, 98
examination of conscience, 163
excommunication, 17, 185
Extreme Unction: definition of, 194;
  duty to receive, 204; effects, 197;
  in New Testament, 195; in Tradition, 196; matter and form of, 203;
  minister of, 207; purpose of, 197; reception of, 199; repetition of, 206;
  sacrament of, 194

faith, act of, 22
Fathers of Church, 54, 85
Florence, Council of: Baptism, 54;
  Confirmation, 85
form of: Baptism, 62: Confirmation,
  84; Extreme Unction, 204; Holy
  Eucharist, 96; Holy Orders, 215
formula of Confession, 188
Fox, George, 50

goal, man's ultimate, 6, 12, 48
God, proofs for existence, 3
godparents, 72

Gospels: manuscripts of, 7; authorship,
  8; critics, 8; historicity, 8; integrity,
  7, 8; sacraments in, 26; Synoptic, 96
Grace: actual, 31, 48, 58; effects of,
  36 f.; necessity of, 22; properties of,
  36; sacramental, 32, 59; sanctifying,
  12, 31, 38, 40, 48; title to, 29
Gregory of Nazianzus, St., 123

Harnack, 9
heaven, 127
Henry VIII, 16
heresy, 2, 21, 67
Hermas Pastor, 157
hierarchy, 213
Hilary, St., 102
Holy Communion: benefits of, 144;
  duty to receive, 135; frequent reception, 142; grace, 145; requisites
  for, 146 f.; under One Species, 140
Holy Days, 130
Holy Eucharist, 26, 33, 74, 93 ff.:
  archeology and, 103; institution of,
  96; notes as sacrament, 104; promise of, 94; substance and accidents
  in, 105
Holy Mass 111 f.: beneficiaries of, 127;
  consecration of, 123, 131; duty to
  attend, 129; ends of, 126; essence of,
  123; identical with Last Supper,
  117; integrity of, 124; matter of, 119;
  of Catechumens, 121; offers of,
  120; offertory of, 122; relative to
  cross, 118; true Sacrifice, 112, 114;
  value of, 125
Holy Orders: deaconship, 223; definition of, 210; episcopacy in, 214;
  grace of, 213; impediments to, 227;
  mark of, 212; matter and form of,
  218; minor orders, 223; priesthood
  in, 217; required age for, 228; sacrament of, 211; subdeaconship, 223
Holy See, 64, 65, 74, 185
Holy Spirit, 77
Human Act, 42
Hus, John, 173

Ignatius of Antioch, St.: deaconship,
  222; episcopacy, 215; Holy Eucharist, 101; Holy Orders, 214; marriage, 233; Mass, 113; priesthood, 218;
  universality, 16
impediment to: marriage, 242; ordination, 227
indissolubility of marriage, 239

indulgence, 190
infallibility, 3, 19, 89
integrity of Gospels, 7
integrity of Mass, 124
intellect, 4, 22, 35
Irenaeus, St.: Apostolicity, 15; Baptism, 52; Gospels, 8; Mass, 114; marriage, 233; unity, 17; universality, 16

James, St., 185
Jerome, St., 52
John, St., 78, 95, 136
John Chrysostom, St., 101, 107, 158, 173, 196
John Nepomucene, St., 185
Judaism, 8, 130, 210
judgment, particular, 39
justification, 53, 58
Justin, St., 101, 113, 121

Last Supper, 119
Lateron, Council of, 138, 187, 231
Latin rite, 64, 84, 119, 130, 141, 207
lay apostolate, 81
Leo, Pope St., 173, 178
Leo X, Pope, 173, 179
Leo XIII, Pope, 226
life, supernatural, 30, 34, 48, 57, 58, 144
Luke, St., 8, 95, 136
Luther: Baptism, 56; Holy Eucharist, 94; Holy Orders, 210; Matrimony, 231; sacraments, 25; venial sin, 179
Lutheranism, 15, 18, 25, 29
Lyons, Council of, 83

Malachias, 112, 125
Mantanism, 231
Mark, 8, 50, 95, 136
Mark: of Baptism, 55; of Confirmation, 78; of Holy Orders, 212
Mass, 112 ff.
Matrimony: closed times, 259; definition of, 232; duties of, 236; form of, 245; grace of, 240; impediments to, 242; in Scripture, 232; in Tradition, 235; mixed marriages, 249; preparation for, 241; properties of, 239; purpose, 235; reception of, 248; witness to, 246
Matthew, 8, 95, 136, 153
Melanchthon, 25
Methodism, 15, 18
Milevis, Council of, 51
minor orders, 223

miracles, 10, 79
mixed marriages, 252
motion, proof from, 3
Mystical Body, 14, 75

Nestarianism, 210, 216
New Testament, 20, 26, 77, 106
Newman, Cardinal, 21
Nicea, Council of, 113

oath, 24
offerers of Mass, 120
Offertory of Mass, 122
Old Law, 24, 112, 116, 125
Optatus, St., 15
ordinary, 64
Oriental rites, 64, 85, 119, 130, 141, 209, 246
Origen, 17, 52, 114, 158, 173
Orthodox sects, 64, 69, 89, 131

Papias, 8
Pauline privilege, 255
Paul, St.: sacraments, 24; celibacy, 225; Gospels, 8; grace, 35; hierarchy, 215; Holy Eucharist, 98; matrimony, 232; Pauline privilege, 255; priesthood, 220; sacrifice, 115
Paulus, 9
Pelagianism, 32, 52
Penance: a juridical act, 182; amendment needed for, 163; contrition needed for, 163; definition of, 152; forgives all sins, 159; grace of, 186; in Scripture, 156; in Tradition, 157; matter of, 162; minister of, 173, 176; necessity of, 161; repetition of, 186; requisites for, 158; sacrament of, 152; satisfaction imposed in, 182; St. Callixtus, 160
perfect good, 6
persecution, 83
Peter Lombard, 25
Peter, St., 8, 61, 78, 210
Petrine privilege, 256
Pius XI, Pope, 82
Pius XII, Pope, 220
prayer, 58
priestesses, 226
priesthood, 217
primacy of Peter, 15
Protestantism, 2, 21, 25, 50, 77, 93, 112, 196
proofs of God, 3
purgatory, 127

Quakers, 50
qualification: of godparents, 72; of sponsors, 89

Real Presence, 96
redemption, 58, 80
Reimarus, 9
religion, 5, 18
Renan, 9
revalidation of marriage, 248
revelation, 2
revival of grace, 29
rites of Church, 64, 84
Ritschl, 9
Roman Pontiffs, 15, 17, 19, 71, 175, 212

Sacramentary of Serapion, 196
Sacred Scripture, 2
Sacred Tradition, 2, 20, 50, 107
Sacraments: administration of, 30; attacks on, 2; decrees of Church on, 21; definition of a, 24; instituted by Christ, 26; intention to confer, 29; matter and form of, 26; means of grace, 28; reception of, 39, 41
sacrifice: elements of, 111, 114; Mass as a, 117
sacrilege, 41
Sanhedrin, 10
seal of confession, 181, 184
seminaries, 228
separation of spouses, 250
sin, 39, 40, 42, 52, 55, 68, 81, 86, 138, 163, 164
sin, forgiveness of, 153
Siricius, Pope St., 225
sorrow for Penance, 165
soul, proofs for, 4
sponsors, 89
Stephen, Pope St., 70
stipends for Mass, 129
Strauss, 9
subdeaconship, 223
Synoptic Gospels, 95, 136

Tatian, 231
Tertullian: Extreme Unction, 196; marriage, 231; Mass, 114; Penance,
157; Real Presence, 102; sacraments, 25; universality, 17
Theodore of Mapsuestia, 2, 102
Thomas Aquinas, St., 224, 228
tonsure, 224
transubstantiation, 97
Trent, Council of: Baptism, 49; Baptism by infusion, 61; benefits of Mass, 128; confession for Penance, 179; Confirmation, 77; effects of Baptism, 54; effects of Extreme Unction, 199; episcopacy, 215; essence of Mass, 125; Extreme Unction, 194; form of Confirmation, 85; grace, 33; Holy Eucharist, 93, 107, 109; Holy Orders, 210; indulgences, 190; infant Baptism, 51; justification, 53; mark of Baptism, 55; mark of Confirmation, 78; Mass, 112, 115; matter of Baptism, 60; matter of Confirmation, 83; matter of Mass, 119; matter of Penance, 162; Matrimony, 232; minister of Confirmation, 88; minister of Extreme Unction, 207; minister of Penance, 173, 176; number of sacraments, 26; One Species in Communion, 140; Penance, 152, 159; priesthood, 217; priest's powers, 219; satisfaction for sin, 182
Trinity, Blessed, 48, 62

uniate rites, 64, 89
Urban II, Pope, 221

value of Mass, 125
Verona, Council of, 231
viaticum, 139, 149
Virgin, Blessed, 52
virtues, 18
Vow: of celibacy, 226; of chastity, 225

Wesley, John, 16
Wiseman, Cardinal, 101
works, good, 58
Wycliffe, John, 173

Zwingli, 29, 94